PRIME TIMES

PRIME TIMES

Snapshots from Three Indelible Decades

Joe Murphy

PRIME TIMES
SNAPSHOTS FROM THREE INDELIBLE DECADES

iUniverse books may be ordered through booksellers or by contacting:

iUniverse
1663 Liberty Drive
Bloomington, IN 47403
www.iuniverse.com
1-800-Authors (1-800-288-4677)

Because of the dynamic nature of the Internet, any web addresses or links contained in
this book may have changed since publication and may no longer be valid. The views
expressed in this work are solely those of the author and do not necessarily reflect the
views of the publisher, and the publisher hereby disclaims any responsibility for them.

Any people depicted in stock imagery provided by Getty Images are models,
and such images are being used for illustrative purposes only.
Certain stock imagery © Getty Images.

ISBN: 978-1-5320-4144-0 (sc)
ISBN: 978-1-5320-4145-7 (e)

Library of Congress Control Number: 2018902193

Print information available on the last page.

iUniverse rev. date: 06/26/2020

CONTENTS

To my brother Pat, who was always right there to help.

ACKNOWLEDGEMENTS

MANY GOOD PEOPLE TOOK THE time and trouble to help me with this book. Their comments and encouragement helped me stay on track and keep going. My brother Jim furnished careful proofreading, as did helpful friend, Kathy Bergee. Writer pals Jim O'Brien, Doug Smith and Dave Klaproth helped with content and style. Longtime friend John Kerrigan checked the veracity and sanity of my ramblings as well. Graphics maven Mike Figarelli contributed much to the cover design. I also want to thank Kathy Young and other staff members at Loyola University's Cudahy Library in Chicago for their diligent fact checking And last but not least, a mega Thank You to Tim Lee and Christina Sutherland, owners of TNT's Coffee and Café in Madison, who put up with years of my visits as I dug through my memory while sipping dark roast. All of the stories that follow are true; those about home, family and education are easily verifiable. Others, relating to my career, describe events that actually happened. Names, dates and locations, however, have been changed to protect innocent and guilty parties and to keep me out of trouble.

INTRODUCTION

THREE DECADES IS A DAUNTING chunk of time to pack into one book, at least it is for me. But throwing caution to the wind, I'm taking a stab at it. The span of days between 1961 and 1990 took me from first-year college in Chicago to a job writing catalog pages in rural Wisconsin. Amazing history was made within that period: John Kennedy was assassinated, the civil rights movement surged ahead, oil embargoes brought grief to the gas pump. The Vietnam conflict escalated, Watergate erupted and the Berlin Wall was demolished. Then came war in Iraq. Fast-forward to right now. A firestorm of media bombards us with mindless tweets, false news and unrelenting reports of conflict and strife. Mercifully, a calming thought manages to cut through the flak now and then, bringing temporary relief. Maybe it's a flashback to a favorite vacation, a line from a Beatles song or a catchy slang word you haven't heard in decades. Scraps from the past like these don't count for much in the grand scheme of things, but if one of them brings a ray of sunshine to a dark day it's earned its keep in your memory. In this spirit I'd like to share a few choice moments from three unforgettable decades of my past.

This memoir picks up where my first book, *Echoes In The Gangway*, left off. On the last page I headed off to Loyola University in the fall of '61. From that point on, my recollections continue until 1990, when my family and I moved from the Chicago area to rural Wisconsin. Of course, it would make sense to take a straight, chronological path through the years leading up the big move, but that approach would drive me nuts. So instead, I'll forge ahead, sidetracked now and then by hot cars, pretty girls, photography and other welcome distractions. Hopefully, the episodes will make for pleasant reading, rekindle a few of your own happy memories and leave you with a good feeling.

When I was a carefree college freshman in 1961, the Vietnam war was still a few years off, but by the time I graduated, classmates of mine were sweating the draft. Just beyond the campus the real world was screaming for attention. It got harder and harder to ignore the mayhem out there. The Cuban missile crisis brought us to the brink of nuclear annihilation, and soon afterward friends of mine were heading to Southeast Asia to "stop the spread of communism." The "conflict," as the media called it, crept closer and closer to my safe little world. The nearest real threat to my wellbeing back then was the harrowing "S-curve" on Chicago's Outer Drive. Halfway between home and Loyola, that sinuous stretch of concrete could be a car-crunching monster on icy mornings. And while college postponed my real-world education, it taught me to pay attention and persevere. Two Loyola highlights were playing intramural football and getting a couple of poems published in *Cadence*, the college literary magazine.

Still immune to reality after graduation, I took guitar lessons and started singing folk songs. Out in San Francisco, hippies were dropping acid and chanting peace and love, man. They tripped on LSD while American astronauts trekked the lunar sands. In 1968 I loved tooling around town in my new muscle car. Life after 5 p.m. was mellow, but my job was not going well. Sears had hired me as a catalog copywriter but I couldn't type. I had to learn fast or get the axe. On a lighter note, Sears was teeming with nubile lovelies aplenty – Betty, Sue, Natasha and others. I managed to get a few dates while learning to type hunt-and-peck style on a manual typewriter. But writing catalog pages was not much fun and the job looked like a dead end.

I left Sears after 18 months and spent the next few years working at a mishmash of hack writing jobs. Those were rough-and-tumble times but they served as a springboard to happier days. I met a pretty girl named Mary who laughed at my jokes. We got married and were blessed with two delightful daughters. Mary made sure they took every kind of lesson known to man. We enjoyed their music recitals, ballet performances, ice-skating shows, baseball games and gymnastic meets. Like other young families, we faced hardships. One was surviving two years in our first house, a dilapidated wooden shack in Downers Grove, west of Chicago. A few years later we bought a nice old home in Oak Park that was still wired with its original 30-amp service. Using a hair dryer plunged us into darkness. But that place had potential and it was just a block from the train. Getting downtown to my job was a breeze.

I worked off and on at advertising agencies in the Loop for a decade, writing ads, radio commercials and TV spots. Finding new ways to sell things was challenging and fun. So was the variety of writing about everything from beer and frozen desserts to microphones and multiplexers. After ten years of agency work I went the freelance route, working out of my basement and taking on any writing job I could find. Mary shored up our cash flow by working at the local bank, then at the senior center and then at the hospital. We stayed in Oak Park for a dozen years. In nearby Chicago a black man was elected mayor and the Bears won Super Bowl XX. Mary and I had the house re-sided and the lawn re-sodded. We planted seven trees. Our place was starting to look good. In summer we enjoyed block parties, long walks and Shakespeare in the park. But after five years of self-employment, a pressing need for financial security steered me toward a job writing catalogs at Lands' End, the mail order clothing outfit. It was 1990 and the company was all set to move its creative staff from Chicago to Dodgeville, Wisconsin. So my family and I pulled up roots, departed the Illinois flatlands and resettled in the land of beer, brats and cheese. A new chapter of our lives was beginning. Much more was yet to happen – maybe enough to fill another book – but I'll worry about that later.

ONE

SERIOUS LEARNING AHEAD

*"I have never let my schooling
interfere with my education."*
– Mark Twain

"WHAT A VIEW!" I BLURTED as we cruised north on Chicago's Lake Shore Drive. It was late August 1961. My cousin Mike was at the wheel. We were incoming freshman headed up to Loyola University for our first day of orientation week. The passing scenery was new to me and everything looked exciting – the hairpin "S" curve at Grand Avenue, the shoreline bordering Lincoln Park, Montrose Beach, the elegant Edgewater Beach Hotel. A long sweeping curve ended at Sheridan Road, where we turned right. From there it was a short scoot to Loyola's Lake Shore campus.

Every freshman received an orientation packet that included a map of the campus showing where all the buildings were located. With my lousy sense of direction I found it quite helpful. I knew Lake Michigan was east. The Cudahy Library sat right on its shore, so spotting that building set my internal compass. On our first day of orientation Mike and I walked over to check it out. Sitting at a table near the shore, we enjoyed a refreshing view of Lake Michigan tinted deep blue by the late-summer sky.

Throughout orientation week we listened to speaker after speaker. They extolled the value of a college education and lauded Loyola grads that had gone on to enjoy distinguished careers. Most of this stuff bored the hell out of me, but a few of the speeches – those that were delivered outside – were easier to take. We freshmen sat on bleachers set up alongside the gym. Above us El trains trundling north and south rumbled past. Talking about our future contributions to mankind, a late-afternoon speaker suggested that one of us might discover a way to silence noisy commuter trains. Another lecturer asked us to look at the people sitting to our right and left. "Before fours years are up, both of those people will be gone," he stated. "Only one in three of you will graduate." *Thanks for the encouraging words!* I thought, wondering if I had the brains and guts to make it all the way through.

The Beanie Bounce

At the end of orientation week, we freshmen were invited to the "Beanie Bounce," a mixer held at the student union to help us newbie guys and gals get better acquainted. Throughout the prior week, we'd all worn little "beanie" caps on campus. Now, on Saturday night, it was time to shed this silly headgear. I hopped a ride up to the event with cousin Mike. Entering, I heard the husky voice of Brook Benton singing "Shadrach Meshach and Abednego" blaring from the PA system. It was the same song I'd heard in the union throughout the week. At the door, Mike and I wrote our names on the insides of our caps. There were two bins. Girls tossed their beanies into one bin; guys threw theirs into the other. Each girl drew a guy's beanie; each guy drew a girl's beanie. We were supposed to find the person whose cap we'd drawn. Mike and I separated as we set out to find our beanie mates. I asked several girls for their names, but none had the name I was looking for. What a waste of time! I abandoned my search and danced with a couple of coeds before bumping into my cousin. We went outside for some air and decided to head back to the South Side. A quarter century later, I was referred to a naprapathic physician in Chicago named Rosita Arvigo. After a few sessions, our conversation took a turn toward college days. The doctor said she had been a freshman at Loyola Lakeshore in the fall of '61 and had enjoyed the Beanie Bounce. I told her that I was there as well. "Who knows?" she said, "we may have danced together."

The right attitude

Despite my lackluster pre-college grades, I knew from an early age that higher education was the ticket to success. An early TV sitcom painted a rosy picture of high school that I loved. Entitled *Trouble With Father*, the show focused on a fumbling high school principal played by Stu Irwin. Each week he faced some minor crisis that he managed to survive with help from his understanding wife and two lively daughters. All the characters were clean cut and likeable. I was in first grade but I wanted to go to the high school where that nice man was in charge. A few years later I got similar feelings while strolling the spectacular campus at the University of Notre Dame; my Uncle Mike had taken me with him on a summer retreat. Besides the religious lectures there were trees, shrubs and winding paths – even a small lake. It was glorious. And enhancing this idyllic scene was the Irish Catholic tradition of Notre Dame football. The "Fighting Irish" always had a great team. I knew ND was for rich kids, but the atmosphere on campus made me feel that college would be worth a shot.

All through my four years at Leo High School the Irish Christian Brothers urged us kids to make a habit of buckling down to study, especially if we wanted to go to college. "Avoid distractions! Stay focused!" they told us. Even back in grammar school the Sisters of Providence stressed the importance of good study habits. As a college freshman I had not yet taken their sound advice to heart. The profs at Loyola expected us to show up for class and keep up with the required reading. Tests were infrequent but covered oceans of material. Staying with it required good time management.

Union man

The student union at Lake Shore was a modest, one-story affair. From the front it looked like it had been excised from an old strip mall. Entering it for the first time, I was surprised at its deep interior, where scores of long tables were arranged just far enough apart to allow access. Each table was home base for a particular group of students, mostly commuters like me. The scene was very territorial. The kids occupying a certain table always sat at that table. You couldn't encroach on their home turf. On a couple of occasions I tried without success to invade their space. Striking up a conversation was impossible; the table's regulars were engrossed in their own concerns. Getting the cold shoulder at lunchtime did not aid my digestion. Luckily, the union included an annex to one side called the Rambler Room, where the atmosphere was more democratic. You could sit at an empty table without feeling like a trespasser. And if you found room at an occupied table, the folks were pleasant and welcoming. I might spot my commuter pal, John Kerrigan, at a table playing poker with a group of guys. Knowing zip about cards, I never joined in these games. Besides, sitting through a long card game struck me as a boring waste of time. I opted to study at the library or take a hike.

The union's speaker system was set on permanent LOUD! Entering the building I could almost count on hearing Brooke Benton singing, "Well, there were three children from the land of Israel, Shadrach, Meshach and Abednego...." A counter at the far end sold sandwiches and coffee. It was lousy coffee but it was hot and a cup only cost a dime. When the vendor raised the price from 10 to 11 cents it caused an uproar. Students picketed the building and an article in the campus newspaper made the price hike sound like a major felony. After a week or two of boycotting and strife, the coffee concession caved in and rolled back the price to an affordable dime a cup.

On bitter-cold mornings getting from the Loyola El stop to the student union was a bone-chilling trek. Ignoring my mom's advice, I braved the elements bare-knuckled and hatless. I hadn't yet shed the notion that hats and gloves were for wimps. With a pile of books under one arm and my ears stinging, I waited at the stoplight on Sheridan Road, possibly the longest in the world. On any given morning the lengthy wait was annoying. On a sub-zero morning it was an eternity. When the WALK sign finally appeared I strode briskly across Sheridan Road and onto the Loyola campus. Passing the Alumni Gym, my shoes crunched crisply on the cinder running track as I hiked toward the union. Entering that building, the instant warmth felt wonderful, even though my thawing fingernails ached. I headed straight for the rear counter for a warming jolt of java in a paper cup.

Sharper focus

College demanded much more reading than I was ready for, and the small print in some textbooks was straining my eyes. A page in my history book turned so blurry it looked like I was seeing through shimmering Jell-O. My left eye had always been weak, but now the right one was faltering. I told Dad about it and he took me to an optometrist for an eye exam – the first one of my life. I learned that my right eye was 20/20 and my left one was 20/400 (legally blind). Following the docs's suggestion, I was fitted with a single contact lens for my left eye. I figured it was better than sporting a monocle.

Better vision improved my outlook on everything. I started studying in the Cudahy Library. Huge and cavernous, it intimidated me at first, but before long I became a frequent visitor. That library was filled with row after row of long wooden tables. Their reddish hue and soft sheen had a calming effect on me. I could sit and study for an hour or two before needing a break. Then I might go outside and skip stones into Lake Michigan. Focusing on one subject for a while, then switching to another worked best for me. Trying to stay with one textbook for too long made me groggy. Occasionally I'd fold my arms on the table, lower my head and fall asleep. But before long, an elderly security guard would tap me on the shoulder to remind me: "You can't sleep in the library," he'd whisper apologetically. Cudahy Library was the perfect place to write essays for my freshman rhetoric course. Knowing that only minutes remained before class began provided miraculous inspiration. I liked my teacher, Mr. Cavanaugh, a pleasant young fellow with a dry sense of humor. And I liked that girl with the chestnut hair who sat behind me.

Easy come, easy go

Forty-five bucks a week was a sweet deal. I was well into my first semester at Loyola and still getting a weekly $45 Workman's Compensation check. I'd been hit by a truck in June while delivering groceries on a bicycle and it was now October. My employer's insurance company had been generous, and I had taken advantage of their largesse by buying all kinds of cool stuff, including a gorgeous Durst photo enlarger from Italy. In the basement I developed rolls of black-and-white film and made blowups of family members, friends and neighbors, cars with fins, airplanes at Midway Airport – even the tiny figurines on Mom's bric-à-brac rack in the parlor. Unfortunately, Dad felt that my compensation checks were a bit stingy. He phoned the insurance company and voiced a complaint. Their claims adjuster was astonished to learn that I was out of the hospital and still getting paid. Dad's call put a stop to the stream of ready cash I'd grown accustomed to. But in his own words, "Nobody gives you anything for nothing in this world."

Duh!

As a freshman I wondered what made some kids in my classes so damned smart. They asked questions and joined in class discussions. Some of them quoted Shakespeare and Henry David Thoreau. How could they know all this crap at age 18? When they spoke up I sat there feeling like a dunce. I wondered if there might be a course I could take that covered just the names of authors and the titles of their works. Knowing that much might help me fake it for a while – until I could catch up on my reading.

I was amazed at how these brainiac kids could keep so many balls in the air at once. They had such a constant supply of mental energy. How did they keep their batteries charged? Sometimes I'd catch snippets of their conversation: "Heading for Milwaukee?" "You bet! We're debating Marquette. See ya Monday." "Hey, I heard you're in the musical." "Yeah – we're doing *Little Mary Sunshine*!" *Good for you*, I thought, wondering how these kids ever found time to sleep.

After a winter of commuting it was obvious to me that dorm dwellers enjoyed advantages that were not in the cards for kids like me. They were tuned in to the moods of various profs – what they'd be likely to ask on upcoming tests and when they were apt to give pop quizzes. Dormies had easy access to the library and more time to get at books that were on reserve for classes. And beyond that they didn't have to brave slippery roads and freezing sleet trying to reach school. They didn't get stuck waiting for delayed El trains. They didn't have to worry about their bladders holding out until they got to school, let alone to class. The fraternity boys enjoyed special perks too, like access to the storied "frat files" (a rich source of papers covering every academic field) from which to borrow.

Pipe dreams

On a September evening in our freshman year Mike and I were browsing at Sears when we lost each other. Suddenly I smelled a delicious aroma coming from the nearby tobacco counter. A young salesman had just opened a can of pipe tobacco for a customer. Hmm ... I asked if I could take whiff; my wish was granted. I inhaled. Ahhh! What a wonderful aroma, rich and robust, with notes of oak and cherry. The salesman suggested that I buy a small pouch of the blend and sample it. Sure, but first I'd need a pipe, I told him. He gestured toward a display rack at the end of the counter stocked with pipes aplenty.

I chose one made of reddish burled wood with a curved neck and added it to my tobacco purchase. Riding home with Mike I pictured myself sitting in the Rambler Room at Loyola, casually puffing away. Everyone would see me as a bright, mature young fellow – probably working toward some advanced degree. In reality, I was a 17-year-old kid and pretty young for my age. My lungs were on the mend following the accident I'd had a few months earlier. And my knowledge about smoking was zilch. I didn't even realize that smokers inhaled smoke down into their lungs.

My fantasy that smoking a pipe made me look mature and sophisticated lasted only a few weeks – until Dad discovered my pipe. I got up one morning, dressed and grabbed a couple of ballpoint pens. *Something's missing*, I thought. *My pipe!* I asked Mom if she'd seen it. "Your pipe? Well, I'm afraid that's gone," she answered softly. "Your father took it to work with him." "He took it to work? Why?" I demanded to know. "He's giving it to a friend, a pipe smoker," she said. "John and I both think smoking will hurt your lungs." I made a loud stink that woke up two of my brothers and left for school in a huff.

My mind was set on buying a new pipe, but with so much happening so fast, I never got around to it. My thoughts were focused on textbook details galore: barbarian tribes of medieval Europe, the life cycle of a mosquito and the P's and Q's of symbolic logic. There was one big distraction however – an automotive design contest sponsored by Chevrolet. I had only a few weeks to finish the model car I was building and send it in.

Highway to Heaven

This is unbelievable! I thought. My little roadster might win first place! I was seated at the Fisher Body Craftsman's Guild awards ceremony in Detroit. The model sports car I'd built for this General Motors competition had made it to the finals. With luck I could win a $5,000 college scholarship! I'd taken a Greyhound bus to Detroit for the event and found myself in a fancy hotel seated amid a sea of tables occupied by finalists from several age categories.

As the winners were announced, photos of the cars they'd built appeared on a huge screen above the speaker's platform. One by one, kids from the junior divisions walked up and accepted their trophies and scholarships. Finally, it was time to announce the winners in the senior division "open" category, the one I'd entered. The third place award went to skinny fellow from Oklahoma. He'd entered an angular little coupe with dashing, dart-like styling. Wow! A sharp pang of jealousy stabbed me in the gut. And now it was down to just me and a guy from Oregon for first place. His name was called next; he got second place. I froze! *Did I win first? There must be some mistake!* I gawked at the screen showing his curvy convertible with cool, scooped-out doors and sleek mini-fins. *My car beat that?* I was so excited that I didn't hear my name announced. "Hey, that's you!" the kid sitting next to me said. "Go up and get your award!" I wobbled toward the speaker's platform on rubber legs. The president of General Motors handed me a gilded trophy resembling the rocket hood ornament from an Oldsmobile. Shaking my hand, he smiled and said, "Congratulations, young man, you can't sleep in here!" *Can't sleep? Can't sleep?* I felt an insistent tap on my shoulder. "You can't sleep in here! No sleeping in the library!" "What?" I gasped. Lifting my head from the study table, I saw an elderly security guard standing over me. His wake-up call brought my dream to a screeching halt. I sat up straight, slid my zoology textbook toward me and looked up at the clock. Uh-oh, I had barely enough time to make it to class.

Truth be told

My interest in building a model "dream car" started when the Craftsman's Guild's national award ceremony was televised one summer night in the mid-fifties. I was probably ten years old at the time. Clicking from channel to channel, Dad settled on that broadcast, and we watched it together. Model car builders aged 12 through 19 were winning college scholarships. Shown up-close and rotating on mini-turntables, the winning entries took my breath away. It was hard for me to imagine that kids – even teenagers – could be skilled enough to build cars like that. Over the next few years I constructed lots of models, some of my own design. Then, propelled by a sudden surge of energy in my senior year of high school, I decided to give the car-building contest a shot. I picked up an info packet at a nearby Chevrolet dealer, took it home and got to work. I made it as far as the clay model stage before getting hit by a truck and spending my summer in the hospital. Then the project hit a second major detour when I started college and had to really hit the books. Before long, the deadline for completion was just two months away. I'd have to work like hell to transform my car from clay into wood, paint it and ship it off for judging.

I bought a block of poplar, traced my car's profile onto it and took it over to the woodshop at nearby Foster Park. The kindly old man in charge cut out the car's outline on a band saw. Progress. After a few weekend sessions with wood chisels and gouges, my car was shaping up nicely. Then came semester exams; time to hit the books. Thoughts of styling details were replaced by the study of unicellular critters in zoology, conundrums in symbolic logic and writing a final essay for my rhetoric class. Unattended, my little car coasted slowly to the junkyard of forgotten dreams. Maybe its rough-hewn body is still parked in a dark corner of a cabinet in the woodshop at Foster Park.

Education from the Jesuits

The Jesuits at Loyola taught classes in all areas – from English Lit to physics, but they required full-time students to take a theology course every semester. Theology classes were only two credit hours each, but after four years that added up to 16 hours, a full semester load. And though they weren't overly stimulating, these courses expanded my knowledge of Catholicism. I wanted to learn more about the Bible because Mother Church did not stress The Good Book in her teaching. Instead, she relied on church-approved volumes like the Baltimore Catechism. I remembered readings from Matthew, Mark and Luke at Sunday Mass, but not much else. So learning more about the New Testament was fulfilling. And I thought St. John's Four Horsemen of the Apocalypse were a hoot; they'd look great thundering across the screen in Cinemascope. I wondered which stars Hollywood would have cast to play their parts. Maybe Charlton Heston, Gregory Peck, Kirk Douglas and Burt Lancaster would have made a fearsome foursome.

I was surprised to learn that the Bible has so many books; some of their names (Leviticus, Deuteronomy, Ecclesiastes, Revelation) aroused my curiosity. Studying the Old Testament helped me put some names and facts in chronological order. Other theology classes included church history – The Council of Nicaea, The Diet of Worms, The First Vatican Council, etc. The prophets were fun – Elijah and his chariots of fire and Ezekiel who lay on his left side for 390 days, then on his right side for 40 days at God's command. Isaiah was intriguing. He claimed that God told him to walk around naked and barefoot for three years. In the sixties he could do the same thing at Berkeley and complete his junior year without creating much of a stir. In Ecclesiastes the narrator insists, "All is vanity." This made me think about what's important in our materialistic world. The Psalms were comforting as well – and not just in college. Years after I graduated, my confessor, a parish priest, gave me the penance of reading the Psalms. Their calming wisdom helped soothe my restless spirit.

Absorbing little critters

Zoology 101 was a revelation. My teacher, Father Peters, was a Jesuit priest with aristocratic style and swagger. He smoked using a cigarette holder as he lectured. It gave him an air of sophistication that added authenticity to his descriptions of the nine major phyla, hydrolysis and free radicals. Peters gave the impression that he had discovered everything he was teaching us. This man was entertaining; his sense of humor kept me awake.

From the very start I was fascinated by the tiny unicellular animals we studied under the microscope – amoebae, paramecia, euglena and such. We freshmen worked our way up the evolutionary scale to the amazing Planaria worm. (You could cut it in half and it would grow back to normal.) We moved onto the common earthworm, where we had to do some cutting. Oops! I slit my worm's gut wide-open, creating quite a mess. "I hope you're not going in for surgery," joked Miss Kuda, the pretty lab assistant. A few weeks later everyone received a live crayfish to study. At my lab table we decided to race our specimens from one end of the table to the other. The fun was just starting.

TWO

BETTER BUCKLE DOWN

*"You've really got to start hitting the books
because it's no joke out here."*
– Harper Lee

THE NEXT SEMESTER I ENROLLED in Dr. Boris Spiroff's zoology class, which went beyond amoebae to animals with backbones. Spiroff was a stocky fellow with a shock of unkempt black hair and wire-rimmed glasses. If you boned up for his quiz sections you could score extra points. He'd shoot a question at you and if you coughed up the right answer he'd put a check in his little black book, then fire a second question at you. This continued until you got something wrong. Miss Gayda, who sat in front of me, was amazing. She came back with one correct answer after another after another. At four or five questions, Spiroff had to move on to give some other kid a chance. Otherwise, he and Miss Gayda might still be going back and forth in Cudahy Hall to this day.

Spiroff had a reputation for being a tough teacher. He was demanding but hardworking, sometimes holding extra sessions after regular class hours on areas that he deemed important. "Don't let this get away from you," he warned us. (I thought of the briefing sessions in movies where bomber pilots get final instructions before dangerous missions.) In one of these gatherings we covered the parts of *amphioxus*, a fishlike critter with a "notocord" instead of a backbone. Spiroff was dead serious. On the blackboard was a carefully drawn schematic of amphioxus. The professor asked for a volunteer to track the circulatory system of this little creature. A well-dressed kid raised his hand and approached the blackboard. Picking up a long, wooden pointer he started in. I could see that he was very bright and knew his stuff, but he stuttered something awful; it was painful to watch. "Di-di-di…" *Diverticulum! Spit it out!* I said to myself. Even though it took forever, he named every structure correctly. When he finished I felt like applauding. I was glad that Spiroff didn't jump in and take over for the kid to save time. He showed a touch of class that I didn't forget.

In one of our lab sessions, every student was supposed to "pith" a live Northern Leopard Frog (*Rana pipiens*). Pithing involved inserting a needle into the frog's brain and mashing it up, like the lobotomy procedure once performed on unfortunate psychiatric patients. I don't remember why we were supposed to pith these poor little guys – maybe they were suffering from serious depression – but it never happened. Someone slipped into the lab at night and stole all the frogs (about 300 of them) from their holding tank. Who knows what they had in mind? Oh well, on to bigger and better species.

Dissecting a giant bullfrog (*Rana catesbeiana*) was a major operation that would involve weeks of lab work. Each student was issued a frog under the watchful eyes of two lab assistants, whose white smocks gave them hygienic, clinical credibility. Recalling how I'd botched my earthworm the previous semester, I made a point of asking for help right away. We slit the bellies of our frogs open to expose their organs: heart, stomach, kidneys, etc. All very interesting, but the closer I got to my specimen, the stronger it smelled. The formaldehyde it was pickled in irritated my eyes. My frog, a male, was injected with colored latex that turned his arteries red and his veins blue – bright as the colors in a comic book. Finding all the required frog parts was slow going. There were scores of them to learn for the frog lab practical. Some of them, like the mouthparts, had strange names, like *lateral substrossal fossa* and *pulvinar rostrale*.

Tricky business

With my dissection going slowly, I got the OK to take my frog home so I could work on it there. The lab assistant handed him to me in a plastic bag, half-filled with formaldehyde and cinched with a drawstring. With my books tucked under my arm and the frog slung over my shoulder, I waited on the frozen Loyola El platform for a southbound train. Once on board, I found a window seat with a heating vent near the floor. Setting my books on my lap, I let my frog sit on the floor. With a long ride ahead of me, I was soon fast asleep. But before long, I woke up choking in a cloud of acrid fumes that was escaping from my frog bag. Lifting it, I saw that the formaldehyde inside was boiling. Yikes! I moved quickly to a seat at the far end of the car, away from heaters and other passengers. This time I sat the frog next to me on the seat.

At home Mom greeted me as I entered the kitchen. "What's in the bag?" she asked. I told her it was my frog from school. "Get that thing out of here!" she shouted. "Put it on the porch!" I stepped outside and tossed my specimen into the mop pail. Mom let me back inside, telling me to wash my hands. After supper I took my frog to the basement and worked on him until I was bleary-eyed from the formaldehyde. I dropped him into the pail and added some water. Upstairs, I left it on the porch, went inside and hit the sack. In my sleep a lady lab instructor drilled me brutally on the parts of my frog and their function. I spat back one correct answer after another until the end. Then came the difficult bonus question, "Do you take your froggy to bed with you at night? *What?* I woke up with a start, got dressed, wolfed down a bowl of corn flakes and hurried out the kitchen door. On the porch I found my frog encased in ice. The water in his pail had frozen solid. Only his eyes and the tips of his front flippers protruded above the surface. With no time to waste, I chipped him free with a screwdriver and slid him into his bag. When lab period started I removed my frog from his bag to find his innards horribly shriveled and distorted. The lab assistant told me I needed a new frog. He said I could buy one from a biological supply outfit on the South Side.

The next day I purchased a replacement male frog. I took him down to the basement, laid him on the Ping-Pong table and opened him up. There was no time to waste. A big chunk of my lab grade would be based on how neatly I'd excised the heart and brain. Removing the heart wasn't too hard. I put it into a glass vial from the lab that was half filled with water. The brain was a different matter. Since it was totally encased in bone, freeing it involved the careful shaving away of that bone. After an hour or so, I was coaxing the delicate, noodle-like organ from its lodging. Oops! One of the occipital lobes fell off. That would cost me points, but at least I got the job done. Slipping the brain into the vial. I thought that maybe I could carve a perfectly shaped bogus brain from a wet lasagna noodle. *No dumbass – you'd just get yourself kicked out of the class!* With my surgery completed, I wondered how things were going with my cousin Mike and his frog. We hadn't touched base in a week.

Zero hour

The moment of truth arrived at the next lab period. Flanked by his two assistants, Dr. Spiroff collected the frog brains and hearts we freshmen had extracted from our specimens. When he approached me I nervously surrendered my vial. Moving to the next table, he stopped in front of my cousin. Looking a bit embarrassed, Mike handed him an empty vial. "Didn't you do the assignment, Mr. Doyle?" the professor groaned. "I meant to," Mike replied, "but I just never got around to it." I could hardly keep from laughing. At that point the big practical on our frogs was only a week away. In a lab test like this all the tables were converted into test stations. Next to the specimens on display were little cards that asked for the names of highlighted structures and their functions. We freshmen moved from station to station, writing down answers on our test sheets. Ideally, these stations were clearly numbered and located in a logical sequence, but this didn't always happen. Depending on who set them up, stations could be arranged in any scatterbrained fashion. I remember one hellish lab practical where everyone kept bumping into each other trying to find the next station. By the time I got to the correct table it was time to move on – there was no time to think. We could have used a traffic cop to keep things organized. I tried to put that experience out of my mind as I prepared for the all-important giant bullfrog practical.

D-Day arrived all too soon. What a scene – the lab tables were covered with dozens of dead frogs on their backs with their bellies torn open and their guts exposed. It looked like the aftermath of some epic amphibian battle. We freshmen moved from table to table, scribbling down our answers as we went. When I finished my eyes were red and stinging from the formaldehyde. Whew! It felt good to be done with frogs. The lab assistant returned my specimen to me in a plastic bag, assuming that I wanted it back. Sliding it on top of the books under my arm I exited Cudahy Hall and hiked to the shoreline behind the library. Here I removed my giant bullfrog from his bag and flung him into Lake Michigan.

The prolific fruit fly

Second semester zoology included a dose of genetics that focused on the teensy-weensy fruit fly (*Drosophila melanogaster*). Each student was handed a glass vial containing a male and a female fruit fly with a supply of some concoction they could feed on. We had to wait till they propagated, then bring them back to the lab. I stowed my vial in the top drawer of our dining room buffet. When I took it out two weeks later I was astonished at the number of flies crawling around inside. Back at the lab we prepared to count the offspring to see how many males and females had been produced and what characteristics they had, such as eye color. But first we had to anesthetize them with ether.

At a glance, it looked like Patterson, the star of our table, had the most prolific mating pair. Of course, everything he touched turned to gold. He got 100% on every lab quiz, and usually got the bonus question right as well. With help from a lab assistant, I knocked out my fruit fly family. Patterson was watching me keenly, leaning forward to get a closer look, it seemed. But his drooping head kept moving downward . . . plop! It hit the lab table and bounced off. His body slid out of sight and crumpled to the floor. His unopened vial shattered, setting his fruit flies free. Our instructor opened a window and a kid from another table helped me drag Patterson over to it. After a few minutes he came to, looking dazed. I rejoined the folks at my table, where we tallied our flies and their genetic traits. Meanwhile, Patterson was shaking his head trying to clear out the ether he'd inhaled. As I left, the lab two assistants were helping him to his feet. Smiling, I wondered what grade Mr. Know-It-All would get on his fruit fly project. *It doesn't matter*, I thought, figuring that he'd already locked in an A for lab.

Recurring headache

Getting the classes you wanted each semester was a challenge. It was wise to make out your schedule and get in line early to improve your chances of landing the right teachers. The line to the registration office in Dumbach Hall stretched all the way through the main corridor to the far exit. The kids waiting patiently in line looked like souls suffering in Purgatory. I couldn't motivate myself to join those intrepid early birds. And being a commuter, I lacked the dorm dwellers' knowledge of which profs were easy and which ones were bad news. For me it was hard enough just to find classes on different days at different times that didn't conflict with each other.

My poor schedule-making skills resulted in school days with vast stretches of time between classes. I'd have an 8 a.m. ethics class with a five-hour wait until my 2 p.m. class in English Lit. To fill the hours in between I'd start by visiting the library. Seated at a well-lighted study table, I'd stay focused for a chapter or two before needing a break. Then I might walk off campus and head south on Broadway. At Devon, right near school, I'd pass an authentic movie palace, the Granada. Built in the twenties, it was one of the largest movie houses in town, with furnishings taken from palaces, churches and villas throughout Italy and Spain. That spectacular theater showed movies into the seventies, then hosted rock concerts in the eighties. When it closed in '87 the Granada was still in great shape – a prime candidate for restoration.

But after a few years of total neglect it was demolished in 1990. What splendid progress! But I digress…

Crossing Devon, I'd soon reach an old-fashioned cafeteria with an interior of white ceramic tile – very antiseptic. It wasn't the Pump Room but it was a place to warm up on a cold day. I ordered coffee and mashed potatoes with gravy. The heavy, ceramic mug held an honest helping of java and its thick walls kept it warm. I rarely saw another customer in that place; my off-hours visits made me feel like I was their only customer. I remember a gray morning when I sat on a stool, staring at the floor of tiny hexagonal tiles and thinking about how to kill time before my next class. The raw feeling in my gut told me I was going nowhere. I could see why so many young guys went into the service. Hitting the sidewalk again, I might walk south another half mile or so before turning back. The lackluster hodgepodge of storefronts and old buildings along Broadway didn't urge me on. The Uptown area farther south was in sad shape.

Strolling north from Loyola was a different experience. On Sheridan Road I could see the marquee of the 400 Theater a few blocks ahead. I knew there wasn't much of interest beyond that movie house for quite a stretch, but my imagination kept me going. Sheridan followed the curve of Lake Michigan's shore, and I fancied that something of interest might lie around the bend – maybe a secluded beach I hadn't noticed before or a coffee shop that I'd missed on my last trek. Fantasy aside, I knew that the lush, green campus of Northwestern University lie only five miles north. A long way to walk, but it would be a pleasant drive if I had a car. Returning to campus on a bitter-cold afternoon, I'd be welcomed by the comforting warmth of the Cudahy Library.

Lost at Loyola

The scene looked vaguely familiar. I was on the sidewalk between Dumbach Hall and the Cudahy Science Building, but I still felt lost. It was a few minutes before 8 a.m. I knew I should be sitting in class, but I couldn't remember *which* class. Embryology? Logic? English? And what building should I go to? What was the number of the classroom? I was clueless, off balance and scared, but a sense of duty urged me onward. I'd written the schedule for all my classes on the inside cover of my thick, multi-subject notebook, but I didn't have it with me. *Where the hell is it?* I wondered. *Did I leave it home? Lose it on the train?* I was getting more anxious as the clock ticked its way toward 8 a.m. *The semester's almost over*, I fretted. *I should know my damned schedule by now!*

Then it struck me: I didn't know what classroom to go to because I'd forgotten all about that morning class months before. God knows how many lectures and quizzes I'd missed; how many papers I hadn't turned in. Panicking, I wondering how I could possibly catch up and earn a passing grade. I decided to go to the office in Dumbach Hall and get a copy of my schedule. At a counter just inside the door I pressed the button on a domed, ring-for-service bell. It sounded with a sharp DING! A little bald man appeared and asked how he could help me. I started to explain my situation. "Stop!" he said. "First give me your name and student number." I blurted them out. "OK, what do you need?" he asked impatiently. Embarrassed, I asked him for a copy of my class schedule, showing the classes I'd registered for and when and where they met.

"I'll have to make a photocopy," he told me, disappearing into a small side office. He returned a minute later with a sheet of paper and a blue book, the kind used for written exams. "I'm sorry," he said. "Before I can give you a schedule you'll have to pass this test covering all the material in your classes to date." "What?" I screeched. "That's ridiculous!" "It's a new school policy," he insisted. Pointing to a student chair in the corner, he handed me the test and walked away. Looking at the questions knocked the wind out of me like a punch in the solar plexus. Whoever came up with them fiendishly focused on the parts of each subject that I hadn't fully grasped; the stuff I'd been meaning to review but hadn't got around to: Avagadro's number, the categorical imperative, *Gemeinshaft* and *Gesellshaft*, the endoplasmic reticulum and the mysterious Finnsburg Fragment from *Beowulf. I've died and gone to Hell*, I concluded … BRRR! A blast of cold air hit me in the forehead, waking me up. I saw the open door of the El car I was sitting in. It wouldn't close, and a motorman was jiggling it, trying to force it shut. Beyond the door I saw LOYOLA printed on a large sign. *My stop!* I sprung from my seat and darted past the struggling motorman onto the platform.

Go Ramblers!

I had the good fortune to attend Loyola when the school fielded a phenomenal basketball team. My pre-med studies and commuting hindered me from being a devoted fan, but the campus newspaper and constant b-ball buzz at Lake Shore kept me updated on the Ramblers. They were the top offensive team in the country, winning their first 20 games and scoring 100 or more points 11 times during the regular season. Even more impressive today, they were pioneers in integrated sports. Four of the starters were black: Jerry Harkness, Les Hunter, Vic Rouse and Ron Miller. John Egan was the only white first stringer. These starting five got game time galore. After losing two good bench players due to academic issues, Coach George Ireland rarely took any of the starters out of a contest. In most games the fearless five had to hang in there till the final buzzer. Chicago sports writers dubbed them "The Iron Men." The '63 Ramblers finished the regular season with a 24-2 record making it to the NCAA finals.

Loyola kicked off the tourney by trouncing Tennessee Tech, 111-42. Their second-round opponent, Mississippi State, almost didn't show up because at that time Mississippi's college teams were not allowed to play against integrated teams. But coach Babe McCarthy and his Bulldogs slipped out of town under the cover of darkness and headed north. They barely escaped before a court injunction prohibiting them from playing Loyola could be served. The Ramblers defeated Mississippi State 61-51 led by forward Jerry Harkness who put up 20 points. That contest is now considered a landmark in the civil rights movement.

Next, the Ramblers bested Illinois 79-64 in the Mideast Regional, moving on to the Final Four in Louisville. In the semifinal against Duke, center Les Hunter scored 29 points in Loyola's 94-75 victory. The stage was set for one of the most sensational championship games in NCAA history. On March 23th, 1963 the underdog Loyola Ramblers took the floor at Freedom Hall in Cincinnati against the two-time NCAA champion Cincinnati Bearcats. Cincinnati's controlled offense and strong defense slowed the Ramblers down. With 13:56 left in the game the Ramblers trailed 45-30. Harkness, Loyola's best player, had not yet scored a single point. Then he suddenly sprang to life, putting up 14 points – 11 of them in the final five minutes of play. His 12-foot jumper with four seconds left in regulation tied the score at 54.

Then in overtime, with 1:49 left and the game tied at 58, Coach Ireland called a time-out to set up a play that was forced into a jump ball. Guard John Egan, 5" 10", went against the much taller opponent to see who would play for the last shot. Egan leapt at the right instant, tipping the ball to Miller who moved it up court for the last shot. With seconds left, Harkness fed the ball to Hunter. He took a jump shot. It hit the rim, spun around and bounced off. But Vic Rouse tipped it in as the clock struck zero. Loyola won! Rouse was mobbed by ecstatic fans and teammates. Red Rush, the voice of Ramblers radio, screamed "We Won! We Won! We Won!" The Loyola Ramblers were the 1963 National Basketball Champs. "I knew I was going to get the ball," Rouse later told reporters, "and I took my time once I was in the air. I never thought we'd lose it. We came too far to lose it!"*

A huge sign boasting Loyola's achievement was installed along the side of the Alumni Gymnasium facing the El tracks. It read, **Loyola Ramblers 1963 NCAA Basketball Champions**. Riding the CTA I read that message with pride countless times as the years rolled by. It made me wish I could go back to that magic time and be a better fan. The Ramblers played their final game in the old gym in 1996 and then moved to a new sports arena on campus. The Alumni Gym was demolished in 2011 to make room for a new student union. When I bought a car in the summer of '63 it was a new '63 Rambler – mainly because of my Dad's advice, but partly because Loyola's team had given me such good feelings toward the word, "Rambler." Going to Loyola

---

*   Game details from Loyola University Chicago Official Athletic Site.

in '63 and owning a '63 Rambler was a great conversation starter. That car changed things for me in a big way. It gave me the freedom to go wherever I wanted without counting on buses and trains. I could ask girls for dates knowing we wouldn't have to ride the CTA. And I could get to second or third shift summer jobs without taking buses or El trains at risky, off hours. Hell, I could even drive to school if I felt like it. I was able to go boldly where I'd never gone before – way beyond the city limits – north to Wisconsin, east to Indiana.

THREE

SUMMER JOBS

*"Hard work never hurt anybody
but why take a chance?"*
– Edgar Bergen

WHAT LUCK! I'D JUST FINISHED my first year of college when a job downtown fell into my lap. A friend of my dad recommended me to a law firm in the Loop. Exiting the State Street subway on my first day, I walked west on Jackson, hurrying my step to get there by 7:30 a.m. The streets were strangely quiet at that hour, and crisp, cool breezes bolstered my grown-up, independent feeling. At the office a nice lady assigned me the task of filing folders in the basement. Cardboard boxes scattered on the floor were filled with client records, and more folders were piled high on chairs. My job was to arrange these disheveled files into alphabetical order and box them up neatly.

The work was boring and lonely, but occasionally an attractive young gal came down with some documents for me to photocopy. Speedy Xerox machines were not yet in general use, so I had to use the quirky device this outfit had purchased. It was chrome plated and rounded like a Sunbeam toaster. I inserted the original and a piece of photo paper into separate slots. After several seconds the original eased its way out of the top and a wet, soggy copy squeaked as it struggled from the machine's rear end. I laid the limp copied sheets onto a flat surface. It took each one of them 10 or 15 minutes to dry; the finished copies were crisp and lumpy. Copying a lengthy document made the room look like washday. Sheets were drying on desktops, chairs, cabinets – everywhere. After a long session of making copies my lungs stung from the machine's fumes. It felt good to go upstairs and outside for some fresh air. At lunchtime I strolled around the West Loop. Once in a while I'd visit Shop and Stop on Washington. It was a unique market that sold upscale foods, including all kinds of exotic fruits. Everything was amazingly fresh and big; one of their apples was lunch.

The law firm job lasted only a few weeks, but I found ways to kill time for the rest of that summer. My new harmonica helped. It was a Hohner with 12 holes and a slider that made sharps and flats. In a quiet corner of the house I practiced *Moon River* and *Deep Purple*. Downstairs in my basement darkroom I enlarged black-and-white photos. Another summer project was reading *The Phenomenon of Man*, by the French philosopher Teilhard de Chardin. My freshman biology teacher recommended it to the class, so I bought a copy and thought I was reading biology. It shows how little I knew about anything at the time. By September I was bored and ready to get back to college.

NOW HIRING

After my sophomore year at Loyola it didn't take me long to land a factory job. Times were good in the sixties; there were plenty of opportunities for summer employment. As soon as final exams were over, my brother Dan and I hit the industrial districts on Chicago's South Side. We applied at outfits that made stuff – everything from lawn mowers to cardboard boxes to candy bars. The number of candy companies we came across was remarkable: Mars, Brach's, Ferrara Pan, Curtiss and Tootsie Roll, just to name a few. Within a week we'd each filled out applications at a dozen different places. Before another week had passed we both had jobs. And college friends from the neighborhood soon found employment as well. It was easier to look for summer work after my sophomore year of college because I had a car to help me get around. Instead of riding the CTA or pounding the pavement, I scooted from one potential employer to another – from Hotpoint to National Can to Cracker Jack to Stone Container.

The application forms I filled out were very much alike: a single two-sided sheet asking for my height and weight, Social Security number and what shifts I'd be able to work. I soon had the needed information memorized. The questions often included: *Have you ever been bonded? Have you ever been convicted of a felony? Can you operate a forklift?* A couple of manufacturing outfits tested my manual dexterity. A person with a stopwatch timed me while I took little metal slugs from the holes in one tray and put them into the corresponding holes in another tray. It seemed like a test for someone who would do assembly line work. I still wonder how I scored on those tests.

A brief stint in Hell

The Stone Container plant made big cardboard boxes to hold major appliances like refrigerators, stoves and air conditioners. After fabrication, the flattened boxes were stacked onto dollies. My job in their big, dark plant was to pile those boxes onto the dollies and secure them with two or three steel bands. A co-worker and I would push a loaded dolly over to a curvy slot in the floor that snaked its way through the plant. Corroded steel hooks moved slowly through this slot like the fins of prowling sharks. One of them would snag a waiting dolly and drag it along a sinuous path that ended in the shipping room.

I was teamed up with Pete, a barrel-chested, young hulk who liked to work fast and "make bonus." I didn't like him one bit. He was a dark, sullen character who prodded me into doing hazardous dirty work. The hooks gliding through the floor were so old and worn that they sometimes failed to snag the dollies as they passed beneath them. To make sure that this didn't happen, Pete told me to ram a round core of wound-up cardboard over the hook just before it hit the dolly. I did this once and felt stupid and angry afterward. If my timing had been just a hair off, that hook would have mashed my fingers to a bloody pulp.

When I complained to Pete that this was really dangerous, he said he didn't like my attitude. That was my last day at Stone Container.

The picture plant

A week or two later I landed a job at the Kodak film processing facility just south of the Loop. The building was immaculate from stem to stern; it was the cleanest plant I'd ever seen. Large, diorama-sized photos in vivid color decorated the entrance lobby and walls throughout the building. My job was in the film alley where 35mm color film emerged from the developing tank. I tended two machines whose faces were big glass panes. Through them I could see a continuous belt of freshly developed slide film traveling up and down around a series of rollers as it moved slowly from left to right. Gentle blowers aided the drying process while the film continued its sinuous trek. Breathing room engineered into the machine's design allowed the roller assembly to expand and contract like an accordion.

Separating one customer order from another was a round, metal splice that got stuck between two steel bushings. It kept the next order from winding onto the take-up reel while I removed the previous order. To keep things moving, I slapped a round plastic core onto the empty spindle and attached the next order to it. Meanwhile, the film transport mechanism was cutting me some slack as its rollers slowly separated – the top bank of rollers traveling toward the ceiling and bottom bank heading toward the floor. If I didn't work fast, the mechanism would reach its limits and stop with a loud CLANK! This happened on two occasions. Yards of film snapped off the rollers and flopped onto the floor in a slithering mess. Lights flashed. Alarm bells sounded. All hell broke loose. "Get a bucket! Get a bucket!" my boss screamed. An emergency crew showed up with water-filled buckets, stuffed the flailing film into them, and took off for God knows where. It was pandemonium!

After three weeks of this mayhem I left Kodak and found an easier job at Continental Can Company. Here I found myself working with Phil Carollo from my neighborhood. Small world. Phil was a year behind me at Loyola. Our jobs at Continental were simple enough: we loaded pallets stacked with empty cans into boxcars. The company turned out all kinds of cans – from huge, gallon-sized ones destined to hold string beans for restaurants to tiny ones that would be filled with tomato paste. Cans in other sizes would eventually hold peanuts, putty, hairspray or motor oil – who knew? Empty cans clattered their way through the plant via overhead tracks night and day, headed for somebody like me, who would collect them, stack them onto a dolly and push them into a boxcar waiting at the shipping dock. Working at CCC, I caught glimpses of how cans were made. They began as thin sheets of steel that received a protective coating on one side, which would become the inside of the finished cans. The sheets were cut, formed into cylinders and finished with a solder seam. Cans left the factory topless; they'd get their lids after being filled by Heinz or Del Monte or Sinclair.

Once in a while I worked on the "dog food" line, where small cans pouring down the track came to a halt in front of me. Using a tool that resembled a wide garden rake, I picked up several cans at a time and laid them on a wooden pallet sitting at the bottom of a cube-like bin that was tilted toward me. I laid down a row of ten cans and then another row on top of it and so on – until ten rows of ten – one hundred cans – created the first layer on the pallet. I covered this first layer with a sheet of cardboard and added another layer of one hundred cans, then more cardboard, then more cans and so on until I had eight layers of one hundred – eight hundred cans in all. Next, I pulled a handle that tipped the bin upright, releasing the can-packed pallet onto a roller track. And finally, I gave the whole shebang a shove that sent it ten feet along the track to guy who was just sitting there waiting for it. His job was to cover the whole thing with cardboard flaps and tie a string around it. On the night I pulled flap-tying duty I read half of *Wuthering Heights* before punching out.

Field's warehouse

During the summer of '65 I worked for Marshall Field & Co., Chicago's legendary department store. My job was loading "gift" boxes into warehouses on the West Side. These festive boxes were printed with colored renderings of holly, reindeer or some other cheery holiday theme. Starting in June, truckloads of boxes began pouring into Field's warehouse complex. I was responsible for three warehouses, all located on the same block. Each building had a dock entrance in front where trucks backed in and deposited their box-filled trailers, mostly 40-footers. They returned several hours later to pick up the trailers, which I would have unloaded by then. The boxes were bundled together, wrapped in brown paper and tied up with string, just like in the song, "My Favorite Things." The strings on these packages made them easy to grab, and I grabbed thousands of them throughout the summer. By the end of August the backs of my hands were shining with calluses.

I stacked the bundles onto dollies and pushed them into the warehouse. Boxes in various sizes from several sources were stored in designated spaces on the floor. These fancy gift boxes were sized to hold everything from blankets to sweaters to handkerchiefs and jewelry. Some opened to reveal other boxes inside that were a tad smaller. This helped save space at the stores. I loaded three or four wooden dollies, piling them high with bundles. Then I stacked the bundles in rows on the warehouse floor, leaving aisles between them. They weren't too heavy, but there were hundreds of them each day. Some were stored on the first floor; others were assigned space on the second or third floors. My boss told me that by end of summer my three warehouses would hold some three million individual Christmas boxes. Sometimes he'd call to inform me that a 40-foot trailer was on its way or already waiting to be unloaded at one of my warehouses. It was wise to keep working and stay on top of things.

Even so, there were afternoons when I had an hour or two of downtime. On the third floor of the largest warehouse I'd sit on an empty dolly behind the elevator shaft and study Dostoyevsky, Chekhov, Racine or some other author on the reading list for my comprehensive exam in English Lit. It irked me that I had to read so many foreign authors for this test. The required courses in English at Loyola only covered writers up to the early nineteenth century. *So what's the deal with all these foreign authors?* I lamented. It would have been more interesting if we'd read a few 20th century American authors, like Dreiser, Steinbeck or Dos Passos.

That third-floor retreat was enchanting at times. Part of it was a storage area for colorful Christmas decorations and miscellaneous store window props. On one bright afternoon sunbeams shot through the big windows, highlighting the chiseled features of a female mannequin that leaned crazily from a storage bin. And there were dozens of dark captain's chairs stacked on top of one another. I'd seen them in the Walnut Room at the downtown store surrounding Field's Christmas tree. That majestic tree stood 40 feet high, filling a two-story atrium. It was a special holiday treat when moms and dads took their kids see Santa Claus. The whole family waited in line for hours so Tommy and Tammy could tell the jolly old elf what they wanted for Christmas. Other folks waited patiently to dine beneath the big tree in a setting of glistening white snow, reindeer and elves. I recently learned what Shirley Temple said about her visit to Santa: "I stopped believing in Santa Claus when I was six. Mother took me to see him in a department store and he asked for my autograph."

My on-the-job studying was often interrupted by the sound of the elevator. *Oops! Somebody's coming – time to look busy.* Sometimes the boss walked over from across the street with special instructions regarding an incoming shipment. A truck could arrive at any moment – there was no set pattern. On a few occasions I was ready to head home only to find a 40-foot trailer sitting in the shipping bay. *Shit!* I'd have to empty that sucker before quitting. After filling up my all dollies, I'd offload the rest of the boxes onto the dock and tend to them the next morning.

Live and learn

One sultry afternoon after a truck had just pulled out of my dock, a middle-aged lady wearing a tank top and shorts walked into the bay. She said she was looking for employment. *Why is she telling me this?* I pondered. "The employment office is across the street," I told her. She looked askance at me and repeated that she needed employment – as if I hadn't understood her the first time. Shaking her head, she walked back to the sidewalk and headed up the street. I wondered why she didn't go across the street to the employment office. Years later it dawned on me that the employment she was seeking was very short term – maybe five or ten minutes.

I usually brought my lunch from home and ate it while sitting on a dolly. But once in a while I hiked over to the main warehouse and dined in the employee cafeteria. The food was good and didn't cost much. And I might bump into some other loading guys my own age. I helped them out on rare days when no Christmas boxes arrived for me to handle. The main warehouse held an incredible variety of merchandise, including major appliances, like stoves and refrigerators, packaged in big cardboard boxes. Picking them up with a forklift was awkward, so Field's used a different vehicle for this chore. We called it the "Squeeze Jeep." It looked like a forklift, but instead of having steel tines protruding in front, it had two textured rubber walls that closed in on the sides of a box and then lifted it. This little workhorse did a great job, except on one morning after a heavy rain. An inch of water had covered the warehouse floor, making the bottoms of the boxes wet and soggy. A maintenance crew had pumped out the water, but those boxes were still pretty mushy. When the Squeeze Jeep lifted a refrigerator it fell through the bottom of its box and crashed to the floor. It stood there on a awkward angle like the Leaning Tower of Pisa.

On another day I was recruited to help a young guy named Larry unload a boxcar full of stoves. This husky kid loved to make up dirty lyrics and set them to the music of songs like "Yankee Doodle Dandy." He was really good at it. We sized up the job and decided to set up a ramp leading to the boxcar's door. But the forklift was too wide to pass through. We'd have to slide the stoves over to the door, but how? They were stacked on top of one another – two rows high. We'd have to remove the stoves on top before we could do anything else. To see if it would be possible to slide the stoves forward, we both pulled hard on one of them. It moved about a foot. Sliding was definitely doable.

With nobody around to advise us, we figured that we could simply yank a stove all the way out and let it fall. Nah, that wouldn't work. Well, maybe it would if we put something on the floor to cushion the impact. Larry and I looked around for some shock-absorbing material and found several unopened bales of brown paper bags. In their bound up state they looked pretty springy, so we arranged the bales on the boxcar floor where we guessed that the stove might land. With one of us working on each side, we pulled a stove all the way out. FWOMP! It landed squarely on the bags, bouncing a couple of times before settling. "Way to go!" I shouted. "Scratch one stove!" Larry yelled. I thought we'd given it more than a scratch. We pushed the stove over to the open boxcar door where Larry got the tines of the forklift under it. He backed down the ramp and deposited the stove on the warehouse floor. Back in the boxcar we pushed the bottom stove over to the door and the waiting forklift. Repeating this process all afternoon, we emptied the boxcar. The bags (if not the stoves) held up remarkably well. Late in the afternoon, the boss stopped in to check on our progress. He was elated that the dynamic duo of Larry and Joe had unloaded the entire boxcar so quickly. I wondered what some of those stoves would look like with their boxes removed.

Where have all the toasters gone?

I was surprised to learn that theft was an ongoing problem at Field's main warehouse. This issue came to light one afternoon in front of several spectators. One of the stock workers had been taking old refrigerators home in his pickup truck, supposedly to refurbish them. (These fridges were ones that Field's had removed from kitchens when they delivered new ones.) To the casual observer it looked like this man had been helping the company get rid of unwanted junk. Safety laws required that door handles on old refrigerators be removed, so Mr. Fixit had been taping the doors shut on ones he took home. One afternoon he was exiting the front of the building with a huge refrigerator on a hand truck. As he lowered it down the stairs, the taped door flew open, releasing a cascade of new radios, blenders, hair driers and other small appliances. With dozens of people watching, this clever thief was caught red-handed. It turned out that he had been stealing stuff with this take-home repair scheme for months.

Summer of '65, a real workout!

"Just leave it to Brown," the glib TV spot for United Parcel Service told us confidently. The commercial was designed to reassure us that UPS delivers the goods on time and in good condition. I'm sure that happens most of the time, but I know it doesn't happen every time. Having worked at United Parcel during the summer of '65, I helped load a few trucks that left the Chicago terminal hauling damaged goods. I was ecstatic when UPS hired me. The man in the employment office shook my hand firmly and wished me luck. His assistant took me downstairs to the loading area, which occupied the acreage of a city park. A giant carousel moved packages around the perimeter to the dock area. Here empty trailers were backed up with their rear doors agape. Strong young men called "pullers" yanked boxes and bales from the ever-moving carousel and heaved them into the backs of big trucks. My job was to pick the stuff up and load it ASAP. There were always two loaders on a 40-foot trailer. I'd grab the boxes and toss (or slide) them to my co-loader. It was backbreaking work and dangerous as well. The puller might throw something at you like a plowshare or a chain saw that could cut or bruise you. Trying to keep up with the carousel, he couldn't worry too much about your safety.

The dimensions of a box could fool you. Big ones could be filled with pillows; small ones could be packed with steel bolts. One day a brown cardboard box about the size of a toaster landed near my foot. I tried to lift it but it wouldn't budge, and kicking it didn't help. I asked my partner for help but he couldn't move the box either. It took both of us to drag it out of the way so we could contend with the flood of other stuff flying at us. When things slowed down I kicked the box again. Tiny brass nozzles started oozing from its bottom. I pointed this out to my co-loader, who kicked the leaking corner, forcing more brass nozzles to spill out. "Somebody's not gonna get what they bargained for," I said. "Yeah," he answered, "but that ain't our problem."

I often found myself loading the forty-footer bound for Escanaba, Michigan. I liked that name, "Escanaba." It sounded like a Native American word. Someone told me that Escanaba was in the U.P., which means the upper peninsula of Michigan. That night I checked an atlas at home to get a mental picture of this locale. Ah, there it was – way up there on Lake Superior. I imagined lumberjacks, Indian maidens, brown bears and tuna-sized salmon. Loading the Escanaba trailer the next day, I wondered what could be in the boxes bound for those hardy Escanabians.

Know-how and work ethic varied greatly from one loader to another. Some of them had a knack for making boxes fit neatly together with bricklayer precision. Other loaders seemed to have no sense of order. One character I worked with had a small square hole to fill and couldn't find anything to fit into it. Then he spotted a long skinny box containing fluorescent tubes. He broke it over his knee and stuffed it into the hole. Sometimes, at the start of my shift, I was greeted by a flat wall of neatly stacked boxes standing at the midpoint of the trailer, making it look half filled. In reality this meant that the loaders on the previous shift were loafers. Pushing on that wall made it topple, revealing a big mess of items scattered all over the floor. Ha-ha! Some people really worked hard to slack off. I would have laughed at this prank if it hadn't made extra work for me. Truth is, it helped to have a sense of humor at UPS. Every other day someone was taking up a collection for a worker who got hurt and had to go to the hospital. Truck loaders came and went fast. I rarely had the same partner two days in a row. And not knowing my co-loaders from Adam made me nervous. Some guys were careful and some were reckless, so I kept my eyes open.

The work at UPS was so exhausting that we were only allowed to work four-hour shifts. After the first two hours we'd get a 12-minute lunch/bathroom break. Everyone hurried to the lunchroom, which was a good half block from the dock. I hit the john first, then went into the lunchroom, injected a hotdog into my throat and washed it down with a carton of milk. Time to get back to the truck bound for Escanaba. After my first day of loading trucks I staggered to my car and slipped the key into the ignition. My ears were hot and my head felt numb. My arms ached. I was so exhausted and dazed that I sat staring at the dashboard for ten minutes before I could summon enough energy to turn the key. After two months on the job, however, my body strength was much improved. I was in great physical shape as I returned to Loyola to take the last few courses I'd need to graduate in January. Jobs like loading trucks and boxcars and working in factories made me glad that I was also working toward a college degree.

FOUR

STAY WITH IT

*"Push yourself because no one else
is going to do it for you."*
– Dr. Bohdi Sanders

Small world

SECOND-SEMESTER SOPHOMORE PRE-MEDS WERE SUPPOSED to take comparative anatomy. It was a tough course; there were hundreds (maybe thousands) of structures to memorize. But by the time I tried to register for that class all the sections had been filled. Standing at the registration counter with a long line of anxious kids behind me, I felt pressured to make up my mind. Scrambling, I found a zoology class that fit into my schedule – histology, the study of different organs, tissues and cells. It was a graduate-level course, but I signed up for it anyway. Dr. L, who taught this class, was a tall, humorless lady in her mid-thirties who lectured at a clip that cramped my fingers. Most of the students in this class were seniors; some had already been accepted into med school.

In the lab we looked at blood cells, skin cells, cells in the heart, liver, kidney, etc. The names for some of them were hilarious. *Polychromatophil erythroblast*, the name for a developing red blood cell, was my favorite. We viewed cells using "oil immersion." This involved squeezing a drop of oil onto the glass slide under the scope and lowering the highest power lens right into it. We had to use the fine focus and be careful, but the world we entered was fascinating.

With four students per lab table, my partner turned out to be president of the biological society on campus. I couldn't believe my luck. Too bad he dropped the course after two weeks. Being abandoned like that was daunting, but the two seniors on the other side of the table took me under their wings. Each of us was issued a box of about 100 slides. Studying them was tedious and demanding, but there were lively moments when one of us found something that showed up with eye-popping clarity. When I showed my pituitary cells to Alexandria, who sat across from me, she was completely blown away. She called the lab instructor over to look at them. He, in turn, invited the whole class to view them. What rave reviews: "Wow, look at that color!" "Great definition!" A few weeks later my testicle cells looked just as sharp, but I decided to keep them under wraps.

The open book incident

One day our lab assistant, Mr. Spurgeon, dimmed the lights and gave us a slide show quiz. A few kids scooted up to my table for a better view. One of them opened a textbook and stretched a gooseneck lamp over it to spread some light. After a few questions, Spurgeon noticed the lamp. He darted to our table and shut the book, which turned out to be *my* book! He demanded to know who its owner was. I admitted that it was mine, feeling that I'd been framed. With a few well-chosen words he brought the quiz to a halt. I tried to explain things, but he was in no mood to listen. A week later I pleaded my case to him again, hoping he'd cooled off. He told me not to sweat it.

Going the extra micron

Later in the semester, a senior at the next lab table told me that the microbiology lab downstairs was available on Saturdays for our use. He planned to sign out his histology slides for the weekend and hit the micro lab. Surprised to learn that we could borrow our slides, I decided to try it. A little nervous, I signed out my box on Friday afternoon. It had to be back by 8 a.m. Monday morning. I figured that our prof's penalty for failure to meet this deadline would be an F for the course. That lady scared me.

Saturday morning I rode the El up to Loyola with my box of fragile slides balanced on my lap. As I exited the station the sidewalk looked blank and lifeless. I was the lone commuter crossing Sheridan Road. Then three guys emerged from beneath the El tracks viaduct laughing and joking. *Were these guys out all night?* I wondered. As they came closer, I recognized one of them – Eddie Manske, who played on Loyola's basketball team. I knew him from Leo High School, where he played B-ball for four years and was varsity captain as a senior. In passing, Eddie waved and advised me that heading to school on the weekend is working too hard – a statement I couldn't disagree with.

Entering the campus, I hiked to Cudahy Hall and went downstairs to the micro lab. The sun's morning rays cut sharply through the ground-level windows. I removed a slide from my box and placed it onto one of the microscopes. A few minutes later the guy from my class showed up. We decided to pool our resources by using our slides and all the scopes in the lab to give each other practice tests. I tried to identify structures on his slides; he tried to name them on mine. Peering into scope after scope we both found things that we hadn't seen before. It was a good drill. I left the lab late in the afternoon feeling that I'd accomplished something. At Cindy Sue's Pancake House beneath the elevated tracks I ordered a cheeseburger to fortify myself for the trek back to the South Side. Early Monday morning I returned my slides to the biology department, relieved that I'd brought them back on time and intact.

Save souls or kill trees

Discouraged about my pre-med progress, I thought about the mandatory, once-a-week orientation sessions I'd attended as a freshman. We first-year students took perception tests like the Rorschach Inkblot Test.

Another exercise involved looking at drawings and writing down our impressions. One showed a young woman sitting in a chair and staring into space. She looked lost and lonely, as if she might be recalling happier times. That's the way I felt in junior year. By then I was adrift in the wrong program, treading water and wasting my time.

Seeking advice about what direction to take, I made an appointment to see a student counselor. He looked pretty young to be proffering advice, but I told him that I was flunking chemistry and trigonometry and in need of direction. He gave me a battery of tests that included the Strong Vocational Test and the Kuder Preference Test. I waited in his office while he went off to evaluate my efforts. He returned a short time later with the results: I might make a good lumberjack or clergyman. "Are you joking?" I gasped in disbelief. There was no way in hell I'd ever be a churchman or a guy who chops down healthy trees. I asked if he could offer me any alternatives.

Looking a bit nonplussed, he picked up a manual from his desktop. As he thumbed through it, I told him about some of my interests – photography, playing the harmonica, woodcarving, etc. Glancing up at me, he suggested that I might want to look into pharmacology. "What's that?" I asked. He read the definition from his manual. It turned out to be the science dealing with the uses of drugs and their effects on people. It was obvious that he had never heard the word "pharmacology" before in his life. *This clown doesn't know what he's talking about,* I concluded. Exiting his office I felt more depressed and disillusioned than ever.

At that point I wanted to pick an easy major that I could grasp and stick with until graduation. I told my older sister Joan that I might switch my major to sociology. "Sociology?" she groaned. "That's a dummy major! Why don't you switch to English?" "I'll think about it." I said, heading for the door. I was so embarrassed about switching majors that I didn't want to talk about it. Then I wondered why it had never occurred to me to major in English. I'd done well in my required English classes. Thinking it over, I decided that English Lit would be something I could get a grip on. So halfway through junior year I said goodbye to slide rules, pig embryos, macrophages and tissue stains, like eosin and Janus Green. I thought there had to be a great-looking

blonde somewhere named Janus Green who'd never guess that she was
the perfect stain for mitochondria.

Carpooling to Lake Shore

When I started my junior year at Loyola I drove my car up to the Lake
Shore campus a couple of days a week. I'd pick up John Kerrigan, Jim
Hay and Phil Carollo – all neighborhood Leo High School grads who
took the El to school on most days. They were lively talkers whose
conversations covered everything from sports to politics to who was the
best-looking babe on campus. John had a good fix on the international
scene and a quick wit that made me laugh out loud. Jim joked about
Art Buchwald's column in the morning *Sun-Times*. And Phil was always
eager contribute his two cents' worth on any topic. On a few winter
mornings Ed Russell joined our merry band. He was on Loyola's cross-
country team and had been a great long-distance runner at Leo.

"Hey, Murph! Turn on the radio!" I'd hear from the back seat. Every
station on the dial was AM – WIND at 560, WLS at 890, WCFL at
1000, WJJD at 1160…. Clark Weber, morning man at WIND, played
"Surfin' USA," "He's So Fine," and the Beatles' "She Loves You." The
Lads from Liverpool were on a roll with one hit after another – "Can't
Buy Me Love," "I Saw Her Standing There," "A Hard Day's Night"…. On
some mornings we listened to *The Adventures of Chickenman* on WCFL.
This fanciful character was billed as "the most fantastic crime fighter
the world has ever known!" During the week Chickenman was mild-
mannered shoe salesman, Benton Harbor. But on weekends, donning a
chicken suit, he continued his crusade to "fight crime and/or evil." Dick
Orkin, who produced the series, turned out nearly 300 episodes.

The treacherous "S-curve"

As the days grew colder and foul weather snarled up Lake Shore Drive,
I drove north in the morning with my carpoolers, wondering what
fresh hell awaited us on the infamous "S-curve" at Grand Avenue.

Joining the crawling caravan of vehicles I had to stay alert to negotiate this serpentine road hazard. While pumping my brakes lightly one morning to stay a safe distance from the car in front of me, I went into a 360° spin and miraculously wound up pointed in the right direction and without a scratch! As winter wore on, my riders and I saw dozens of cars lose control on that crazy curve, including one that did a *double* full-circle spin in front of us. Incredibly, it wound up facing straight ahead and without any damage! Once we'd made it past Grand Avenue the worst was over. If we reached Loyola early enough we might find a space in the undersized parking lot. But we usually had to park on the grass between the gym and the cinder track. Disembarking, we went our separate ways. Some of the group, those with late-afternoon classes, might have to take the CTA home. The next morning I'd ride the El to school and possibly run into one of my carpoolers.

"Didn't you see us?"

Driving through the Rush Street area on my way home from Loyola Lake Shore I felt sad and lonely. I can't recall why I was taking this convoluted route. Ordinarily I'd take Lake Shore Drive to the Dan Ryan and bypass the whole downtown area. I was heading south on McClurg Court as I reached Ohio Street. Uh oh! I blew the stoplight. WHAM! A car slammed into my Rambler, crumpling the right front fender. *Oh boy!* I got out to survey the damage. The folks from the other car – a middle aged man and his teenage son – were standing on the street shaking their heads ruefully.

"Didn't you see the stoplight?" the father shouted at me. I remained mute, absorbing the gravity of the situation. The son was beside himself with grief. Looking from his dad to their wrecked vehicle, he lamented, "We spent years restoring that car!" The Chicago police soon arrived and asked lots of questions. Still in a daze, I surrendered my license. An officer told me I'd have to go to the police station. I gathered my schoolbooks and climbed into the back seat of the squad car. We drove to the station, where I had to remove everything from my pockets. The officer on duty escorted me to a cell, which was small and dark. He said I'd have to stay there till someone contacted my parents and one of them came to secure my release. The steel door clanked shut with a slight echo, just like in the movies.

Sitting on a cot in that dingy little cell, I felt strangely calm. *All of this is out of my hands,* I thought. In this reflective state of mind I picked up a book I'd purchased for a difficult philosophy course I was required to take: Kant's *Critique of Practical Reason.* I opened it and started reading. It was amazing – the difficult text was almost making sense to me. From another room I heard the voices of two policemen who were obviously going through my coat pockets. "Look at this – the kid was carrying a rosary!" "And he's got some pills here – maybe he's sickly," a second voice added. "I better check to see if he should take one of these." An officer soon appeared outside my cell, asking me if I needed to take a pill. I explained that I was okay for the rest of the day. He offered me a bologna sandwich, which I gratefully accepted. Then he told me that my dad had been contacted and was on his way to get me. Waiting for him, I munched on the sandwich. Its crunchy crust was delightful. I went back to reading Kant. The policemen's voices mingling with the flavor of bologna made his *Categorical Imperative* easier to digest. After an hour or so, Dad arrived and sprung me. On the way home he asked me why I was driving through the Rush Street area and what made me blow a stoplight. My answer to both questions was a dreary "I dunno." I clammed up for the rest of the ride, wondering what the damages to my car would cost and what I'd tell my friends who were counting on me for a ride to school the next morning.

The only sadder day during college was November 22, 1963, when John F. Kennedy was assassinated. I was at Loyola walking from one lecture hall to another when alarmed voices behind me nearly stopped me in my tracks: "Assassinated! The president was assassinated!" "What? Oh my God! I don't believe it!" I heard "Dallas" and "motorcade." Slowing my pace, I let the group catch up to me. "Is it true?" I asked. "Yeah, Kennedy was shot in the head! They took him to the hospital but he died." Stunned, I stopped and looked at the flag flying above the athletic field. I jogged toward it, intending to lower it to half-staff.

A couple of other guys had the same thought. Without saying a word to one another, we pulled the cord until the flag was halfway down the pole and secured it. That day is stamped indelibly into the memory of every American who was old enough to understand right from wrong. Each one of us remembers where we were, whom we were with and what we were doing when we got the news. Thanksgiving Day, five days later, was a pretty somber affair at home.

Midnight madness

By junior year I was doing most of my studying at Loyola. The libraries at both campuses were quiet and distraction-free unless a good-looking coed was sitting nearby and facing me. I figured that undisturbed hours studying at school would pay off on my report card. On some nights, especially ones before final exams, I'd stay until closing time, 10 p.m., sometimes cramming for three tests. Finals were a logistical nightmare. At Lake Shore campus or downtown, they were always scheduled too close together. It seemed unfair at the time, and looking back it *was* unfair. One night when I was a junior and my brother Dan was a freshman, we crammed together at the kitchen table, popping No-Doze tablets to stay awake. I said goodnight to Dan at three a.m. and grabbed a few hours of sleep before my 8 a.m. exam. I was on the train at seven, studying all the way to school. Finishing my last final felt like getting out of prison. Midyear semester break was a welcome vacation; time to goof off – take some pictures, play the harmonica, browse the hardware store…. During the break in my junior year I played with my new camera, taking close-up shots of glass blobs and abstract plastic shapes strewn across a stretch of sand I'd poured onto the Ping-Pong table. Very soothing.

FIVE

DON'T LET UP NOW

"I could have been a Rhodes Scholar except for my grades."
– Duffy Daugherty, Michigan State football coach, 1954-1977

CHANGING MAJORS AND CRAMMING A ton of English Lit courses into a few semesters was daunting. And having to study for the comprehensive exam added to the fun. At Loyola in the sixties, we seniors had to pass this monster test covering all the required courses in our major. What's more, the reading material for English comps included a lengthy list of works by American and European authors, plus writings going back to Euripides and Plato. This single test would determine whether or not we'd graduate.

The day of my comprehensive exam was a doozy. It was late November, near the end of the extra semester I'd tacked onto my college career. A torrent of facts blasted through my brain as I drove to school in the morning: the titles of novels and poems, essays and plays, the names of authors and their works.... Pulling into the campus at 7:30 a.m., I was surprised to find a space in the regular parking lot. *A good omen?* With no books to carry I felt naked. Hopefully, six months of study had packed my brain cells with enough of the right stuff to pass this grueling test. I exited my car and paused, sensing that I'd forgotten to check something. *But what?* Nothing came to mind, so I walked over to Dumbach Hall.

My brain was boiling with esoteric details about literature from the time of *Beowulf* to the end of the Victorian era: *The Canterbury Tales, Paradise Lost, The Pilgrim's Progress* ... poets aplenty – Donne, Pope, Swift and Dryden ...Tennyson and Browning ... English novels galore: *Tom Jones, Vanity Fair, Pride and Prejudice* ... plays by Shakespeare, Marlowe, Goldsmith and Sheridan ... American authors from Cotton Mather to Herman Melville ... *Moby Dick, The Scarlet Letter, Portrait of a Lady*.... And there was all that stuff on the reading list: Greek tragedies, works by Racine, Ibsen and Dostoyevsky ... contemporary authors – E. M. Forster, Evelyn Waugh and others ... the list just wouldn't quit.

Zero hour was at hand. Pass and graduate. Fail and wait another semester to take the comps again. I located the correct room and took a seat among my fellow comps takers. They were all complete strangers. Searching my shirt pocket for a ballpoint, I found nothing. I tried my pants pockets. No luck there either. *Oh boy!* There had to be one in my coat pocket. But there wasn't. *You dumb shit!* I cursed to myself. *You go to take your comps and you don't bring a pen?* Embarrassed as hell, I asked the guy sitting across from me if he could lend me a pen. "What the hell," he said, "You go to take your comps and you don't bring a pen?" Looking annoyed, he handed me a cheap Bic ballpoint. *Good enough if it doesn't run dry*, I thought.

Our proctor handed each of us the weighty test (eight or ten pages thick). We were given two hours to complete it. When time was up my head was spinning. Driving home I felt completely spent, the way I'd felt the previous summer after loading a 40-foot trailer for UPS. I walked to my car and opened the door. Aha! Lodged between the seat and the seat back and protruding pointedly were three ballpoints. I must have stuffed them into my back pocket before leaving home. My brain was stuck in neutral as I headed south, figuring that my chances of success on the test were about 50/50. A week or two later I was relieved to learn that I had passed my comps – one of nine English majors out of 23 who had succeeded.

More memorable teachers

Dr. Martin Svaglic was a classy prof with a witty but friendly sense of humor. I signed up for his class in Romantic literature on a recommendation from my friend, John Kerrigan, who said Svaglic's lectures were terrific. John was right. Listening to that man talk was captivating. His tests, however, were probing and exhausting; I wished there were more time to write my answers. I remember how disappointed Svaglic was when the class performed poorly on a big test. Thoroughly flummoxed, he asked us for the cause of our weak grasp of the material. Was it sex? Booze? Drugs? He seemed genuinely hurt, like a frustrated parent. I felt ashamed of myself and was eager to redeem myself on the next test. Svaglic was an authority on the nineteenth-century Oxford Movement in English literature. He taught at Loyola from the late 1940s until his retirement in 1983. On his death, in 1988, he left a generous bequest to Loyola that funds undergraduate scholarships in the humanities. Svaglic was first class all the way.

My best college grades were in Español. Mr. Ortíz, my first Spanish teacher, was a slightly built Jesuit novitiate from Spain. His diminutive stature belied his remarkable energy. Ortíz taught with missionary zeal, grilling students with pointed questions. Despite his pronounced accent, he got his message across loud and clear. Ortíz taught Castilian Spanish, a dialect in which the "s" sound is pronounced as "th," as if you had a lisp. At the end of the semester he threw a party for the class. This thoughtful gesture produced a memorable event. I took Eileen, the girl I was crazy in love with.

My second course in Spanish got off to a sputtering start. Our teacher, Miss D, was a tall blonde in her late twenties. This lady's deep tan was almost brown. She always showed up for class late, carrying a rolled-up towel, like she was on her way to or from the beach (which was a stone's throw from campus). Pleasant but preoccupied, Miss D was allergic to teaching and determined to keep her classes under 15 minutes. She reviewed our homework assignments at warp speed, took a few questions and then took off. This routine lasted only a couple of weeks, however, when she was replaced by an actual teacher. Word had apparently reached the dean's office about her accelerated teaching style. Miss D was suddenly free to enjoy more fun in the sun. I pictured her lying on the beach clad in a bikini and oversized sunglasses, her bronzed body coated with glistening suntan oil. Hasta la vista, baby.

Our class was taken over by Mr. Martín, another Jesuit novitiate from Spain. He was taller and more relaxed than Mr. Ortíz, my first-semester Spanish teacher. Martín had a warm, friendly sense of humor that put the class at ease. He happened to be teaching my brother Dan and me during the same semester, but on different campuses. This situation prompted some good-natured kidding about which brother was doing the homework assignments. Truth is, Dan occasionally bribed me to translate the stories we were studying.

Marcel Fredericks was a tall, gaunt gent with a mysterious accent. I took his sociology class in my junior year. He looked like a stretched Omar Sharif, which made me think he was from the Middle East. I soon learned, however, that he was born in British Guiana. His lectures were interesting, but they often covered material that wasn't in our textbook. Fredericks put books on reserve at the library for us to consult. They were filled with terms like *secularization, exogamy, entrée* and *rapport*. When he asked the class a question about biology one day, I responded with the correct answer. Encouraged by this, he asked me to write out the Krebs Citric Acid Cycle on the backboard. I told him that I didn't even know what it was. Doctor Fredericks is now a Professor Emeritus, after teaching for 50 years at Loyola.

And there was Miss Orloski, my algebra teacher, a sweet young thing and very cute. Luckily for me, this girl was blessed with the patience of Job. She tutored me all the way through her class and generously awarded my efforts with a C. I really wanted to take her out when the semester was over, but didn't have the nerve to ask. She was probably two or three years older than me, which dampened my spirits. That age difference made her seem like my big sister.

BS I love you

I graduated from Loyola in January of 1966. Commencement exercises were held on a gray, bitter-cold Sunday afternoon at McCormick Place, the mammoth convention center on Chicago's lakefront. And much to my delight, Dad was going to be there. It was the only one of my graduations he was free to attend; Dad finally had a job that didn't demand much overtime. Anyway, this graduation was the one that really counted.

With Mom and me on board, Dad piloted his aging Ford north on the Dan Ryan Expressway and east to the lakefront. We pulled into a parking lot the size of Kazakhstan and found a spot about two blocks from the building. I felt bad watching my elderly parents fight their way through a driving wind toward the entrance. Mom shut her eyes against the arctic blast and Dad limped, favoring the leg he'd broken decades earlier on a construction job. Once inside the massive structure, we hiked another two blocks to the auditorium. The ceremony seemed to drag on for an eternity. Department heads were dressed in multi-colored robes that, no doubt, had some arcane academic meaning. They looked like guests at a geriatric Halloween party; I couldn't keep from laughing. The sluggish proceedings soon put me to sleep, so I missed some of the lofty sentiments that had been crafted to give me a rousing sendoff. When I finally got my diploma, it was a dummy – a big white envelope stuffed with a cardboard insert. (The authentic sheepskin would come later.) Another surprise was having to surrender my tassel or pay cash for it on the spot. Dad gave me the two or three bucks I needed. The official degree arrived at my folks' house a few weeks later via the US mail.

But seriously...

I wonder how colleges decide on the courses kids *have* to take. As a freshman premed I *had* to take zoology, algebra, rhetoric, logic, history and theology. My logic teacher, Father Ford, taught symbolic logic from a tiny text smaller than a toddler's Golden Book. But it was packed with hair-tearing problems without the slightest suggestion of how to solve them. It amazed me that such a miniscule volume could demand so much time and gut-wrenching effort. Venn diagrams, syllogisms, tautologies, Boolean expressions ... the fun just kept coming. That course was like a second math class, and I already had my hands full with algebra. Passing symbolic logic took up about a fourth of my study time, and I had five other classes that needed attention. I got through the course, but any improvement in my logical thinking came at the expense of my other studies. Maybe some of the courses listed below would have left me better prepared for the real world. In fact, today's graduating seniors (even the most cyber-wise and tech-savvy of them) might have a better chance of success with a few of these classes under their belts.

Required	Elective
Freshman year	**Freshman year**
Spelling	Using the library
Writing in words and sentences	Cursive writing
Sophomore year	**Sophomore year**
Writing a letter	Getting organized
Single tasking	Corporate jargon
Junior year	**Junior year**
Making presentations	Conducting a meeting
Self-promotion	Dealing with difficult people
Senior year	**Senior year**
Creating a résumé	Basic office politics
Interviewing techniques	Street smarts

SIX

WHAT NEXT?

"The future isn't what it used to be."
— Robert Graves

NOT GOING TO SCHOOL TOOK some getting used to. I didn't have to get up early, scarf down my breakfast and dash off to catch a bus. The freezing winter weather gave me little incentive to venture outside. But my brain kept churning. Thinking about all the English majors who flunked their comps gave me survivor's guilt. I thought about the scores of questions on the Graduate Record Exam that left me clueless. That long, computer-scored test covered a vast, deep ocean of reading that I hadn't dipped my toes into – Greek myths, French poets, German novelists…. It didn't count for anything in my life, but as a graduating senior I had to take it. The exhaustive exam left me feeling stupid and obligated to learn more about classic literature and mythology.

So now, with plenty of free time and no classes to attend, I started visiting the Mount Greenwood library on 110th & Kedzie, where I read *Masterplots* of novels and plays. But after a couple of weeks of reading outlines and plot summaries I felt like an intellectual phony. It was time to return to Earth and find a job. I checked with the Board of Education about becoming a substitute teacher in the Chicago Public School system. To be eligible I had to sign up for some education classes, so I registered for correspondence courses at Loyola, figuring I'd complete the lessons in my spare time. The Board of Ed hired me as a substitute teacher at the elementary level, issuing me a book of tickets to bring with me to school. Each ticket represented one day's work. On my first morning as a sub I presented the book to a lady in the principal's office, expecting her to tear off one ticket and hand the book back to me. Instead, she kept it, saying she'd return it to me on Friday. Hey, I'd locked in a week's worth of work. Not bad for starters.

Arriving at my classroom, I was greeted by a noisy bunch of fourth graders milling about in the aisles. With their regular teacher out, they were expecting a picnic. Pointing, shouting and gesturing, I managed to get everyone seated. Then there were questions: "Where's Miss Cassidy today?" "When is she coming back?" "Can we watch a movie?" I asked the kids what subjects their teacher covered in the morning. The volley of answers left me confounded. "How about English?" I asked. "We don't have English!" an oversized Latino boy reported. "How about reading?" "We don't have that either!" he shot back at me. "Spelling? Do you have spelling?" "All that stuff is language arts!" volunteered a girl with blonde pigtails. I took a book from the shelf near the window and started reading. This had a quieting effect so I stayed with it. One of the boys stood and said he had to go to "assembly." I had no idea of what assembly was; the word was never used in the Catholic grammar school I attended. I asked him what he did at assembly. "Rehearse," he answered. "Rehearse what?" I pleaded. "Rehearse for assembly!" We were like Abbot and Costello doing *Who's on First?* I soon learned that there was always a big "assembly" show coming up in the auditorium that certain kids were always rehearsing for. They seemed like a troupe of professional entertainers.

Welcome back!

A few weeks later, my sister Joan and her baby girl came to live with us while her husband, a young M.D., was going through Army basic training in Georgia. Joan was a certified elementary school teacher with experience in the Chicago Public School system. She applied at the Board of Ed and was soon substitute teaching like me. I was driving to work one morning with Joan as my passenger. My plan was to drop her off at her assigned school and continue on to mine. The car ahead of me stopped quickly. I slammed on my brakes. KATHUNK! The car behind me slammed into me. I plowed into the car ahead of me. Joan was thrown into the dash; my chest hit the steering wheel hard.

A lady got out of the car in front of us, which had sustained some rear-end damage. She was waving her hands frantically and ranting about her baby. I thought there must be an injured infant in her car. The driver behind me got a crumpled grille and buckled hood out of the encounter. My Rambler was crunched front and rear. The police were soon on the scene. An officer directed all three cars over to the curb, issuing a ticket to the accident's prime mover. The hysterical woman kept carrying on about her baby, which was nowhere to be seen. As it turned out, she was a few months pregnant. After everyone exchanged insurance information, Joan and I crawled home in my doubly dinged car. Two Chicago schools had to find substitutes for their substitutes that day. *Things could have been worse,* I thought. *At least all the drivers have insurance.*

The next day, I got a phone call informing me that everyone was insured except me! *What?* It turned out that my coverage had expired two weeks earlier. *Oh no!* At that point things got complicated fast. The woman whose car I'd hit was holding me liable for possible damage to her unborn child. Before I could even buy more auto insurance I had to purchase a surety bond that cost me $500! Money borrowed from Dad got me back on the road. And since I was working, I was able to pay him back soon. Getting a weekly check from the Board of Ed was great, but I didn't enjoy subbing and the job didn't involve any writing. *I should be writer,* I kept telling myself. *I don't know many guys who wrote all their own papers all the way through college like I did!*

Bygone Boulevard

One day I was assigned to Park Manor School on the East Side, where my family had lived until 1951. It was fun to drive along Garfield Boulevard through the Grand Crossing area. I remembered scooting across that broad-shouldered thoroughfare with my brother Jack 20 years earlier when I was a young kid. I recognized the broad lanes and the big viaduct we used to burrow into. What happy memories! At school I was assigned to an eighth grade classroom that was really a recreation room – very large with a linoleum floor, an accordion room divider and movable student desks.

Things went well in the morning, but a different group of kids showed up after lunch. Michael was one of them. I remember him because he had unusual eyes: one was blue and one was brown. He was one of the more animated kids in the group. I spotted a projector and put on an educational film to calm the class down. It took a bit of work, but I threaded the Bell & Howell machine and got it rolling. After a few minutes the screen went white and we lost sound. I flicked on the room lights to see what had happened. The film was spewing onto the floor. Somebody had yanked it out of the projector. I trimmed the film with a scissors, retreaded it into the projector and switched it on, keeping an eye on the film feeding into the take-up reel. In less than a minute, the screen went white again and film was slithering across the linoleum. So much for the movie. I switched on the room lights and rolled the projector into a closet.

I told the kids to turn their chairs to face me. But Michael and one of the girls didn't hear me. Standing on opposite sides of the open floor, they were shouting at each other. The girl accused Michael of spoiling the movie for everyone. He came back with denials and nasty cuss words. "At least my mother ain't livin' with no other man!" the girl screamed. Michael started toward her. She picked up a chair and hurled it at him. He ducked. She charged, knocking him flat on his back. In a flash she was sitting astride his chest choking him. A volley of filthy expletives erupted from her mouth as she bounced his head off the floor. All this happened in seconds! I rushed in to break things up, followed by the whole class. A couple of strong boys helped me separate the combatants. I sent them to the office as the period ended. *Saved by the bell!* Driving home that afternoon I pondered the fresh memories of Park Manor I'd just acquired. They were just as unforgettable as my older ones, but not nearly as pleasant.

Whacha readin' kid?

At another South Side school I started my Monday with an eighth grade class. I was working on a math problem at the blackboard and glanced over my shoulder to see if everyone was paying attention. Spotting a kid way in back with his nose in a book, I questioned him about the problem on the board. His clueless answer prompted me to see what was diverting his attention. As I approached, he stuffed something into his desk. I asked to see what it was. After a long pause he handed it over. To my surprise it was a four-color "girlie" magazine. *Where would a kid his age get something like this?* I wondered, dropping it into a deep drawer in my desk. When he stood up at the end of class I was amazed at his size; he was over six feet tall and had to weigh at least 200 pounds. Then, after school let out, I flipped through the magazine. *Vavoom!* Exiting the rear of the building, I tossed it into a dumpster in the alley.

Monday morning it looked like I'd have the same classroom all week, but on Tuesday I was assigned to a different room. On my way there I ran into that hulking kid in the hall. He asked me what I'd done with his magazine. *Uh-oh!* I said it was in a safe place and kept moving, thinking that this was just a chance encounter. I'd probably never see the boy again. But that's not the way things worked out. Exiting my car on Wednesday morning, I encountered the huge man-boy again. Just like the day before, he asked me what I'd done with his magazine. This was getting downright scary. I tried to wave him off but he caught up with me and said he wanted his magazine back. I walked faster, entered the school and made a beeline to the principal's office, where I got in line behind half a dozen folks. When my turn came I asked for my book of vouchers, explaining that I wouldn't be available for the rest of the week. Opening the office door, I looked left and right. The kid was nowhere in sight. I made a quick dash to my classroom.

My stint as a substitute teacher was full of little surprises like this that exposed my immaturity and lack of experience. At another public school I got into a verbal sparring match with an eighth-grade boy, who kept making smartass comments. Unable to shut him up, I walked to his desk and slapped him across the face with a paperback novel. He sprung from his seat and stomped toward the door. "Your ass has had it, Jack!" he shouted, exiting the room. A few minutes later a lady from the principal's office appeared on the scene and informed me that I was being transferred to a different school, and should go to the office for directions. Things like this were happening too often, but I stuck with subbing until the school year ended. Over the summer I collected my thoughts and started looking for a writing job.

The quality goes in before the name goes on

In mid-June a downtown employment agency sent me on an interview to Sunbeam Corporation in Cicero. I drove out to their headquarters way west on Roosevelt Road. One sprawling building housed offices and a huge manufacturing facility that produced irons, toasters, hair dryers, can openers, lawn mowers and dozens of other products. All my life I'd heard their corporate mantra: *The quality goes in before the name goes on.* The receptionist in the main lobby directed me to an office area across the hall. The huge open space was filled with secretaries and other clerical workers. Offices lining the perimeter were plywood cubbies topped with three feet of frosted glass. A young secretary escorted me to the office of Don McClair, head of internal communications. In his early thirties and balding, McClair struck me as an honest, hard-working guy.

He asked me about my writing experience. I told him that aside from papers I'd done for classes in college, I didn't have any. This didn't seem to bother him. Then he explained that he was responsible for turning out a weekly newsletter and a monthly newspaper, *News and Views.* These were the main things I'd be helping him with if I were hired. He also said that the newspaper work would involve shooting some photos. I told him that I loved taking pictures and had studied photography at Ray-Vogue in Chicago. McClair then ran through some other aspects of the job. I assured him that the position sounded like a terrific opportunity. "If you really want the job," he concluded, "tell me in a letter." I left Sunbeam feeling excited and a bit nervous.

I phoned my employment guru downtown and told him about the letter. He said I should type it up and bring it to his office the next morning so he could look at it before I mailed it. It slipped my mind that I'd promised to drive Fran Kelly, a college friend, to a downtown restaurant that night. He needed to make arrangements for an upcoming frat party. I figured there was time enough to run that errand and then go home and write the letter. As I drove Fran back to his apartment in Roseland, he suggested that we work on the letter together. I wasn't nuts about that idea, but in the spirit of fraternity I said, "OK."

Fran sat me down at a card table in his living room and plopped a portable typewriter on it. "Take a crack at that letter and then we'll look at it together," he said confidently. I typed a few soulful lines about the dignity of work and how important a job was to a person's self esteem. Kelly looked over my shoulder and laughed. "Lighten up man," he said. "They're not looking for a philosopher." His crass reaction to my efforts was a bit disheartening, but I perked up and tried a less formal approach. Kelly didn't like my second letter either. While he made phone calls trying to set up his frat rally, I typed letter after letter. It got so late that Kelly invited me to sleep on the couch. He hit the sack around two. I typed letters for another hour or so before stretching out on the couch. Waking up at daybreak, I folded my favorite version of the letter and exited. Fran was still asleep. I had to get home, suit up and get downtown to the employment agency.

At 9 a.m. I handed the crucial letter to my counselor. He read it quickly and looked at me blankly. "Hang on a sec," he said, exiting the office. A few moments later he was back with a different letter. "Read this," he said, handing it to me. "This is the letter you need to land that job at Sunbeam." I looked at the letter. It sounded very crisp, to the point and businesslike. "This looks great," I told him, "but I didn't write it." Smiling, he advised me to use it as a guide. "You can customize a bit, but not too much." He said. I sat down, made a few edits and handed the letter back to my job coach. "Spot on," he said. "I'll get this clean typed and send it out to Sunbeam by messenger."

I phoned McClair the next morning. He said he liked my letter and wanted to talk to me again. After lunch I drove out to Cicero for a second interview. Don and I chatted for a half hour or so and, to my delight, he offered me a job. I accepted with glee. Wow, I was a writer! Well, at least I had that title. Come Monday morning I punched into work at 8 a.m. McClair said I should call him "Don," and I was happy to comply. He put me to work on the company newsletter, gathering facts from different departments throughout the plant. The subject matter ranged from assembly line improvements to employee contests and anniversaries. To help me get a feel for the plant, Don arranged for me to put in a couple of hours on an assembly line, using a power tool to drive screws into plastic hair dryer handles. Dropping screws and getting them stuck halfway into the handles, I didn't show much promise as an assembler. It felt good to get back to the manual typewriter in my office.

All in a day's work

Inside our modest cubby Don and I pecked away at our manual typewriters. Like me, he had never taken a class in typing, but he was remarkably fast and accurate. I thought if Don could teach himself, so could I. We kept cranking out the work; the only thing that slowed us down was the approval process. A mock-up of the newspaper was routed to department heads and other corporate biggies. If it didn't come back to us in a week, it was time to make phone calls or do some legwork to keep it moving.

It bothered Don that I rarely got up and left our cube. "You have to walk around and talk to people more," he insisted. In particular, Don kept pressing me to talk to the shy young secretary named Sharon who sat in the bullpen outside our office. She was sweet and pretty, but the effect that Don's goading had on me was the opposite of what he intended. I said as little as possible to her. Without all McClair's prodding, I probably would have asked her out. I felt that if I dated her Don would broadcast it all over the office. He liked to recall his salad days when he was a Young Turk on the prowl. "I don't feel that I missed out on a thing," he boasted. With very little experience in the sexual arena I couldn't add much to the conversation. It bugged Don that I was such a babe in the woods. "We gotta take you out and get you dirtied up a little," he said. Then one Friday after work, when he and some of his office pals were going out for a few brewskies, Don invited me along.

I followed his car to Richard's lounge on Harlem Avenue, a couple of miles west of Sunbeam. Our group sat at a long bar. Directly above it and spanning its entire width was a bigger-than-life painting of a naked lady. Stretched out prone and lazy, she looked downright pudgy and out of shape. One of Don's pals described her as "Rubenesque." I thought that must be a nice word for "fat." The paint glowed iridescent against its black velvet background. At first glance that flabby female left me cold, but after a couple of beers she began to radiate a mature, seductive charm. And she stimulated some spirited conversation; Don's buddies began swapping tales about their amorous adventures in offbeat settings such as stairways, closets, office supply rooms, rooftops and canoes.

One of the guys joked about my Rambler, encouraging me to take advantage of those handy reclining seats. I ordered beer after beer, absorbing the alcohol along with the lively stories. About eight o'clock Don said he'd better hit the road, so our group headed for the parking lot. I was dizzy – way too drunk to drive. I plopped into my Rambler, reclined the driver's seat all the way back and fell asleep. When I woke up darkness had fallen. The clock on my dashboard said three something. *Three in the morning! Mom must have the police out looking for me!* But as my head cleared, I remembered that my car clock had been lapsing in and out of consciousness for weeks. Turning on the radio, I learned that it was only a little after ten. I pulled out onto Harlem Avenue, turned south and headed for home.

Where the hell am I?

Getting around inside the plant was confusing at first – there were so many different areas and aisles. It was easy to take a wrong turn and end up in parts unknown. But getting from department to department was a breeze in one of the electric carts. They were reserved for men in white shirts, and one of them was usually parked at the entrance to the shop floor. Scooting around the plant, I'd roll past banks of punch presses, polishing machines, degreasers and automatic screw machines. Those screw machines were amazing. The set-up men could program them to turn out screws, bolts, bushings, flanges, and fittings, plus an infinite variety of gizmos, doohickeys and thingamabobs. These sweat horses never got a rest. They just kept cranking away.

The monster, 200-ton punch presses were awesome. They could turn a thick slab of aluminum into a fry pan with one punch. WHAM! It's a fry pan! Once in a while I had occasion to visit the die-casting department in a far corner of the plant. That's where the housings for lawn mowers and the sole plates for irons were molded. It was hot and very smelly back there. I feared that a glob of molten metal would somehow squirt out of a machine and land on me. At that time Sunbeam was having quality issues with the sole plates for irons. After they were buffed, they didn't look clean and shiny. Instead, they were pitted, like a tool that had rusted and wouldn't clean up to its original luster. This problem seemed to be driving the die-casting folks nuts.

In retrospect, I can see that I should have put in a few extra hours at Sunbeam to show some enthusiasm for my job. But hanging around at night in a dark, empty office was the last thing from my mind. I'd be safe within Sunbeam's gated confines, but beyond the chain link fence the night scene was pretty seedy. Don jokingly warned me against picking up girls from the neighborhood. At 5 p.m. every day I punched out and headed straight for my folks' house as if I were going home from school. By the end of summer I yearned for some time off from the real world just to sort things out. So I gave my notice at Sunbeam and registered for a couple of night classes in English Lit at Loyola's downtown campus.

As luck would have it, a girl named Eunice (a friend of my brother Dan) was in one of my classes. She had a lively, perky personality and was fun to talk to. Sometimes after class we'd stop at the Interlude Lounge on Rush Street for a cocktail or two. Eunice was a quick study. One night before class she confessed to me that she hadn't read the novel we were going to be quizzed on. I spent a few minutes filling her in on the plot and characters. When our blue books were returned to us a week later, I noticed that Eunice got a higher mark than I did.

SEVEN

BRAND NEW START

*"There are far, far better things ahead
than any we leave behind."*
– C.S. Lewis

THE FALL SEMESTER ENDED IN January and 1967 was off to a nasty start. A long spate of subzero weather was starting to wear on me when some sudden stimulation brightened the scene. The Blizzard of '67 hit Chicago, locking the city into a deep freeze. Cars and buses weren't going anywhere. The sudden change of scene was just what I needed. I grabbed my camera and went outside to shoot pictures. It was slow going as I high-stepped my way through a foot and a half of the white stuff. Cars were stuck in the middle of the street; some were lodged into snow banks at crazy angles. I trekked south on Kedzie toward 111th Street. The bright blue sky and white snow made my eyes ache.

As I approached the busy intersection more and more people came into view. Some were pulling little kids on sleds; others were using their sleds to haul groceries. Everyone seemed happy and carefree despite the paralyzing weather. It looked like blissful chaos. I took shots of everything in sight – cars, snow piles, kids – great fun! None of my subjects complained about having their pictures taken. I walked around snapping photos until I ran out of film. Then I trudged home for a long, hot soak in the tub. Ahh ... I basked in the good, warm feeling of accomplishment, a feeling I hadn't enjoyed for quite a while. Meanwhile, my car sat buried in a snow bank across the street from our house on 107th, thanks to quick work by a Cook County plow. It stayed there for weeks until we got a thaw. Then my brothers helped me dig it out. We charged the battery and drove slowly through puddled streets that hid deep, dark potholes. At Kedzie we took a left and headed north to the Colony Theater on 59th Street. That great, old movie house was screening films like *Lord of the Flies* and *David and Lisa* — old flicks that were new to us. And the one-dollar ticket price was a gift from the past.

Press on

I was pumped to launch an aggressive job hunt, but as it turned out, opportunity was lurking right around the corner. Stretching my legs one morning, I discovered a small employment agency on 111th Street. I interviewed with a dynamic young man who phoned Sears headquarters while I sat beside his desk. He just wouldn't take no for an answer. "Give this guy a job!" he demanded. His commanding performance got me an interview at Sears headquarters. The lady I spoke with was pleasant and direct. She explained the open position and handed me a take-home copywriting test, which I completed and mailed back to Sears.

Trying to stay focused, I got right back to job hunting. A downtown employment outfit sent me up to Minneapolis to interview with Northwest Orient Airlines. They were looking for someone to work in their own personnel department interviewing prospective stewardesses (now known as flight attendants). *Am I dreaming this?* I wondered. Better yet, Northwest was willing to fly me up to the Frozen Apple and back at no charge. Arrangements were made for me to interview the next day. I phoned a Murphy cousin, Marilyn, who lived in Minneapolis, and asked her if I could visit. She assured me that she and her hubby would be delighted to see me, and insisted that I stay at their place overnight.

As I boarded a mid-sized jet at O'Hare, a stewardess mumbled something about "non-rev" as she checked my ticket. Seated in the coach section I felt sophisticated and grown-up. I was excited too — this was my first flight in a jet. On takeoff the kick of those big engines took me by surprise. And the steep angle of ascent was exhilarating. The hop from Chicago to Minneapolis took only 40 minutes or so. With no time to spare, my stewardess served dinner as soon as we leveled off. When I asked her why I hadn't been served she said it was because I was "non-rev." "Non-rev?" I asked. "That means you didn't pay for your ticket." "Oh, sure," I answered, as if I'd known that but it had slipped my mind.

Back on terra firma, I didn't have far to go for my appointment. Northwest Orient's personnel department was right at the Minneapolis airport. I still couldn't believe I was being interviewed for a job interviewing attractive, young females who wanted to go places. Maybe they got résumés from two applicants named Joe Murphy and phoned the wrong one. I was a very young 23 years old with my job experience limited to stocking shelves, loading boxcars and three months of writing at Sunbeam. The closest thing to interviewing I'd ever done was talking to distant relatives at wakes and weddings.

A nice, friendly chat

Within the personnel department I was directed to a tidy office, where a graying middle-aged gent showed me to a chair facing his desk. He looked down at my résumé, then up at me and asked if I had any experience interviewing people. "No." I answered. He didn't seem the least bit surprised. I told him I was amazed that the employment agency in Chicago was able to set me up with this interview. Just as surprised as I was, he started laughing. I couldn't help laughing too. It was like were we were doing a humorous episode of *The Twilight Zone*. Assured that the interview was a total bust, the personnel man asked me what some of my interests were. I mentioned playing the harmonica and taking pictures. Noting that I was from Chicago, he said he's be visiting there soon, and asked me to name a few hot spots. I recommended The Art Institute, the Museum of Natural History and the Shedd Aquarium. I'll bet he thought a wild-and-crazy guy like me was far too jaded to interview wholesome young stewardess applicants. The entire encounter was over in 20 minutes. The kindly interviewer shook my hand and wished me well.

It was suppertime when I cabbed it to my cousin Marilyn's place, which was huge, old and classy. She was married to a lawyer; they had a little boy about a year old. Marilyn arranged for a babysitter and we grownups went out to Shakey's Pizza, a cavernous sing-along place where the lyrics to old-time tunes were projected onto the wall. We ordered a pizza and a pitcher of beer. The loud music made it hard to converse, but by shouting, gesturing and writing on napkins we managed to have a few laughs. Back at Marilyn's place, I adjourned to the guest room and went right to sleep. But before long I was awakened by a scorching heartburn. (I'd forgotten what the beer-and-pizza combination could do to me.) Seeking relief, I stole downstairs to the kitchen, found a box of baking soda and stirred some into a glass of water. One loud belch and the fire in my gut subsided. Then, after a few hours of sleep, I got up, dressed and went downstairs. With hubby already off to work, I played with the baby and chatted with Marilyn before she packed him up for our ride to the airport. When I got home, Mom told me that a lady from Sears had phoned and wanted to hear back from me. I returned her call; she invited me back for a second interview. This time I talked to Vern Frank, a longtime employment manager who specialized in creative folks. He said I'd done well on the writing test and offered me a job as a catalog copywriter. I accepted eagerly, asking nothing about salary or benefits.

Lots to learn

I went to work for Sears in March of '67 at their corporate headquarters on Chicago's West Side. Producing their hefty general catalog (The Big Book) involved hundreds people following cut-and-dried steps that had been set in stone decades earlier. The atmosphere was stodgy; every male employee was required to wear a white shirt and a tie. "Casual Fridays" were light years away. Along with scores of other new hires, I sat through orientation sessions that familiarized us with the corporate culture at Sears. In one of the sessions for new writers, Frank Livermore, the creative head over the entire catalog operation, talked to us about creating well-focused, hard-selling catalog pages. He also touched on the Sears guarantee: "Satisfaction guaranteed or your money back." Frank was a true company man. He had started out as a copywriter at Sears and had risen through the ranks to become the head honcho in cataloging. Livermore struck me as a dedicated, straight-shooting guy. His talk impressed me, although I couldn't imagine pledging my undying loyalty to a big outfit like Sears.

New scribes received basic training from a friendly, middle-aged fellow named Pat Fricano. He made sure we were issued big pads of paper and other supplies we'd need for making rough layouts. These were pencil layouts for two-page spreads that indicated where the artwork, headlines and text should go. Using a clear plastic grid I measured the area it would take to describe an item. Then I drew a block to hold the words (known as "copy" in catalog parlance). Inside the blocks I penciled in the area in square inches (1.4, 3.5, whatever) to help the layout artist. With my plastic pica stick I measured how many lines deep a copy block would run. The rough layout process was very cut and dried; everything lined up with T-square precision. After two weeks of training and practice, a flock of us fledgling writers were released to various merchandise departments.

Baby steps

My first writing stint began one sunny morning when Vern Frank escorted me to the farm department. He introduced me around and shook my hand before heading for the elevator. The cleats on his heels clicked crisply on the linoleum floor as he walked away. That sound was his trademark; it told us writers that he was in the area. Time to clear our desktops and look busy. I shared an office with Jerry, a nervous guy in his early thirties. He had a few years of writing experience and typed fast, getting his pages done ahead of schedule. This gave him free time to chat with folks in the office or take a short walk to the Sears retail store on Homan Avenue and browse awhile. I envied him for his speed and the solid grip he had on his job. Jerry could be irritating, however; he was always blowing his nose. It seemed like he had a permanent cold. He grossed me out by honking into sheets of typing paper, wrinkling them up and tossing them onto the floor. This continued all day long. One morning he leaned a yardstick against the wall and promised me that when his wrinkled sheets reached the top of it, he'd clean them up. Jerry's sense of humor escaped me at times. Luckily, he didn't inject it into the copy he wrote.

Trying to keep up with Jerry, I was working through lunch one day when a secretary entered my cubby and asked me if I knew how to drive a "stick." When I assured her that I did, she told me that the office manager's car had rolled out of its parking space. The manager, a pleasant, middle-aged lady, was nowhere to be found and I didn't mind helping out. I moved the car and put on the parking brake. No problem. When I entered my cubby the next morning I was flabbergasted to find a big, mahogany desk sitting where a gray, steel one had been the day before. The office manager's repayment bolstered my sagging faith in humanity.

My weekly paycheck enabled me to pay Dad back the money I'd borrowed to buy that damned surety bond. Things were going well until a letter arrived in the mail informing me that I could no longer drive. My surety bond company had gone belly-up. To get back on the road I'd have to find a similar outfit and pay them half a grand for a new bond. *Enough!* I decided to put my driving privileges in PARK and walk. Of course, this left me totally landlocked. *Walking will do you good,* I told myself. *You can take the bus to work.* Yeah, right! Luckily, our house was a short walk from Kedzie Avenue. And from there it was 100 blocks straight north to Sears. A CTA bus would deposit me just steps from my job.

SEARS HAS EVERYTHING!

"I never think that people die.
They just go to department stores."
– Andy Warhol

HERE I WAS TRANSPLANTED TO the farm department, when a week earlier I didn't know there was such a place. I was amazed at the broad array of items in their catalog: brooders for tiny chicks, electric fence chargers, post hole diggers, tractor hitches and castrators, just to name a few. If an item was new to the catalog or really complicated I consulted with one of the buyers, who were all men. Listening carefully, I took notes on the merits of solid-state fence chargers, Timken® tapered roller bearings and posthole diggers with optimum torque. In those days the company's advertising motto was "Sears Has Everything." And looking at all the specialty catalogs they put out, I believed it. In the farm department I learned that Sears even sold little fish fingerlings to farmers for stocking their ponds. In fact, I got to write a page about pond-stocking, describing rainbow trout (*Oncorhynchus mykiss*), large mouth bass *(Micropterus salmoides)* and other familiar species with obscure Latin names. The finished layout showed a fish leaping out of the water. I was astonished! That crisp graphic illustration had begun with my faded pencil scribble. I was pumped to create the most dynamic selling copy ever written at Sears.

My basic, pencil-on-paper layouts had to be OK'd by a copy chief upstairs in Department 744 before they could be sent to a layout artist.

The first copy guru I encountered was Bob Barclay, a plump middle-aged man with a red face and wire-rimmed glasses with small round lenses, He looked like a character from *The Pickwick Papers*. Bob perused my layouts carefully, peppering me with questions about product features, display prices, disclaimers, logos and such. His stern, schoolmaster aspect intimidated me at first. Blessed by Barclay, my layouts went off to the art department, which could have been located on Neptune. We writers had no contact with the art folks whatsoever. They were cranking out finished layouts in one of the red Sears buildings; I never found out which one.

Within a week or so, my first tissue layout came back to me transformed, as if by magic, into a black-and-white finished layout. I was impressed by how clean and crisp the artists' renderings looked. They made the farm items stand out with sharp contrast. Delivered to me in a huge envelope known as a "pouch," the layout was stapled to a large piece of stiff manila stock. A sheaf of blank white sheets (known as "pica sheets") was pinned to it. Now came the real challenge – typing! I'd never learned to type and now it was part of my job. I slipped a pica sheet, backed by carbon paper and a second sheet, into my manual typewriter. Typing my words onto those sheets, I tried to keep them within the area enclosed by a typographer's red lines. (Like the layout artists at Sears, typographers inhabited their own distant planet.) Each pica sheet corresponded to a specific copy block on the layout – A, B, C, etc. A block of copy might be ten lines deep by 14 picas wide (a pica measuring 1/6th of an inch). When all the copy blocks on all the sheets were filled with words, I pinned them onto the layout, stuffed everything back into the pouch and sent it on its way.

The Donnelly Expedition

One day in the spring of '67, Sears chartered a bus that took us new copywriters from work to the R.R. Donnelly Company on Chicago's lakefront. This giant printing outfit had been churning out the Sears catalog for four decades. I brought my camera along, hoping to snap a few pictures. Inside the plant, we were guided through all the departments involved in producing the general catalog. Copy was first set in monotype, a method that cast every letter of every word in its own tiny lead slug. (Each of us neophyte copywriters was given our very own piece of monotype to take home.) Words and pictures were transferred to printing plates wrapped around massive cylinders. Ink was applied to paper through a process called "rotogravure," in which tiny depressions on the plate pick up ink and deposit it onto the paper. The din of thundering presses and the endless belt of paper speeding through giant rollers made for total sensory overload.

Our tour stopped for lunch in the company cafeteria, which served some of the worst food I ever tasted. Afterward we watched printed catalogs rolling off the line and being stacked onto pallets. Some would be mailed to customers; others were bound for Sears stores and catalog sales offices throughout the country. When our tour was over late in the afternoon it felt good to get outside into the sunshine. I hadn't popped a single picture all day, but I was glad I'd brought my camera anyway. I decided to hike north along the lakeshore and shoot photos of yachts and sailboats. The vast expanse of blue water soothed me. The scene helped me shrug off the angst of being lonely, horny and unsure of where the hell my life was going. Near Monroe Harbor I stopped to look at a carpet of alewives floating in the water. The dead fish had drifted into a corner formed by adjacent walls of rusty steel pylons. That floating mass stretched for an area as large as two football fields. The unsuspecting alewives had made their way from the ocean through the St. Lawrence Seaway into Lake Michigan only to die there. I clicked a picture of them that completely filled the frame. Packed tightly together they looked like a swatch of tweed fabric.

I hoofed it north to the Prudential Building and walked inland a block to Paulson's Coffee House on Wabash. I ordered coffee, which arrived in a glass hoddle nestled snugly in my cup. Its fat neck held almost an extra cup of java. Sitting at the counter I tried to imagine what parts of the Loop would be fun to visit. With the late afternoon sun glowing gold behind the downtown buildings, I strolled up to Lake Street and walked under the El tracks over to State Street. I drifted south to Randolph, which was booming. To the west I could see the marquees of big movie houses. The United Artists, Woods and Oriental were all going strong. In the front window of Flo's restaurant a pretty girl swayed back and forth on a swing.

I headed two blocks south to State and Madison, the intersection that's often called "the busiest corner in the world." From there I wandered west a few blocks to the Forum Cafeteria, an immense eatery that my parents took us kids to several times. Built at the end of the depression, it was art deco all the way, with huge saucer-like overhead lights and colorful glass murals depicting mosaic scenes of the Midwest. One whole wall was a mirror, doubling the space's dimensions to the eye. Escalators took diners up to a mezzanine level. On this visit to the Forum I chose chop suey and cherry pie – my favorite combination since age eight. Then I went next door to the Today Theater and caught the "One-hour Movie," consisting of the Movietone newsreel and a funny film short narrated by Pete Smith. The whole scenario was a replay of a happy childhood experience.

Bar hopping

Without a driver's license throughout that winter of '67, my mobility was zilch. I was glad to have John Kerrigan for a friend. On many a Friday night, he drove out south and rescued me from an evening of TV. We'd go out and tip a few, sometimes at one of the bars west of Kedzie along 111th Street, but more often we'd head for the Mayfair Tap on 63rd & California. That cavernous Irish tavern was John's favorite watering hole, and Willie was his favorite bartender. He had such a thick brogue and talked so fast that I never had the slightest idea of what he was saying. John, however, enjoyed lengthy, lively conversations with Willie, even with the jukebox blasting away at full volume. Songs like "The Black Velvet Band" and "Johnson's Motor Car" were always playing. But the most popular selection of all was Mario Lanza singing, "Drink, Drink, Drink" from *The Student Prince* operetta. Sometimes I wondered if the management kept playing that song to boost business.

John drank draft beer and bottles of Guinness Stout while I sipped vodka martinis. I don't recall what got me started on hard liquor at such a tender age, but those silver bullets got me zonked in short order and kept me hung over for most of the next day. After a few months I switched to whisky sours; they tasted good, but gave me a scorching heartburn that a whole roll of Tums couldn't quell. A hangover/heartburn combo was more punishment than I deserved, so I started ordering Rhine wine on the rocks. Meantime, John was happy with his beer. We were both determined to succeed, but John had a definite goal: earning a PhD. My ambitions were more flexible – I wanted a writing job that would let me use my imagination. Staying abreast of the news gave John a global perspective that I lacked; conversing with him updated me on what was happening in the world at large. We liked to talk about getting ahead, and commiserated about things that got in the way. But whatever our topic of our banter, John always infused some witty barbs and comic observations that made me laugh. I rode shotgun on our Friday night expeditions, while John did all the driving. He piloted his baby-blue 1960 Ford slowly and cautiously, assuring me that he'd get us both home safely. Having to rely on my friend for transportation gave me occasional pangs of conscience. The longer I was without my driver's license, the more I felt like a freeloader.

*John Kerrigan lost in a reverie of lofty thought at
Chicago's U of I Circle campus, 1968.*

New threads

Early in the spring of '67 John decided to buy a new suit for his upcoming
graduation from Loyola. He said he was going down to Sam Taxman's
place on Maxwell Street to get himself measured. I asked him why he'd
chosen such a honkytonk area for his wardrobe needs. John assured me
that this was the right way to go. A friend of his had convinced him
that Taxman's was a shop where you could get a new suit, including
alterations, cheap and fast – faster than an Earl Scheib paint job for your
car. And hell, I was in need of a new suit myself. The blue sharkskin I'd
worn for three years was losing its luster.

John picked me up and we took the Dan Ryan north to Chinatown.
We headed west to Halsted and hung a right. After a mile or so we
parked and hiked north, discussing our chances of finding a bargain or

two. Our breath turned to white mist as we talked. After a few blocks
we came to a district filled with vendors of every ilk hawking their wares
on the street. The scene was ragtag and raw. All the merchandise was
displayed on blankets and tables or strewn right on the asphalt. John
and I browsed displays of watches, ties, shirts, tools, hubcaps, small
appliances and day-glow paintings on black velvet.

We wandered through a landscape of electric motors, toys, lawn
mowers, jewelry, power tools and office equipment. An elderly man was
selling IBM Selectric typewriters out of the trunk of his car. Nearing
Taxman's place we stopped at a busy street vendor selling hotdogs and
coffee from his steamy cart – the perfect combination on that cold, gray
day. Munching and sipping as we walked, that little meal seemed like
the best one I'd eaten in a year. Shop owners came out to the sidewalk,
hustling us to come inside and look at their goods. Their chutzpah was
astounding! It dawned on me that I'd visited this stretch of sidewalk
when I was a kid walking with my Dad. I remembered seeing a huckster
with a cane actually hook a man by the shoulder and try to pull him
into his shop.

Sam Taxman had started out on Maxwell Street in 1922 selling caps
from a pushcart, and before long, he opened the store that John and I
were visiting. Climbing the creaky stairs to his loft was like going back
in time. The place looked like something out of *Oliver Twist* – small,
dark and dingy. A little gray man greeted us and showed us some fabrics.
We each chose one and were measured in short order. The tailor told us
to come back in a couple of hours, so we had a leisurely lunch at a nearby
deli. When we returned John's suit was finished. He tried it on and liked
it. Minutes later my spiffy new threads were ready. I was pleased, but
the pants were missing belt loops. When I mentioned this, the tailor
said they'd cost me extra. *What?* He'd be charging me more for my suit
than John was paying. When we started to haggle, John, who had not
yet produced his wallet, interrupted. "My friend asked for belt loops
right up front just like I did." "Okay, okay!" the little guy groused. It
took him just a few minutes to make and attach the loops. John and
I emerged from Taxman's toting brown paper packages bulging with
our new glad rags.

We made it! *My brother Dan and John Kerrigan congratulate each other on graduating from Loylola University, May 1967.*

In tune with the times

One of my chats with John at the Mayfair launched my guitar-playing career. He mentioned that a friend of his was taking guitar lessons at the Old Town School of Folk Music. His comment registered with me because I'd been toying with a guitar at home that nobody knew how to play. A week or so later I took the CTA to the Old Town School and checked it out. The folk guitar lessons were group lessons with one teacher up front and thirty or forty people playing and singing in unison. Seated on a sea of folding chairs, they fingered basic chords and thumb-strummed their way through "The Crawdad Song" and "Go Tell Aunt Rhody." The directness and simplicity of this system appealed to me, so I signed up for night lessons during the week. I thought they'd be fun, but getting to Old Town after work without a car proved to be a challenge.

Departing Sears on Wednesday night, I caught a CTA bus that took me east a short way and then turned north onto Ogden Avenue. It trundled along that diagonal street for miles. The route gave me wide-open views of the inner city. All the way to Old Town the shops and businesses along Ogden appeared to be thriving. Stepping off the bus at

Wells Street, I had to walk half a mile to the school on North Avenue. But there was plenty of time to kill before lessons started. Wells Street was Hippie Central in 1967; its shops sold peace signs, tie-dyed T-shirts, astrological charts, beads and bandanas. Head shops offered a fanciful assortment of pipes and other smoking paraphernalia, even hookahs.

Many places displayed psychedelic posters illuminated by black light that intensified their Day-Glo colors. Crescent moons and stars abounded. Peter Max, the star-happy illustrator, was in his glory. Sometimes I stopped at the Pickle Barrel on Wells Street for a sandwich. I liked the informal atmosphere and the peanut shells on the floor. Sitting at the bar killing time in this big, echoic eatery was lonely, but it was better than waiting in an empty room at the school.

My first guitar teacher in Old Town was Norm Cantor, who showed beginners like me how to finger basic guitar chords. We weren't reading notes, just trying to direct our digits to the right frets while singing "The Crawdad Song" and "This Land Is Your Land." As we progressed, Norm explained "hammering on" and "pulling off," techniques named by Pete Seeger in a book he'd written about playing the banjo. Other groups in other rooms were learning banjo, mandolin or dulcimer. When all the lessons were over I was tempted to join a group headed to the Old Towne Ale House. But without a car I had to concentrate on taking the right mix of trains and buses to get back to the South Side – hopefully before daybreak.

Walt's Workshop

About this time I was transferred to the hardware department at Sears. Veteran farm writers told me that hardware was a smooth-running, profitable department where everyone got a bonus. They fondly referred to the catalog production group as "Walt's Workshop." Walt was Walt Wiegand, an old-timer who had spent his entire career writing copy at Sears. Pushing 70, he had just a few faint wisps of white hair clinging to his head. He wore wire-rimmed glasses and a permanent expression of surprise, as if he'd just received some alarming news. All hardware copy was created under Walt's watchful eye.

Over the decades Walt had written about every hardware item in the catalog. When I worked with him his area of specialty was Craftsman lawnmowers – big profit makers. He knew every feature of every model going way back. As one of his helpers, I wrote about lesser items: radial arm saws, air compressors, socket sets, even plain old nuts and bolts. For some hardware items, the exact same copy might appear from one issue of the catalog to the next. Instead of retyping paragraphs and charts we clipped them out of the current book, slapped their backsides with rubber cement and glued them onto sheets of typing paper. Catalog writers in other departments pasted down old copy now and then, but in the hardware department we did it all the time.

Charts for nuts, bolts, screws and sockets were unchanging and untouchable. Their sacrosanct content had been set in stone years (maybe decades) earlier and was picked up again and again. Walt cautioned me to never retype or alter anything in these hallowed charts. "All the specs are correct," he assured me. "Just glue the charts down." I was happy to comply, but occasionally I had to construct a chart from scratch. It was the best way to show multiple sizes and features. Crafting a chart could actually be fun if things didn't get too complicated. Finishing a big one made me feel like I'd worked the entire *New York Times* crossword puzzle – my head felt hot. Time to stand up and let my cranium chill. One afternoon I confessed to Walt that I just couldn't squeeze everything into a chart I'd been working on. He glanced at my efforts and told me not to sweat it. "The typographers will make it fit. They can cheat a little bit with condensed type."

One-track grind

Page after page rolled through Walt's Workshop. They were like the cars of a long freight train stretching beyond the horizon to infinity. Occasionally a ray of sunshine brightened the scene when something new appeared on a page – maybe a multispeed reversible drill or a garden cart. By November I was getting my work done on time and feeling comfortable in my job. But taking the CTA to work each morning was getting old. Stepping off the bus in front of the Sears campus, I crossed the street and entered a massive red building. I climbed the stairs to the second floor, walked down a long, gray hall and entered my cubby. Walt was already pecking away at his manual typewriter. We exchanged good mornings before I shed my coat and plopped into a wooden swivel chair. The conveyor belt was moving – there were layouts to make, words to type, things to glue down. I felt safe and snug. But not young.

As the morning wore on it felt good to stand up, stretch and look out the window, even though the Sears parking lot across the street was no visual vitamin. On boring afternoons I'd take a coffee break, walking to a vending machine at the end of the hall. I'd insert a dime and view the exciting choices: COFFEE BLACK or COFFEE LIGHT with or without sugar. LIGHT added chalky powder that simulated the look, if not the flavor, of cream. Pushing both the LIGHT and SUGAR buttons was the best way to disguise the brew's cough medicine taste. Back in my cubby I'd sit and let my thoughts drift – from the date I'd lined up for the weekend to photo school to the folk songs I was working on at the Old Town School. All to soon someone's voice or a random office sound would jolt me back to reality.

A Very Searsy Christmas

It was Christmas Eve. Everyone was anxious to get home. We writers in the hardware department were invited to the "Christmas party" upstairs in 744, home of the biggies in catalog advertising. Knowing the Sears culture, I was afraid not to put in an appearance. So I headed upstairs with a couple of production guys from the adjoining cubicle. We followed some folks down a long aisle toward a spot where a few of the catalog heavyweights were standing. The group ahead of us stopped briefly to shake hands with these big shots, then moved on quickly. I was surprised by the perfunctory nature of this routine. Beyond the suited stiffs were tables holding an array of cookies and candies. I shook hands with a couple of gents I'd never seen before, grabbed a cookie and headed for the exit. Maybe there was some coffee nearby but I wasn't in the mood to look for it. I was happy to get off that floor and head for home. I took the electric Kedzie bus south to 63rd Street, my regular transfer point. Before changing buses I dashed across the street to the Cupid candy shop and bought a box of gift-wrapped chocolates for Mom and Dad. A minute later I was seated on a gas-powered bus bound for my home turf.

NINE

THE GREAT AWAKENING

"I've been down so long
gettin' up never crossed my mind."
–Bobby Darin, "Down So Long", 1963

Brave new year

IT WAS 1968 – TIME to make some changes. I told myself to get my
license back and get rolling. I'd had enough of riding CTA buses. It
took $500 plus a few letters and phone calls, but I was able to straighten
out the surety bond mess, get my insurance back and regain my driving
privileges. Dad was only too happy to get my forlorn Ford Falcon out of
his driveway. Lifting the hood, we found a family of possums inhabiting
the engine compartment. After shooing them out with a broom, Dad
gave my engine a jump that brought it sputtering to life. Then, after
hand-pumping air into its flattened tires, I put the Falcon into reverse
and backed out onto 107th Street. It felt great to be in control of my
own vehicle, even if it was a dinged-up heap.

Then one February morning while driving to work I got a strong
feeling that things were looking up. The warm sun felt good on my face.
A pop tune was playing on the radio. "Sell me a ticket for an aeroplane –
ain't got time to take a fast train…." All of a sudden my spine was
tingling. *What the hell is this? I feel good, almost … happy! Yeah! What
have I been so bummed out about for so long?* I thought that if I could
just maintain this mellow mood, the future would be worth looking

forward to. About the same time, The Old Town School moved half-a-mile north to Armitage Avenue and started offering lessons on Saturday mornings. What a fun way to start my weekend! Instruction for all the different instruments concluded at the same time, and everyone gathered in a big room for a sing-along. Led by guitar whiz Ray Tate and fabled folk singer Win Stracke, we strummed along while singing "Good Night Irene" and "Shady Grove," or newer stuff, like "Blowin' in the Wind" or "Scarborough Fair." I was learning to play folk guitar and meeting some fun folks. After class I hung around Old Town and browsed the folk albums in record shops on Wells Street. I developed a liking for Gordon Lightfoot, Phil Ochs, Judy Collins, Donovan and Joan Baez.

Shock and awe!

Within a few weeks the Sears complex was hit by a tornado – a force of nature named Dennis Flavin! This hulking young guy descended on our safe, quiet department with no warning. Dynamic, flamboyant Flavin nearly lifted Walt's Workshop off its foundation. He did everything with a bravado that astonished people and gave them a boost. Standing well over six feet tall, Dennis made a big impression on everyone. He worked fast, joking as he typed, and he laughed like the Jolly Green Giant. Having graduated from Columbia University in New York City, Flavin doted on the Big Apple. In fact, his love of all things New York made him a bit disdainful of the Windy City. I mentioned to him that one of my profs at Loyola was a Columbia grad. "And he taught at Loyola?" Dennis joked. "That guy must have graduated last in his class!"

Approaching an aging little copywriter named Mel Goodrode one morning, Dennis greeted him with a hearty, "MISTER GOOOOD! Hey man, what's the hap?" Shrugging his shoulders, grumpy little Goodrode looked up at Flavin smiling. *Nobody doesn't like Dennis*, I thought. *He's the Sara Lee of Sears.* His exuberance always brightened the atmosphere. It was fun hanging out with this character. Staying abreast of New York fashion trends, Dennis sometimes came to the office sporting a double-breasted suit and a wide tie. He spoke fondly of his Nehru jacket although he never wore it to work. Dennis said he was taking a speed-reading class after work. And to show me his progress, he asked me to quiz him on a chapter from a paperback I'd been reading. He flew through it in about a minute then answered all my questions correctly. I was astonished. On his birthday a bunch of young lovelies from the office gave him a cake and sang "Happy Birthday" to him. I was jealous, wondering why things like that never happened to me.

Flavin would occasionally belt out a line from a country and western song, changing the words to make them describe a piece of hardware. He liked country songs because their lyrics were honest and the singers pronounced the words so you could understand them. Despite his upbeat persona, the tedium of writing catalog copy sometimes got to Dennis. On one hot July afternoon he lowered his forehead onto his typewriter and moaned, "Get me out of here!" Then he split to visit some friends on another floor. Getting his work done fast gave Dennis time to spare, something that I craved. He sometimes mentioned colorful catalog writers working in different departments. There was a sweet young thing named Natasha who liked to clear her desktop and paint it with rubber cement. Then she'd roll up the dried glue into a gummy ball and bounce it off the wall.

Somehow Dennis persuaded management to let him split his time between writing catalog pages and cranking out retail copy on TVs and stereo equipment. I read some of his first-draft copy, describing a stereo system: "All your favorites will sound better than ever – songs like, "If It Takes A Multispeed Sabre Saw, I'll Get To You Baby" and "I'll Go Nuts If You Bolt On Me Again". This nod to us folks back in the hardware department was entertaining. Too bad those song titles didn't make it through Editorial.

Agency urgency

"Agencies" were a hot topic among young writers at Sears. In fact, some of them were hoping to land jobs in agencies. Up to that point, the only agencies I'd ever heard of were insurance agencies, and I couldn't imagine what a young writer would be doing in one of them. Then one day while lunching with Dennis and Steve Turner, another young writer, I asked, "What are these agencies you two keep talking about?" They looked at each other in disbelief. "Ad agencies, Einstein!" blurted Flavin. "You don't know what an ad agency is?" Steve asked with a smirk. My co-writers described the fun and excitement of writing for big-time agencies that turned out TV commercials for consumer products. They used the word "creative" a lot. It sounded like the more creative you were, the better chance you had of getting into a big agency. If you got hired and were really good, you could have a fun-packed career making TV spots for Coca-Cola, United Airlines or McDonald's. You could be earning big bucks and flying out to Hollywood on a regular basis. Flavin and Turner described Leo Burnett, Needham, Harper & Steers and J. Walter Thompson as big creative shops that were looking for people with ideas. That lunch was an eye opener for me.

Knowing that he was looking for a job in town, I peppered Steve with questions about ad agencies over the next few weeks. He told me he'd been interviewing at Burnett and the people there were looking at his "book," a portfolio showing samples of his work. He had come up with selling concepts for several products and developed them into campaigns, including print ads with headlines and TV storyboards with frames showing the video sequence and the audio message. Everything had come from Steve's imagination since he had no actual agency experience to draw samples from. Turner promised to show me his book when he got it back from Burnett. Flavin was acquainted with ad agencies, but his employment goals seemed to be pretty broad. He gave the impression that if he could just get back to New York he'd get his bearings and be on his way to big things.

Trouble in the hood

Just a few weeks later, in early April, the West Side riots broke out after Martin Luther King, Jr. was assassinated in Memphis. It was

Friday afternoon when I heard the word "riot" mentioned in a hallway conversation outside my cubby. Soon everyone was talking about fires raging just a few blocks from the Sears complex. Looking out my window I saw plumes of black smoke rising from the neighborhood. Minutes later all employees were instructed to get to their cars and follow a police escort to the Eisenhower Expressway just two blocks south. I joined the caravan to the Ike and drove west – way beyond the city limits – before turning south toward home. My car radio reported rioting, fires and looting. Mobs were breaking store windows, taking TVs, clothes, food – whatever they wanted. Police were answering emergency calls from merchants along Homan and Kedzie Avenues. People in the Loop could see clouds of smoke rising from the West Side.

The nightly news showed fires blazing out of control. Army units and National Guard troops soon arrived to back up the Chicago police. Meanwhile, snipers were taking potshots at military and fire department crews. By noon on Saturday the military had secured the overpasses along the Eisenhower, but fires, shootings and looting continued through Sunday night. Before Monday morning 162 buildings had been destroyed and 350 people had been arrested for looting. Mayor Daley later told reporters that he had ordered police to "shoot to kill any arsonist or anyone with a Molotov cocktail in his hand ... and ... to shoot to maim or cripple anyone looting any stores in our city."*

On Monday morning I decided to bring my camera with me to work. Approaching 22nd Street I saw black smoke billowing ahead of me. A mile farther north I stopped at a light. Just a few feet from me firemen were hosing the smoldering remains of a building. Behind them the entire block was gone. *Holy shit!* Hiroshima came to mind. I snapped a picture of the scene before the light turned green and drove on to Sears.

---

* "*Riots follow killing of Martin Luther King Jr." Chicago Tribune* article by James Coates, April 5, 1968.

*Chicago firemen were still fighting flames Monday after
the weekend's West Side riots, April, 1968.*

Perilous times

Chicago was still reeling from the King riots when, in June, Robert
Kennedy was assassinated while campaigning for president in California.
"On to Chicago" were three of the last words he ever spoke. Then, in
August, the Windy City was the scene of more violence when it hosted
the Democratic National Convention at the Amphitheater. After a
massive rally in Grant Park, thousands of protesters began a march
to the convention hall. They got as far as the Conrad Hilton Hotel,
headquarters for the candidates, before police stopped them with tear
gas, mace and billy clubs. Demonstrators chanted, "The whole world's
watching." Many threw rocks and bottles. When someone tossed a
beer can, police charged the crowd. Television networks cut away from
the convention coverage to show this mayhem outside the hotel, where
hundreds on both sides were injured.

Abbie Hoffman and Jerry Rubin of the infamous "Chicago Seven"
led protests against the Vietnam War in Grant Park. And fanning the
flames, police publicized reports that demonstrators were planning to

spike Chicago's water supply with LSD. The Illinois National Guard was soon on the scene. Roads to the Amphitheatre were covered with heavy security. Reporters Mike Wallace and Dan Rather were roughed up on camera by security guards, prompting anchor Walter Cronkite's statement, "I think we've got a bunch of thugs here!" The next day, the *Chicago Tribune* called the convention site "a veritable stockade." It would later be described as a "police riot." The Chicago Seven were charged with conspiracy, inciting to riot and other crimes.*

---

*   *Copyright © 2017, Chicago Tribune*

LEAVIN' ON A JET PLANE

"Bizarre travel plans are dancing lessons from God."
– Kurt Vonnegut Jr.

THAT CRAFTSMAN REVERSIBLE DRILL WAS a hell of a tool, but my layout gave me only so much space to work with. After cutting the copy twice I needed a break. I stood up and gazed out the window. A faint haze dulled my view of the sprawling Sears parking lot across the street. In one week I'd be taking in a totally different scene – the verdant highlands of Chiapas – while staying with my brother Jim and his family in San Cristóbal de Las Casas, Mexico. Jim had married a Mexican girl in this picturesque town and was the father of two young sons. He was trying to eke out a living doing accounting and odd jobs. My brother's letters described his surroundings in rich detail. He loved the mountains and green valleys, the lush and varied flora. Even better, the entire region was loaded with Mayan ruins. But for Jim the biggest attraction was the area's extensive network of caves, largely unexplored. His spelunking exploits had taken him to remote passages where no other human, he assured me, had ever set foot. With all this awaiting me, I planned to bring plenty of film. Two weeks before my departure I put in for a week's vacation plus one extra day. The look my boss gave me made me feel like I was pressing my luck. And now, with only a few days left before takeoff, my request still hadn't been OK'd by the high command. *What's holding things up?* I wondered. It wasn't like I'd asked for a raise or an office with a door. Then, the day before my departure, I finally got official permission to take one extra day off – without pay, of course.

Increíble aventura

On Saturday morning I packed a large suitcase, stuffed my camera bag full of gear and tossed some small items into a briefcase. After lunch Dad drove me to O'Hare. Two of my younger brothers and my Uncle Mike came along to see me off. My flight would take me to Mexico City. From there I planned to make my way down to Chiapas via bus. Mike recommended that I stay at the Regis Hotel in downtown Mexico City. When Dad stopped outside the American Airlines terminal, everyone got out of the car and shook my hand. I picked up my bags and walked into the busy terminal.

Setting out on this trip all by myself was exciting, but my lust for adventure was tinged with loneliness. During the flight I tried to picture the scene in San Cristóbal. Jim, his wife Lucha and their two young sons were living in central Chiapas, just a three-hour drive from Guatemala. Lucha's brother was the legendary Catholic bishop, Samuel Ruiz Garcia, spiritual leader for a major chunk of Chiapas. When Jim and Lucha wed two years earlier, she was the housekeeper in the Bishop's huge residence, the Casa Episcopal. And happily for the newlyweds, Lucha kept this position, so at the time of my visit she, Jim and the kids were all settled there comfortably.

Vamanos!

My hotel room at the Regis was unspectacular but tidy. I flopped onto the bed for a little R&R and woke up an hour later recharged and ready to explore the local turf. My loose travel plans gave me the whole next day in Mexico City, but it was Saturday night and I was itching to prowl a bit. Roaming from the Regis, I only went half a block before encountering a young woman seated on the sidewalk holding an infant.

She held out her hand and looked up at me with pleading eyes. I handed her a couple of pesos. Resuming my hike, I didn't travel 30 feet before finding another young woman with a babe in arms. I placed a peso in her palm and kept going. Glancing across the street, I spotted two or three more women on the sidewalk holding babies. *What the hell is this?* At the corner I turned left, passing another mother and child. Out of pesos, I trudged onward.

The sound of trumpets playing was faint at first, but I headed toward it. After a few blocks I came to a city park where a mariachi band was playing. Beneath a big tree strung with lights they were entertaining a sizeable group. This was my first encounter with one of these colorful bands and I enjoyed it thoroughly – the lively music, the huge sombreros and glitzy costumes – great fun! Bright silver medallions on the players' pant legs reflected the overhead lights as they sang "La Cucaracha" and "La Negra."

When the band took a break I drifted a few more blocks to a busy street. It was well-lighted, so I felt safe. Before long I found a neon-clad lounge and walked in through the open door. Sitting at the bar, I tried to recall the Spanish word for beer, but when the bartender approached, I uttered "tequila," the only word that came to mind. He set a shot glass on the bar and filled it. I took a sip. What a weird taste. My server walked away as I sat staring at the glass. He returned a moment later with a saltshaker and half of a lime. He shook salt onto the back of one hand, bit into the lime, licked the salt, then went through the motions of tossing back a shot. Smiling, he gestured for me to give it a try. I mimicked his salt/lime ritual and chugged my tequila. *This is more like it,* I thought. The barman nodded, smiling. I ordered another tequila as the music of distant Mariachis drifted in through the open doorway.

A young couple seated themselves at a table behind me. They had a spirited conversation with the bartender in Spanish. I had no idea what they were talking about, but it was full of laughs. I stood up, left some change on the bar and turned toward the door. "Adios!" shouted a voice from behind me. "Adios!" I replied, looking over my shoulder. A bit tipsy, I made it back to the Regis. At the desk I inquired and learned that there was a Catholic Church nearby. I asked for a 7 a.m. wake-up call, took the elevator upstairs and hit the sack.

El Domingo

In the morning I found the church without any trouble. Its vast dark interior contrasted sharply with the meager handful of churchgoers in the pews. The service was a low mass, with just two candles and no singing by the priest. I was back at my hotel in less than an hour. In the lobby I asked about bus tours of the city. And what luck! In half an hour a coach would be stopping to take folks to the Floating Gardens. I joined a small group of tourists for a trip to Zochimilco, a swampy area just outside of town. Created centuries earlier, these "gardens" were a network of canals and islands blooming with exotic flowers. Our group sat on a large float boat that seemed more like a barge. Other visitors in similar boats were mostly families out for some Sunday fun. I thought of the Sunday drives along Chicago's lakefront that my family took when I was a kid.

I enjoyed the islands full of bright flowers. The pretty floating plants shared the water with debris tossed from the boats. "I can see why they call this place 'the floating garbage,'" a lady in our group commented. I got back to the hotel just in time to catch another tour bus – this one headed for the bullfights at the Plaza de Toros. Sitting next to me on the bus was a man who appeared to be in his mid-fifties. His muscular forearms and high energy made me think of Popeye. He introduced himself as Steve Carrol, a painting contractor from Boston. As it turned out, he had been staying at the Regis but was ready to move on.

At the stadium our group sat way up in the stands, looking down at a steep angle. I thought my telephoto shots would get rave reviews back home. The crowd's intensity took me by surprise; the locals were into every phase of the bullfight ritual. Witnessing the slaughter of big, healthy animals didn't turn me on, so I was delighted when a team of horses dragged the last dead bull out of the ring. For me, the real show had been watching the fans shout "Ole! Ole! Ole!" I chatted more with

Steve on the ride back to our hotel. He said he was a retired widower whose children were all grown up. Somehow we got on the subject of religion. He told me that he and his wife had raised their kids Catholic. As adults, he said, a couple of them drifted from the church for a while but found their way back, like he thought they would.

Acapulco, only one per planet

I told Steve I was headed down to Chiapas, and following my uncle's advice, I planned to see Vera Cruz on the way. "Nah," he said. "That's a tough place – a big dirty port. You want to see a beautiful place, go to Acapulco. That's where I'm headed." He described it as a tropical paradise – very green with palm trees and beautiful beaches. I was sold. My detour would be to Acapulco. The next morning we boarded a first-class bus that took us south through vast stretches of scorching, bleached desert. We must have traveled four hours or so before a few green plants appeared alongside the road. Then our coach began a slow descent. More and more greenery came into view until we were rolling through a lush setting of deep green foliage, with huge fronds arching over the road. "Wha'd I tell ya?" Steve asked with a smile.

Acapulco was gorgeous. Steve and I got off the bus and found a hotel that was cheap but clean. After we'd secured a room, I took a nap. Steve, at least a quarter century my senior, left to check out the local scene. He got back just in time for dinner. Then we sat on the patio watching the sun descend slowly into the bay. In the morning we hiked along the oceanfront till my legs ached. Steve toted snacks, suntan lotion, towel and other essential etceteras in a small net bag slung over his shoulder. It was the only way to travel, he assured me. After lunch he was gung-ho for more hiking, but I begged off, opting to sit in a hammock near the beach. The water beneath the azure sky was deep blue, dotted with the brightly colored sails of small watercraft. With a large, fruity cocktail in my hand I drifted off to sleep.

The next morning we found a cheap flight to Oaxaca on an old DC-3, the storied twin-engine plane that served so well in World War

II. It sat near the runway with its nose pointing up and its tail wheel planted in the grass. Steve and I boarded and walked downhill to our seats. It was only a 40-minute hop to Oaxaca, where we saw the ruins at Monte Albán: impressive terraces, plazas and huge stones carved with images of dancing men. In the center of town we saw the legendary Tule Tree, a giant Cypress thought to be over 2,000 years old, with a trunk measuring nearly 31 feet across. Astonishing.

Chiapas or bust

Oaxaca was a fun side trip, but it was time to press on toward Chiapas. I said goodbye to Steve and cabbed it across town to a second-class bus depot that looked like a deserted store. Near the rear of the place I purchased a ticket for Tuxtla Gutierrez. Exiting the back door, I joined a group of about 40 people standing in an open area next to their makeshift luggage. Half an hour later a yellow school bus pulled up. Everyone ran toward it as it came to a stop. They started throwing their bags and boxes onto its roof. All this happened in seconds. I was left standing by myself watching the driver help passengers load their luggage. "Forget this!" I said aloud, turning back toward the store. "No! Come back amigo!" someone shouted. Folks already seated on the bus beckoned to me through the open windows. "We have room for you!" the driver shouted to me in English. "Give me your bag!" I handed him my big suitcase, wondering if I'd ever see it again. As he tossed it onto the roof I boarded the bus with my briefcase and camera bag.

Every seat was filled; riders were sitting on the floor, some holding clucking chickens in basket-like cages. My co-passengers were extremely gracious, standing and gesturing for me to take their seats. I was busy declining their offers when a strong hand grabbed my wrist and pulled me into a seat. I plopped down next to a portly Indian woman who had a bunch of ceramic bowls in her lap. The largest one was a foot wide; two or three smaller ones nested inside it. She silently slid them onto *my* lap *(Gee, thanks)*. After half an hour of hanging onto them my abs and forearms were aching. Several stops down the road the lady finally exited the bus. I opted to sit in the aisle on my upended briefcase, holding onto a pole. This allowed me to rest my aching gut and catch a few winks – a poor imitation of real sleep. Later in the night, when seats became available, I grabbed one and fell asleep for real.

I was awakened by the sound of laughter. Opening my eyes I saw rows of empty seats ahead of me. Daylight was streaming in through the windshield. The bus was stopped on a steep incline. I heard male voices coming from behind me – and more laughter. Looking over my shoulder I saw three or four Mexican men who looked like they were half in the bag. *What the hell! I'm stuck in an empty bus on a mountain with a bunch of drunks telling dirty jokes!* Peering out the window I saw green, mountainous terrain below; no easement or shoulder – just a steep mountainside – as if the bus were balanced on its peak. Before long, passengers started streaming into the bus carrying armloads of glass jars. I read the label on one of them: Chase & Sanborn. Everyone was loaded down with jars of instant coffee. The driver told me that a truck had gone off the mountain. Nobody was hurt, but the cargo was strewn all over the place. Apparently it was fair game for anyone at the scene. Wide-awake now and occupying a window seat, I was in for a breathtaking but scary ride up the mountain. Throughout that slow, sinuous ascent I never saw the edge of the road – just steep canyons below. When I reached Tuxtla Gutierrez (capitol of Chiapas) I caught a cab that took me about 30 miles and a mile higher to San Cristóbal de las Casas (elevation 7,000 feet).

Casa Blanca

Arriving in mid-afternoon, I was amazed by the grandeur of the Bishop's home; it was bright-white stucco with a red tiled roof and huge, arched doors with ornate hinges. Jim and Lucha greeted me at the entrance as servants attended to my luggage. Lucha served a great lunch that, surprisingly, wasn't the least bit spicy. She listened patiently while Jim and I caught up on family news. When I admitted to being really pooped, Jim and Lucha showed me to a small, tidy bedroom, where

I slept until morning. At breakfast I met their little boys. Patrick, the older one, was a good-natured toddler of two with jet-black hair. Roberto, who was just a few months old, bore a strong resemblance to his dad.

My toddler nephew Patrick chases chickens in the yard,
San Cristóbal de las Casas, Mexico, 1968.

Breakfast featured exotic melons – papaya, mango and a melon with ebony-colored flesh. Jim assured me that it was fresh and tasty, so I tried some. Not bad at all. Jim and I left little Patrick chasing chickens around the yard and went for a ride in the Bishop's Jeep. "Sam," as my brother called him, was out of town so his new, open-top CJ was ours for the week. It handled well on the uneven, rusty-red soil. The vegetation around San Cristóbal was remarkable. Conifers that looked like Christmas trees were growing right next to exotic century plants with tongue-like, sharp-tipped leaves. As we explored the region Jim told me that Chiapas looks a lot more like Canada than Mexico. He said the local tribes clung to many customs and beliefs inherited from their distant Mayan ancestors. The prevailing form of Catholicism, he said, leaned toward Paganism.

Every day with Jim was a new adventure. He took me to the bustling marketplace, where the locals were selling fruits, veggies and colorful handicraft items like straps, belts and dolls. Indians from nearby villages were everywhere. Those from San Juan Chamula were leading donkeys loaded with charcoal. The Chamulas wore coarse drab outfits that looked like potato sacks. But the Indians from Zinacantán donned much brighter attire. The men wore embroidered jackets and straw hats with long, colored ribbons hanging down in back. The women were dressed in white shawls with red pinstripes and navy skirts.

As we hiked up the mountains I was astonished to see airplanes hundreds of feet below us flying over the town. After an hour or so we came to a great sweeping basin, which Jim called "The Valley of Tranquility." Heading down into it, we passed a woman in a tiny, shack-like chapel. She was kneeling on the ground before a mass of glowing candles. I asked Jim if she was she praying to Christian saints or the Mayan gods of her ancestors. He said it was probably a combination of both. The following day we drove to a nearby Chamula village abounding in tropical vegetation. Jim agreed that it was a scenic wonder, but cautioned me that it was an unfriendly place to visit. On our way back to San Cristóbal my brother mentioned the Lakes of Montebello, each a distinct hue of blue or green located near the Guatemalan border.

The main event

The next morning Jim said it was time I saw some of the caves that he'd described in his letters. He guaranteed that I'd be amazed. The caves, he promised, were in pristine condition because the superstitious locals never went near them. I blithely agreed to go with him for a private tour. We took the Jeep a mile or so to the entrance, which looked like a shallow crescent of black in the forested terrain. This was no puny sinkhole in the woods; we both entered standing up. Some crawling would come later as we moved from one large cavern to another.

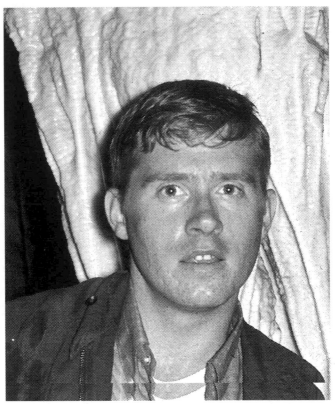

Me in front of "The Towels" trying to put on a brave face.

Jim pointed out all kinds of fascinating formations – stalactites, stalagmites and a startling formation he called "The Towels." It was a vast, glittering sheet of white resembling a frozen waterfall. Moving farther inward, we passed several round, white basins filled with water; they looked like fancy bathtubs for the rich and famous. After a few hours Jim located the vertical slot in the wall he was looking for. It was so narrow we could barely squeeze through it. Voila! We were in a large cavern, standing upright and ready to press on, but the going was slow. As we crept along a narrow shelf our heads broke little glass-like straws that were hanging from the ceiling. Jim said this was proof that we were the only humans to walk this way in eons. After 45 minutes or so he turned to me and confessed, "I don't remember ever being here before." *Uh-oh!*

Scared as hell, I suggested that we head back to the cave's entrance.

We turned around and went back half a mile or so. Stopping to rest, I set my flashlight down at my right side. It rolled into a crevasse and disappeared. *Oh no!* Now, with one flashlight between us, I was near panic. Jim's light was already very dim; the batteries were almost dead. But he had two fresh ones with him, he said. Minutes later we had to stop and change them. Standing on the narrow ledge, we planned every step of the procedure: who would do what and when. It was a life-or-death operation. Jim unscrewed the cap. The inky blackness of total dark smothered us. He dumped the dead batteries and held the handle upright. I gingerly dropped two fresh batteries into the handle. Jim screwed the cap back on and light erupted onto the ceiling of the cave. I started breathing again.

We were trying hard to locate the tiny slot in the wall that would take us back to recognizable terrain. "We should have hit it by now," Jim said. "We'd better go back a ways." We backtracked slowly and carefully. "Here it is!" Jim shouted with glee. He squeezed through the opening into the adjacent cavern with me following close behind. My brother assured me that we were home free, and sure enough, we started passing things we'd seen on our way in. An hour later the way ahead of us suddenly yielded faint hint of light. My heartbeat slowed and my blood pressure dropped as I heaved a sigh of relief. Whew! We were heading toward the mouth of the cave! We were going to get out of this thing alive!

It was suppertime when we arrived back at the Casa Episcopal. Jim and I had been gone for nine hours. Lucha shed tears of joy at seeing her husband in one piece. She had informed the neighboring Catholic Marist Brothers of our long absence, and they were organizing a search party to look for us. We both looked like hell. Our hands were scraped, our faces were scuffed and our clothes were torn. But so what? We were safely above ground. I'd never in my life enjoyed such feelings of relief and well-being. That harrowing experience made a lot of things that had been bothering me seem very unimportant; it gave my brain a needed cleansing. Before flying home I bought an inexpensive guitar from a local craftsman, a switchblade knife and a bottle of mescal with a worm in it. I also packed a few souvenirs for my family and a pendant for Betty, the girl from work whom I was dating. At the Tuxtla airport Jim and I embraced and said goodbye in Español: "Mucho gusto!" "Mucho gusto!"

Back in Chicago summer had arrived. The trees were leafy and green; flowers were in full bloom. I arrived home with a fresh perspective on things. It felt like my mental slate had been cleared. Unpacking, I found that everything had made it through customs except for the pendant. I suspected that a lady customs worker couldn't resist it, or a male worker saw it as the perfect gift for someone special. The next morning I reported bright and early to my workstation at Sears. My desktop was piled high with pouches holding unspectacular catalog pages in various stages of production.

So long, Sears

My near-death episode with Jim in his cave altered my outlook on life. I made some changes, starting with my personal appearance. I started wearing contact lenses and beefed up my wardrobe with a new suit and new sport coats. Then I traded in the humongous Plymouth I'd purchased a few months earlier and bought a svelte, new Javelin – fire engine red with a four-barrel carburetor and four-on-the-floor. On workday mornings I entered the vast Sears parking lot with panache. Making a sweeping airline approach, I swung my car in a broad arch and nosed into a parking spot. Riding a wave of positive energy that seemed out of place at Sears, I was impatient to seek new horizons. *Why stay here where my creative talent is going to waste?* I thought *Maybe I should quit right now.*

Before giving notice I talked to Frank Livermore, head of all things creative, about transferring from hardware to a different merchandise department. I was hoping to land in a clothing category like shirts, sport coats or even shoes. Livermore offered me building materials. I left the company two weeks later without having another job lined up (not the smartest way to quit, but it got the job done). On my last day I worked right up until 5 p.m. Dennis Flavin took me out for a drink at a bar on Archer Avenue. He commiserated with me, agreeing that my pulling out of Sears was the right thing to do. I figured that he'd soon be leaving Sears and heading for success in New York City. After a couple of martinis we shook hands and promised to stay in touch. I drove south on Kedzie, heading toward home and wondering how I was going to keep up the payments on my new Javelin.

ELEVEN

THE DATING SCENE

"I'm dating a woman now who, evidently, is unaware of it..."
– Garry Shandling

THAT GIRL WHO WALKS HER COLLIE AT NIGHT . . . who is she? I wondered. There was something about her . . . no . . . a *lot* about her that I liked. She was pretty and had a calm, elegant bearing that struck me as very classy. I asked Marg, my younger sister, if she knew that girl. As it turned out, she did. Her name was Eileen, and she lived less than a block south of us on Peoria Street. I can't recall how I introduced myself; the experience must have been so traumatic that I've buried it in my subconscious. On our first date we walked over to the Capitol Theater on Halsted, just two blocks east of Peoria, and saw *The Devil at Four O'clock* with Frank Sinatra. Then we went for a bite at the Capitol Annex Restaurant, a few doors north. Walking home, we talked about school and the snow piles covering the parkways along the street. On another date to the Capitol we saw *Lawrence of Arabia* with Peter O'Toole.

Two of our infrequent dates were downtown. Since I had no car at that time (much less a driver's license), we took the El to the Washington subway stop, climbed the stairs to street level and found our way to a movie house on Randolph Street. On one occasion we saw *How The West Was Won*, a musical with Debbie Reynolds and Howard Keel. On another downtown date we dined at Trader Vic's in the Palmer House. The setting was deliciously dark and tropical. And it was quiet. The island atmosphere, created with carved totems, fishing nets, pontoons from outrigger boats and such, was captivating. Browsing the menu I was totally at sea … Macadamia Mahi Mahi … Beef Kew Pake … Bongo Bongo…. There was no way I could recommend something to Eileen. The drink menu listed a fanciful array of large, fruity cocktails. Barely 18, I was clueless in this area as well, and my date was two or three years younger than me.

Live bands right next door

In 1961 young males and females could meet at the Holiday Ballroom near 80th and Halsted. Located a block from my house, the place had been the Cosmo movie theater when I was a kid, so it was hard for me to think of that venue as a dance hall. On a frosty Saturday night in January I suited up and walked over. A live band was playing classy tunes like "Harlem Nocturne" and "Take the A Train." The ambience was dark, but not exotic or alluring. Males and females stood around the edge of the dance floor, some chatting, others just gazing blankly across the open expanse.

To reach the dance area you had to walk down a slanted stretch of floor – a structural holdover from the building's days as a movie house. I danced with a cute girl named Pat. Her first name cut through the loud music, but I had trouble making out her last name. *Isten? Christian?* She kept shouting it – and continued after the music stopped. "Gripson! Gripson!" "Gripson?" I hollered back at the top of my lungs. "Yes! Gripson!" she confirmed, looking a bit annoyed. We danced to a slow tune before her girlfriends wanted to leave – they had to catch a bus on Halsted headed toward the southern boonies. Pat scribbled her name and phone number on a scrap of paper and handed it to me before she took off. I liked the way she'd stayed with me between songs and I admired her persistence in shouting her last name over and over until I finally got it.

The next day I looked at her address – way south and west. I tried to think of places I could take her without a car; my options were limited.

I located a movie house, The Coral, not far from her home. *There must be a restaurant near it*, I figured. I could take a bus south on Halsted to 95th, transfer to a westbound bus, ride a few miles, get off and walk two blocks north to her house. We'd walk back to 95th and west a couple of blocks to the show. Afterward, we'd stop for a bite to eat and chat a bit before heading back to her house. And finally, I'd hike back to 95th, catch an eastbound bus, and transfer at Halsted to one headed north. I'd ride to the terminal at 79th, get off and walk one block home. *Simple!* I wished to God I had a car.

On Monday I phoned the movie house to see what would be playing on Saturday night. It was something safe and tame, as I recall. Tuesday I called a couple of the nearby eateries to make sure they'd be open. My plan was taking shape. On Wednesday night I phoned Pat and asked her if she'd like to go to the show on Saturday. "No!" she said emphatically. Wednesday was too late to call, she informed me. She'd already made plans for Saturday night. I said goodbye and took deep breath. *Oh well, the best-laid plans of mice and men oft turn to shit,* I paraphrased to myself. *Yeah, he who hesitates is screwed.* I didn't feel like calling Pat any time soon, and a week or two later she'd completely slipped my mind. But half a century later I still remember Pat and my elaborate plans to take her out.

Once I had a car, dating became an actual possibility. I wasn't confined to my neighborhood, the South Side or even the city limits. Even better, I could expand my horizons beyond movie shows. With wheels I could take in a concert at Ravinia up in Highland Park or see a play at Pheasant Run out in St. Charles. And after I owned my own vehicle, I pursued a romantic, long-distance dating campaign for several months, but all the driving wore me down. I decided that the ideal first date was a movie or play in the Loop, thinking this was a classy, upscale way to go. This grand, downtown gesture would be sure to make a winning impression. Chauffeuring a gal all the way to the Loop, paying downtown prices for entertainment and dinner, and then getting clipped big time for parking – didn't that show real effort and serious intent? Unfortunately, the longer I pursued this strategy, the farther it took me from reality. The wheels fell off after date number two; I could almost count on it. My big-first-impression campaign was getting me nowhere and keeping me broke.

Cheap date

"You sure you know where you're going?" my sister Marg shouted from the back seat. "Don't worry," I replied, "I've got good directions." We were driving south on Route 45 on a warm Saturday night in July. Our destination was a small town called Posen, where my girlfriend Marilynn was babysitting. We'd already picked up Marg's date, Phil Carollo, who lived in our neighborhood and carpooled with me to Loyola. Now we just had to fetch Marilynn.

Over the phone she'd given me directions on how to get to her aunt's house. We'd already made a date to see a Grant Park concert when she agreed to babysit till 6 p.m. way out in the middle of nowhere. It was already 7 p.m., and I was anxious to find the house. (Maps and directions were never my strong suit.) As we approached a railroad crossing bells rang and red lights flashed as the gates came down. I was tempted to pull around it but there was the safety of my passengers to consider.

I turned off the motor, knowing we'd be in for a long wait. An endless string of freight cars inched by like a funeral procession: boxcars, hoppers, tank cars and low-slung gondolas filled with scrap metal. "This is torture," I griped. "What if I were in an ambulance? I'd die before they got me to the hospital." I started reading the names of different railroads painted on the cars: Union Pacific, Santa Fe, Burlington, Chesapeake & Ohio, Rock Island ... they just kept coming. Phil said there were laws that required long trains to stop on major roads and break apart to allow emergency vehicles through. This road didn't look like one of them. Finally, Marg spotted the caboose down the line. I started the engine, put my Rambler into gear and rolled across the tracks. We didn't have far to go, and with help from my crack navigation team, we got there in short order.

Marilynn was waiting on the porch, clad in tan shorts and a white blouse. A picture of loveliness, I thought. I now had three navigators to help me find Grant Park in time for the concert. With Beethoven on the bill, arriving late would make us look like uncultured rubes, I feared. We slithered our way east to the Dan Ryan Expressway and took it to the Outer Drive bordering Chicago's lakefront. Shooting north, we reached Soldier Field and parked. From there it was just a few blocks on foot to Grant Park and the grassy expanse facing the band shell. We spread out a couple of blankets and Marg settled onto one of them. Phil crashed to the ground and plopped his head onto her lap. "You brazen twerp!" I wanted to shout. The band shell looked spectacular against the darkening sky. Lit from within, its half-moon form projected a delicate iridescence, each of its concentric bands glowing with a different shade of blue. Folks on the blankets around us were nibbling cheese and sipping wine. *Why didn't I think of that?* I wondered. Oh well, I was happy enough with Marilynn, Beethoven's Fifth Symphony and a soft, skin-caressing breeze off Lake Michigan.

When the concert ended we folded up our blankets and hiked about a block east to Buckingham Fountain. The nightly show of colorful water jets was just starting. And what a show – frothy plumes shot skyward as their colors changed from red to orange to pink and blue. Standing near the fountain we enjoyed the cooling spray of tiny droplets blown by the wind off the lake. The show ended when the fountain's big central spout shot a majestic plume 30 or 40 feet into the night sky. After the water show our group just took a few steps to the Lake Michigan shore, where a Wendella tour boat was waiting. The fare was something like $1.75 a head. Our little boat cruised near the shore, giving us views of Chicago's night skyline. The captain pointed out some highlights: the pristine-white Wrigley Building, the Tribune Tower and some of the taller downtown structures. Topping all of them was the 41-story Prudential Building, standing 601 feet high with a broadcast antenna that stretched skyward another 311 feet. Near the roof, red neon letters spanning the building's width spelled PRUDENTIAL. As Marilynn took in the sights I admired her chestnut hair and left earlobe. When she shivered from a sudden lake breeze I covered her shoulders with our blanket. It all seemed so wonderfully romantic.

Back on shore we hiked to the car. Everyone was still full of energy, talking and joking as we drove back to the South Side. I dropped Marg off at home and drove Phil back to his folks' place. Then Marilynn and I headed south on the Dan Ryan past the Ford plant on Torrence Avenue to Lansing. Before I kissed her goodnight Marilynn told me that I had a darling little sister, just like I'd told her. That Grant Park concert and lakefront tour was a cheap date, but my memories of it are solid gold. It felt great to be young, healthy and dating a bright, pretty girl named Marilynn. With two ns.

Betty at Sears

What a doll! I had just been talking to one of the ladies in the pricing department when I noticed a new girl sitting at a nearby desk. A few days later I was in front of my typewriter trying to think up an excuse for talking with her when she walked into my cubby with a question about a price listing. Her sweetness and shyness enhanced her allure. It wasn't long before I asked her for a date. "Sure, Joe," she said, which made me deliriously happy.

On Saturday I washed my new red Javelin before driving north to pick up Betty at her folks' house. I climbed the wooden front porch steps and rang the doorbell. There was no sound, but an overhead light flashed on and off a few times. *What the heck is this?* Betty answered the door, looking a bit embarrassed. "I suppose you're wondering about the lights," she said after we got in the car. "Yes, I am" I answered. "They let my Mom and Dad know when somebody's at the door. They're both deaf mutes." After a long pause I managed to utter, "Really?" Betty continued, telling me how her family had recently moved to Chicago from Tennessee. We dated a few more times prior to my trip to Mexico, where I bought her the crystal pendant that didn't make it through customs at O'Hare. I told Betty about that mishap, which was probably a mistake. I don't think she believed me.

Soon afterward, I asked Betty if I could drive her home from work. She was embarrassed, but gave me an emphatic "No!" Soon afterward she said she couldn't go out with me any more. "You're so much smarter than me," she blurted. "You know all this stuff about literature and philosophy. I feel like a dummy when you talk." Wow! I was speechless and felt ashamed of myself for trying to be bright and clever. That event was real education. Painful but real.

Rollerdater

While employed at Automatic Electric Company I started dating an attractive typist whom I'll call Pam. She was pleasant but a bit childish and sort of wooden. I didn't know what to make of her. Pam lived northwest in Schaumberg, a long way from my home turf on Chicago's far South Side. But looking at her was such a pleasure that I kept taking her out. After several dates I asked her if there were someplace where she'd really like me to take her. "To the roller rink!" she answered in a wink. I told her I wasn't much of a skater, but she didn't seem to mind. *Oh boy,* I worried, *I'll look like a super klutz while she skates circles around me.* I picked Pam up on a Saturday night and we drove to The Elm, a huge indoor roller rink in Elmhurst, not far from O'Hare. We rented old lace-up skates that looked like they'd been around the rink millions of times. After lacing my skates I rolled a few feet toward Pam who was still working on hers. She got to her feet, weaving dizzily. We headed for the rink walking on our skates as if they were ill-fitting galoshes.

Pam stepped onto the rink and veered left, merging with the throng of skaters. She looked paralyzed as folks young and old skated by her. Staggering into the far turn, she tripped and veered off the track. *Jeez! This girl skates worse than I do!* I managed to shuffle forward to the spot where she was stranded. Rolling unsteadily toward her, I reached out for a helping hand. None was extended. I fell hard on my ass. Red-faced and struggling, I managed to get up. Pam just stood there looking blank and emotionless. "Why didn't you help me?" I asked. "Well, I didn't want to fall, too!" she answered vacantly. I reluctantly admitted to myself that this girl was not playing with a full deck. So despite her great looks, I stopped asking her out. It was very hard to leave her behind, but I needed someone I could strike up a friendship with, someone who would enjoy conversing with me. Underneath the whole dating routine – the movies, plays, sports events and social gatherings – lay the serious business of finding Mrs. Right. Looking back at that pretty girl from work, I think she might have had some form of autism, like Asperger's syndrome. I hope she found the right guy somewhere down the line.

A jug of wine, a hunk of cheese and thou

I started taking flamenco guitar lessons on weeknights from Tom Wilson, who played at Geja's Café in Old Town. And before long I was bringing my dates to Geja's on Saturday nights. The atmosphere was dark and exotic. An orange and white parachute suspended from the ceiling formed an exotic, arabesque canopy. Candles on the small tables provided most of the light. I was swept up by the stirring music and romantic atmosphere. My date and I nibbled goat cheese and sipped Lancers Rosé. It was carbonated like soda pop and came in a shapely bottle. I thought it was the height of sophistication. Wilson was introduced as "Tomas," suggesting that he had flown in from Madrid for a limited engagement. His red hair made him look like a displaced Mick. Between sets he'd walk over to my table and say hello. I felt like a celebrity as we discussed trémolos, rasgueados and other flamenco farrago. Luckily, none of the girls I took to Geja's ever asked me to borrow Wilson's guitar and play it.

An idea ahead of its time

I even went on a few computer dates. Every so often a few IBM cards would arrive in the mail. Each one had the name and phone number of a girl who was supposedly a good match for me. I called and had clumsy conversations with girls who sounded awkward and off balance, just like me. The most memorable date was with a nice girl named Julia, who lived in Griffith, Indiana. On the phone she sounded like a bright girl with a good sense of humor. I asked her if she'd like to see a play at Drury Lane, a dinner theater on Chicago's South Side. "Absolutely!" she said without hesitation. I asked for directions on how to find my way to her place. Her instructions were complex. Just getting to the state line was going to be a challenge. She told me to get off in Lansing, Illinois, drive to the first gas station and call her. "I'll talk you in from there" she said. *Is this is an IQ test to see if I'm smart enough to take her out?* I wondered. Following her directions I made it to the gas station and called in for more instructions. A few minutes later I pulled up in front of her house. Julia was waiting on the front porch.

We sped east to the Dan Ryan and drove north to 95th Street, exited and headed west. A few miles later we were at the Martinique Restaurant, home of Drury Lane, which featured "theater in the round."* It felt good to get out of the hot car and into some cool air-conditioning. Things were going well until we approached the spiral stairway leading up to the theater. "I didn't know we'd have to climb stairs," she said nervously. I asked her what the problem was, and she confessed to having a terrible fear of heights. *Hmm.* I told her to hang on to the bannister but that didn't allay her fears. "Hold my arm," she pleaded, so I took her arm and we started up the staircase. Julia gripped the railing tightly and kept pausing to look down at the carpet below. Finally, an usher came to our aid. He took one arm and I took the other. Moving slowly we got her upstairs and to our table. Once we were seated and dining, her quick sense of humor made me laugh out loud. Julia was more entertaining than the play. After the final act an usher helped us down the stairs. My date navigated us safely back to her home in Indiana, where, smiling, we shook hands goodnight.

---

*   Theatre-in-the-round or "arena theatre" is a production where the audience is seated at tables surrounding the stage. Live plays are performed, usually after everyone has finished dinner.

TWELVE

HOCUS FOCUS

"The quickest way to make money at photography is to sell your camera."
– Disgruntled wedding photographer

TWO MONTHS AFTER MY RELEASE from the hospital in '61, I was still getting Workman's Compensation checks and spending them like a drunken sailor. I bought an electronic flash for my camera that could freeze the fastest action. Eager to try it out on people, I asked my cousin Mike if he'd drive me around the neighborhood so I could shoot unsuspecting bystanders. He thought it might be fun, so after dark the next night we drove east on 79th Street. I rode shotgun with my window rolled down, snapping pics of people who were waiting to cross the street. When Mike pulled up to a stoplight I waited till it turned green, then popped a photo. My cousin stepped on the gas and we peeled out laughing like little kids. At one corner a rotund little man was leaning against a trash basket reading the paper. I shot him as he looked toward me. Gotcha! I asked Mike if he'd make another pass so I could shoot him again. We circled the block, stopping at the light once more. When it turned green, I popped the shutter. We peeled out into the night. When I made a blowup of that shot in my darkroom, I was surprised to see that the portly gent was flipping me the bird.

Early photo lessons

Eager to increase my photo IQ, I got a subscription to *Popular Photography* magazine. I enjoyed browsing the photos shot by pros and talented amateurs, especially the black-and-white shots. Unfortunately, Mom screened all incoming mail before anyone else got to look at it. As soon as my magazine arrived in the mail she flipped through its pages, removing any that included racy shots or nudes. So I failed to mature to the point where seeing a babe in the buff was no big deal. Also, Mom's censorship removed major chunks of the articles I tried to read. Continued on p. 64 ... Really? Where the hell is p. 64? The back pages of *Popular Photography* were overstuffed with small-space ads set in tiny type. There were hundreds of them selling cameras, accessory lenses, filters, tripods, flash units, studio equipment, bulk film, photographic paper, developer, even correspondence courses in photography. I answered one of those ads and wound up taking classes from The New York School of Photography.

"Great job, Joe! Send me more soon!"

Yeah, right, I thought. The handwritten note was attached to my corrected assignment. The enthusiastic comment read just like the ones attached to my previous lessons. All I'd done was develop a large negative and mail it to my photo mentor in the Big Apple. His usual pleased-as-punch remarks were beginning to irritate me. They sure weren't teaching me much. My new challenge was to take an underexposed negative and give it some guts by "intensifying" it in a special chemical bath. I started thinking, *Even if I become a professional photographer, I'll probably never have to intensify a negative in my life.* And here I was paying a small fortune for these foggy lessons from afar. At that point I dropped my correspondence photo classes. With no more pricey lessons, I was free to throw my money away on something new. It didn't take me long. At Clark Camera downtown I found a sexy Durst 606 photo enlarger, made in Italy. It was rock solid with a sharp condenser lens and precise metal turret for razor-sharp focusing. Very cool! I paid cash and brought my new toy home on the CTA. In the basement I started making enlargements from black-and-white negatives, blowing up images to colossal size. The prints were crystal clear, making the smallest fleck of dust show up looking bright white.

Projecting the pigs

Embryology was a required course for sophomore pre-med students at Loyola. It was a tough course and the labs were 100% microscope work. Looking at one slice of embryo after another, we had to identify organs, veins, arteries, etc. It was a tricky task; some organs disappeared and then showed up several slides later because parts of them looped and curved. I enjoyed the lectures, by our teacher, Dr. Hisaoka, but his voice faded in volume as he reached the end of each sentence; my notes were filled with question marks.

One day I got the notion that I might be able to blow up the images on embryo slides at home using my photo enlarger. So I purchased a set of slides and loaded them, one by one, into the negative carrier. Swiveling the enlarger head 90 degrees, I projected the images from one end of the basement to the other onto 11x14 sheets of photo paper. Wow! The tiny embryo structures loomed large, and the finished prints helped me study them without sitting on a stool and straining my eyes. My lab scores improved, but that wasn't enough to boost my overall grade. Those IBM multiple-guess tests continued to baffle me.

Single-lens magic

I was a junior taking classes at Loyola's downtown campus when a camera at Standard Photo captured my imagination. I walked by their shop on Chicago Avenue every day on my way to school. The camera was a 35mm single-lens reflex made by Pentax. This wonder of camera design would allow me to focus sharply on distant mountains or on objects as close as one foot from the lens. After peppering the sales folks at Standard with questions about the Pentax for weeks, I came in one day and bought it. But before the salesman would let me depart, he carefully went over the camera's features, showing me how to adjust the lens aperture and shutter speeds. He told me how to get a sharper image by stopping down and using a lower shutter speed, how to shoot in backlighting situations, where to insert a cable release for long exposures….

When he started talking color photography, I told him I'd just be working with black-and-white film. He said I'd get great results with Kodak Plus X film and FR X-44 developer. After ten more minutes of helpful tips he was ready to box up my camera. But returning it to the form-fitting Styrofoam packaging had this guy completely flummoxed. He tried one way, then another, then another. It should have taken him all of two seconds, but it was making him crazy. After explaining all its features in detail, he couldn't get my camera back into its box. "Don't drop it!" I uttered under my breath. Luckily, a young female employee came to our rescue, deftly fitting the camera into place. Intelligence comes in all shapes and forms.

Aurora Glorialis

It was always fun to experiment in my basement darkroom. After reading a "how to" article in *Popular Photography* one night I tried to put colorful light patterns on film by swinging a tiny light suspended over my camera. I nailed a string to the ceiling and a tied it to a small, pocket-sized flashlight. A gentle nudge sent the light into orbit, swinging in random patterns. Setting my camera on the floor facing up, I was ready to try some abstract expressionism. There was a knock at the door "You in there, Joe?" It was Jim Bradley, the kid who lived in the flat below ours. Jim, who was about 13 at the time, was the last person I wanted to see at that moment. But I let him in, knowing that he'd bug the hell out of me until I did.

Switching on the room light, I clued Jim in on what I was up to and said I'd let him launch the flashlight into orbit. I opened the aperture on the lens and killed the room lights. Next, I locked the shutter open for a long exposure and told Jim to give the flashlight a little push. Then, as it swung overhead, I placed a red gel over the lens. After a few seconds, I switched to a blue gel, then to a green one, etc. My goal was to make patterns with colors galore. Jim and I made several images before calling it quits. When I got the finished pictures a week later I was dazzled by the graceful patterns and vivid colors and the way they contrasted with the black background. I showed them to Bradley, who really flipped. "Wow! We made these? They're incredible! Can I have a copy to show my mom?"

Picture-perfect

As I mentioned earlier, writing catalog copy at Sears was not my heart's desire. So to spice up my life I started taking photography lessons at Ray-Vogue. It was a well-known school that taught photography, commercial art and interior design. One night a week I drove downtown to the school on North Michigan Avenue. It was obvious that Ray-Vogue had been in operation for quite some time. The floodlights we used were pretty dinged up and the tripods and booms were nicked from constant use. Despite this, everything was in good working condition. We used 4x5 Graflex cameras like the ones newspaper photographers carried in the thirties and forties. I'd load sheet film into a frame-like holder and slide it into the back of a camera. Those old cameras were bulky, but mounted on rolling tripods they were easy to handle. Professional-grade light meters showed us where to set the aperture and which shutter speed to use. Somehow the settings were always $f32$ at one second. I tripped the shutter by pushing a button at the end of a cable.

The instructors were helpful, making suggestions about composition and lighting but, for the most part, they left us students alone unless we were really off base. It was wise to plan your shots before class so you wouldn't lose time looking for props or figuring out how to set things up. The darkroom was equipped with big, professional-grade enlargers made by Beseler. And there were plenty of them, so we didn't have to wait in line. After making an 8x10 blowup I decided whether parts of it should be lighter or darker. Then, using that first print as a guide, I made second one. But this time I used techniques called "dodging" and "burning in" to manipulate the light coming from the enlarger. In the space between the enlarger and the photographic paper I used both hands to manipulate the light coming through the lens. *Dodging* was a way to lighten things up by blocking light that hit a particular part of the photographic paper. I used a stiff wire with an opaque oval at one end to lighten things up here and there. *Burning in* made certain areas darker. I made a fist with just a small hole in it so only a narrow beam of light passed through to the photographic paper. On a portrait, this technique made a person's eyes look darker and more dramatic.

Texture: Ray-Vogue photo assignment, 1968.

I shot that photo

Paul could really crack me up. I met this young black guy at Ray-Vogue when he asked me for my opinion on a shot he was setting up. He appreciated my comments and joked that he would recommend me for a promotion and a raise. Before long, we were consulting with each other about all things photographic. If one of my photos was on display in the lobby Paul gave me a verbal pat on the back. So did a pretty young blonde named Samantha. And she was no slouch herself. Some of her pictures were good enough to earn a special gold sticker. (It reminded me of the gold stars the nuns used to stick onto our papers back in grammar school.) One night Samantha told me that she was quitting photo school to become an airline stewardess. Training would keep her in town for a few weeks, but after that she'd be flying all over the globe. I was sad to see her leave, and so was Paul. "Hey man, you can't just let her take off like that," he urged. "You oughta get her phone number at least!" This little pep talk was just what I needed. When I saw Samantha a few minutes later I told her that we should stay in touch. She liked the idea and asked me to call her "Sam."

We only had time for a few dates, but they were fun. Not only was Sam pretty, she was very relaxed and liked to laugh. One Friday night we dined at Trader Vic's – my all-time favorite place for a romantic interlude. Sam was in a magic mood – very bubbly and playful. We had passion fruit ice cream topped with little parasols for dessert. It was wonderful. I never saw Sam again after that night. She took off with Pan-Am to see the world. For two years afterward I enjoyed the perky post cards she sent me from all corners of the globe. Her last card, an oversized one, told me how happy she was. She'd met Mr. Right, a soldier in the U.S. Army, and they were engaged. *Good for you*, I thought. *But I let you get away. Maybe I should have booked myself on a flight you were working or flown to one of your destinations ahead of you and surprised you as you stepped off the plane.* Maybe, maybe…

Pictures for profit

My job in 1969 was a long way from home. The ride from Chicago's
South Side up to Northlake and back was putting 250 miles on my
car each week. And my Javelin, with its monster engine and four-
barrel carb, could guzzle gas with the thirstiest muscle cars. I got the
notion that a little extra income would help defray the high cost of my
commute. Maybe I could shoot weddings on the weekends. I checked
out a photography outfit on 57th & Pulaski called Jan's Photo and
talked to the owner, Henry Jankowski, about a weekend job. He said
he could send me out with an experienced shooter for a few weeks to
see if I could handle the job. Of course, I wouldn't be paid anything
during this trial period. I agreed to this arrangement and soon got a
call from a guy named Bob Hacker, an old pro who'd been with Jan's
for years. He told me to meet him at the store on Saturday morning. I
could help him shoot a big wedding, he said. When I arrived Bob was
up front to greet me. He took me behind the counter and into the back
room, where we picked up cameras, film and strobe flash units. Other
photographers were coming in, grabbing their gear and heading out on
their own assignments.

Bob was a colorful character and a good photographer. It was fun
working with him. He taught me some basics, like the right shots to
get inside the church, outside after the ceremony and at the reception
hall. He was good at getting folks to smile, using ethnic expressions I
never could pronounce. At the reception he advised me to shoot the
kids. "People love kid pictures," he assured me. "They order tons of 'em."
In fact, Bob told me to shoot everything. "If the cake falls over onto
the floor, shoot it! People will buy that picture!" Bob and I were each
packing two 35mm cameras – Leica M-4s, with rangefinder focusing
that worked well in dark places. Those cameras had very sharp lenses
and were incredibly reliable. Bob usually carried one camera and stashed
the other one someplace at the reception hall where he could find it
fast, like inside a service cabinet where dishes and silverware are stored.
When we focused on someone, we checked the lens to see how far away

they were from the camera, then set the aperture to the correct f-stop: ten feet was *f*/6, six feet was *f*/10, etc. We had all this stuff memorized.

One of the receptions we shot was a whopper, held at a cavernous VFW hall. There must have been four hundred people there. Shooting folks seated at the tables wasn't always easy. I had to get group shots plus photos of couples. Sometimes there was a shiny wall behind my photo subject to contend with. Bob told me to shoot on an angle to avoid getting a nasty "hot spot" reflection. After half an hour the strap on my ten-pound battery pack was cutting into my left shoulder.

Not for the faint of heart

I found out fast that shooting weddings was exhausting. I had to set up shots and pose people fast, while shouting loud enough to be heard over the echoing din in a large hall. Hacker told me that I would occasionally encounter a drunk who wants his picture taken with every pretty girl in the place. "If this jerk keeps bugging you," he advised me, "don't even focus your camera. Just tap the shutter button lightly. The flash will pop, but your camera won't take a picture." I followed his advice and used this trick once or twice when I was shooting weddings on my own.

After I'd tagged along with Hacker for a few weeks, he told the boss that I was ready to shoot a wedding on my own. When I picked up my gear the following Saturday morning Bob was nowhere to be seen. Being the new boy on the block, I didn't get to shoot the classiest weddings or ones that were close to my home turf. I was dispatched to distant places like South Chicago and Maywood. The receptions, often held in huge halls, were not always elegant, but I enjoyed their casual character and the roomy atmosphere. Among the hundreds of people at these weddings were scores of kids. And, as Bob had told me, folks always ordered lots of kid pics.

Shooting a wedding demanded quick, clear thinking. For starters, I had to find the bride's house, where I'd pose and shoot her in her wedding gown – usually in front of the living room drapes. Then, I had to race over to the church (usually a Catholic church), find the priest and ask him about which spots I could shoot pictures from. The sacristy behind the altar was best, but I always made sure it was okay with the priest.

When the first notes of "Here Comes the Bride" blasted from the organ I had to be in position to catch the couples walking up the aisle. All through the ceremony I'd move around taking shots, then I'd hurry outside to catch the newlyweds exiting through a shower of rice. There were lots of shots to get on the church steps – the bridal party, the bridesmaids together, the groomsmen together, the bride and groom with their moms and dads – it was a workout. One Saturday, when I called Jan's with a question about my flash unit, the boss dispatched me to cover a reception for a photographer who had fallen while backing down the church steps trying to get a shot. The poor guy was taken to the hospital in an ambulance.

Be sure you take some wedding cake!

One night at a VFW Hall reception I had a big group shot lined up and posed. It must have been ten people wide and two rows deep. "OK, pretend like you're having a good time," I shouted before pressing the shutter button. Nothing happened. *Uh-oh! Out of film.* No matter – I had prepared for this predicament by stashing my spare camera in the service cabinet near the kitchen door. I asked the group to bear with me and keep smiling while I switched cameras. I dashed to the cabinet, knelt down and reached in. Ah, there it is! As I gripped the trusty Leica I felt something glide over my right calf. There was a loud banging sound and screams. Turning toward my photo subjects I saw chunks of white wedding cake all over the floor. Not just a few; there were dozens of them. The unlucky waitress I had tripped was getting to her feet. She looked back at me wearing a perplexed expression. The folks posing for their picture had mixed reactions. One man was helping the fallen waitress to her feet. A couple of women were picking up pieces of cake and returning them to the huge carrying tray.

I forgot about the picture and asked the waitress if she was all right.

"I think so," she answered. "But I better get someone to clean up this mess." One of my photo subjects pleaded, "No! Take the picture with the cake in it – it's funny as hell." Not wanting to delay things any longer, I popped a few photos of the crazy scene. By that time two bus boys with brooms started sweeping things up. The family group started drifting away. "Wait," I shouted. "Let me shoot the picture again!" Some of them smiled, but nobody wanted to pose for another shot. I hoped that the boys in the lab back at Jan's Photo would be able to crop out all that cake littering the foreground.

THIRTEEN

MOVIE MAGIC

"There are no rules in filmmaking. Only sins.
And the cardinal sin is dullness."
– Frank Capra

ALL THROUGH COLLEGE I WAS able to put studies out of my mind on Saturday nights. Whether I was dating a girl or heading out with a couple of my brothers, the destination was usually a movie theater. Big-screen entertainment provided welcome escape from worldly cares. Panoramic film epics like *Lawrence of Arabia* blew me away. When I saw *Goldfinger* in college the opening music and graphics knocked the wind out of me. And the surreal action that followed provided escape from the eighteenth-century literature I was studying. Musical comedies were the best escape of all. Movies like *A Funny Thing Happened on the Way to the Forum* made me laugh; they took the edge off my worries about grades, girls and the enigmatic future.

Right after college I got a part-time job downtown at the Morton Salt Company in Riverside Plaza, separating sheets on signed order forms and putting them in neat piles. I'd be done by noon, giving me the rest of the day to goof off. Sometimes I'd hike eastward to the Clark Theater, where a different movie played every day. One afternoon I stopped in and saw *Shoot the Piano Player,* a French gangster film starring Charles Aznevour. Films like these were quite different from the movies I was used to seeing. They evoked a whole new range of emotions I'd never felt before.

Walking past the Monroe Theater after work, I noticed that *Juliet of the Spirits* by Federico Fellini was playing. Out of curiosity I bought a ticket and walked in halfway through the film. It was a bizarre, totally absorbing flick about a daydreaming housewife who fears that her successful husband is cheating on her. The colorful, surreal images were hypnotic. Juliet is haunted by images from the spirit world. Her neighbor is a pleasure-seeking lady who lives in a fantastical tree house. Despite opportunities to enjoy sexual freedom, Juliet resists, remaining dowdy and chaste. I left the theater feeling like I'd been dreaming. Heading for the train, I recalled that just a few months earlier I'd walked out of Fellini's *La Dolce Vita* when it was playing at the Highland Theater in my neighborhood. I thought it was terrific but my cousin Mike, who was driving, wanted to split. So, not wanting to walk home, I didn't object.

A year or so later I took a girl downtown to see *Doctor Zhivago*. In one scene Zhivago is sitting at the open door of a boxcar on a moving train. A woman holding a baby runs beside the train with her arms outstretched; she's trying to hand her baby to him. *Keep running! Keep running!* As Zhivago grasped the baby I saw my own extended arm silhouetted against the screen. "Put your arm down!" my date whispered. Oops! I really got carried away. Afterward, we walked a block to the Italian Village for some pasta. The atmosphere was dark and accented by tiny Italian lights. It put me in a dreamy, romantic mood. Too bad it didn't work the same magic on my date.

Despite all the effort and expense, I loved going downtown after dark. The night scene on Randolph Street was electric. Big movie houses, the United Artists, Oriental and Woods, were aglow in glaring neon colors. Their huge marquees were rimmed in light bulbs that lit sequentially, looking like moving strings of bright pearls. I could hear buzzing and clicking as I walked beneath them. On a few occasions an approaching sidewalk photographer snapped a picture of me and my date. He handed me a small envelope that I could fill out, add a couple of bucks to and drop in the mail. I finally mailed in one of those envelopes. A week or two later I received a small picture of Margie Foley and me looking carefree and happy as can be. Unfortunately, I lost that little photo when someone lifted my wallet on the CTA. Damn!

Making a film

In the late sixties camerawork in American films featured split screens, multiple images and shots looking directly into the sun. At the time this artsy-fartsy stuff struck me as very cool, even though it distracted from a film's story. Figuring that being more film-savvy would help me write TV spots, I took a filmmaking class the Illinois Institute of Technology on Chicago's Near South Side. There were eight or ten students in the class, and we were all young. Our teacher looked even younger. Right off the bat he told us to pick a subject and get to work. We should be shooting before our next class met, he said.

We had a good textbook, *Exploring The Film*, which talked about famous films by Sergei Eisenstein, D.W. Griffith, Cecil B. DeMille and Billy Wilder. We even read about Norman McLaren, a Canadian filmmaker who created the images for his films by scratching them onto each individual film frame. One chapter included a complete Spiderman comic book to show examples of perspective and camera angles. I decided to shoot an abstract film with my Super 8 camera that was nothing but light patterns depicting one day in a person's life. The scenes were a series of soft images ranging from clouds and rippling waves to ultra-close panning shots of everyday objects, even the taillights of cars on the road at night.

As usual, my younger brother Pat was eager to help. He rode around with me looking for things to shoot, like black soot pouring from industrial smokestacks. I spliced the shots together on a small editing machine. Then, using a tape recorder I borrowed from the office, we recorded sounds galore – city traffic, sirens and airplanes flying overhead, just to name a few. Some sections of the film included human chatter, but there were no recognizable spoken words. Dinner sounds were just scrambled crosstalk and the sounds of clanging dinnerware. Music here and there helped keep things moving. Pat edited a sound track to match the scenes. When we played the audio and video together the images matched the sounds perfectly. The little film made sense in a vague way as yellowish morning scenes transitioned into bluish mid-day scenes, then those images gave way to darker ones toward evening.

On the last day of class I racked up my film on the projector at IIT, cued up the sound track on the school's tape recorder and turned off the room lights. Things started out fine, but within a minute the video was running ahead of the sound. The morning sounds were playing under the noontime scenes. Oh boy, everything had matched up so well at home! When the video had run its course, the sound kept going for ten seconds or so. The room lights came on. Everyone applauded. *They're just trying to be nice,* I told myself, convinced that my film had made no sense at all to anyone. I had learned a few things – one of them was that a homemade recording doesn't time out the same way when played on professional equipment. A week or so later my report card arrived in the mail. My film making efforts were rewarded with a big fat A. I was sure that other work I'd done in that class was the main contributor to my final grade.

Big-screen impact

Funny the way movies affect you over the years. As a kid, science fiction movies were my favorites. And over the years I found that films based on stories by early sci-fi masters were some of the best. I loved Walt Disney's rendition of *20,000 Leagues Under the Sea,* based on Jules Verne's famous book. And *The Time Machine,* recalling H.G. Wells' story, captured my 17-year-old imagination. It drew me back to the Capitol Theater for a second viewing. *Forbidden Planet* was a gem, based on Shakespeare's *The Tempest.* (Hard to go wrong with "the Bard" as your main source.) *The Day The Earth Stood Still* was a low-budget wonder from 1951 shot in black and white. A good story, great acting and believable effects worked together to make it unforgettable. Some sci-fi flicks were scarier than others. I remember *Invaders from Mars* with creepy aliens who inserted needle-like projections into the brains of their human victims. Ouch! After seeing that film at the age of ten I walked home from the Cosmo Theater with an ache in the back of my head.

Sci-fi flicks featuring human-like monsters chilled me to the bone. The more humanoid the creatures were, the more plausible they seemed, arousing primal fears in my young brain. These trepidations first visited me when I saw *The Mummy* at a drive-in with my family. I was probably eight years old. Half a decade later, my brothers and I watched the original *Frankenstein*, from 1931, on TV at home. The monster scared the bejeezus out of me. Realizing how strongly horror movies were affecting me, I decided to avoid them, so I missed classics like *The Exorcist, Alien, A Nightmare on Elm Street* and *Poltergeist.* Doing a bit of research, I found that my fear of monsters had a name: *teratophobia.* This fear is common in pre-school-age children and generally lessens during the early elementary years. It's rare by the time a kid reaches middle school, but I still had it. Some of us never grow up.

Luckily, I shed most of these fears over the years. Still, I was surprised at how sensitive some people, like my wife, are to screen violence. Mary and I avoid "action" movies, and if we're watching TV she can sense impending conflict way ahead of time. Edging forward in her chair at the first hint of an upcoming scuffle, she exits the room before things get out of hand. "It's only a movie!" I remind her, but it's all too real to her. Maybe some kind of desensitizing therapy, like the treatments that help people overcome their fear of flying, would help. In *A Clockwork Orange*, Alex, a dangerous street hoodlum, agrees to undergo aversion therapy in lieu of a long prison sentence. He's forced to watch violent movies while under the influence of drugs that make him nauseous, so that he comes to associate violence with personal suffering.

Evening jaunts to the Fine Arts

While we lived in Oak Park Mary and I occasionally drove downtown on a weeknight to enjoy a film at the Fine Arts Theater on South Michigan Avenue near Orchestra Hall. With light traffic on the Eisenhower Expressway at that hour we got there in minutes and parked in the Grant Park underground lot. The theater was the best show in town during the eighties for first-run foreign-language, independent and art films. It was part of the antique Fine Arts Building, which also housed artists' lofts, art galleries and musical instrument makers.

We saw *The Manchurian Candidate*, there – a terrific black-and white film from the early sixties. It was the cleanest-looking film I'd ever viewed – not a black speck or hair to be seen from start to finish, and we saw that movie a quarter century after its original 1962 release. We enjoyed foreign movies like *A Room With A View* and exotic flicks like *Kiss of the Spider Woman*. Unfortunately, the Fine Arts closed in 2000. Competition from updated Chicago movie houses and construction of new North Side theaters helped seal the Fine Arts' fate. More progress, I suppose.

FOURTEEN

THE TIMES, THEY WERE A CHANGIN'

"Turn on, tune in, drop out!"
– Timothy Leary

SOON AFTER LEAVING SEARS I put together a résumé and a sample book, consisting of a few stories I'd written at Sunbeam, some catalog pages and a couple of my poems that had appeared in the Loyola literary magazine. Michigan Avenue looked like a world of opportunity chock full of ad agencies. J. Walter Thompson was about to unleash a powerful ad campaign reintroducing 7-Up as "The Uncola." Before long, posters and billboards for 7-Up were sporting vivid illustrations by artist Peter Max. His psychedelic images with their saturated colors and galaxies of stars were in tune with the times. The TV jingle went, "Seven-up, Seven-up, Seven-up the Uncola!" Beyond its TV and outdoor advertising the campaign included hats, sew-on patches – even thermometers. *So, 7-Up is the Uncola*, I mused. *Fine, but I'd rather have a Coke any day.*

I interviewed at a few downtown agencies without any luck. The "creative" folks I talked with told me that my portfolio lacked any actual print ads that had run or commercials that had aired. Without them, they assured me, I couldn't demonstrate the creative wherewithal to get hired by a good ad agency. Most of these folks advised me to start from scratch on a new portfolio. Undaunted, I pumped myself up to create a dazzling array of savvy advertising concepts – ideas that would sell like hell in print and broadcast. "It's all about appearances," one young interviewer insisted. I had to make my stuff look like the real deal. Agencies were impressed by concepts developed to the point that they looked slick enough to run in *Time* or *Life*. I was advised to get my headlines and copy set in type by a printing outfit. And to make my TV concepts really pop, I should make storyboards. This might involve finding someone to draw and color them. Doing all these things would demonstrate my resourcefulness. Of course, it would have been better to get my ducks in a row while I still had a job. The more comments I gathered about my portfolio, the more I tweaked my samples.

Gatekeepers from hell

Getting past the reception desk at an agency for a job interview was a challenge. And the bigger the agency, the more daunting that challenge was. Huge agencies like Thompson and Burnett had personnel specialists who prescreened aspiring writers and art directors. By some perverse twist of fate these non-creative experts were in a position to judge people with real creative talent. Their evaluation determined who reached the next plateau. Their shaky qualifications could result in the wrong candidates getting through and the right ones being rejected. I interviewed with several of these misguided specialists – three of them at Leo Burnett. One was a lady who told me that I didn't *look* like a person who'd work at Burnett. She added that I *did* look like someone from the client side. At another large agency a pre-screening lady boasted that she had sent two young people to Campbell-Mithun years earlier who were both hired. I was working with them at the time and thought they were both creative zeros.

Even less authentic than the agency pre-screeners are some of the so-called "creative head hunters." They run employment agencies that refer job candidates to advertising agencies. But their skills in judging creative talent are no better than those of the screening interviewers who work inside ad agencies. In the early eighties I was determined to get a job working on better TV accounts. I started working with a lady who was considered to be one of Chicago's premier creative headhunters. She arranged to review my TV reel in the screening room at a nearby ad agency. After we'd watched it together she asked me to leave the reel with her. A few days later I phoned her about getting it back. She didn't have it, she said, claiming that she'd given it back to me. *One of us is nuts*, I thought. When I asked her to please look for it, she insisted that I had it, not her. Oh boy! Fearing the worst, I phoned the agency where we'd viewed my tape. They let me come in and search the screening room for it. It took me five seconds to find it sitting atop their tape player.

Here's your hat. What's your hurry?

During my days on Michigan Avenue I showed my work three times at Foote Cone & Belding, a big agency with some solid TV accounts. Separated by a few years, my first two interviews were with the same pre-screener. The fellow smiled a lot. His pleasant comments and vague questions made me nervous. Although he seemed to like my stuff in both interviews, I didn't get past him to see any creative folks at Foote Cone. That's why I was amazed when, a few months after my second visit to the agency, I got a direct call from their creative director, Mike Rogers, who wanted to look at my stuff. The next afternoon I was sitting in his office. He flipped through my book and viewed my TV reel without comment. But he really sparked to the spots on my radio reel, remarking that there were some great ideas in them. Then, picking up a file folder, he read a few comments that described a writer who didn't have much to offer. The agency's pre-screener had written those notes about *me*! Smiling, Rogers shook his head. I left with the good feeling that somebody up there liked me. And I wanted to kill that douchebag gatekeeper.

Fools rush in...

Getting back to my early days of job hunting on Michigan Avenue, I spun my wheels, oblivious to the fine points of established etiquette. My MO was to leave my résumé with an agency's receptionist and follow up a with a phone call. This exercise usually got me nowhere, but once in a while it prompted a short telephone response. A female voice would inform me that I could drop off my portfolio at the agency. I'd go downtown and hand my bag to a young receptionist who would add it to a stable of identical black bags standing behind her like horses lined up for a race. I always felt skittish about entrusting my portfolio to a total stranger at a place I knew nothing about. And I wondered who would be looking at it. One person? A few? A whole slew of folks? Would any of them be in a position to hire me? And were they being careful with my stuff? I had no duplicates of my samples; if someone lost my bag I'd be sunk. I'd heard horror stories about lost portfolios, so if the girl up front who took my bag struck me as a ditz, I'd worry. On one occasion, however, the routine of dropping my bag off gave me an unexpected jolt when the reception girl stooped over to stash my bag. OMG! Hot pants were at their skimpiest in 1968.

North by Northlake

A week before Christmas 1968, I was driving back to the South Side after a hapless interview downtown when I heard a commercial on my car radio. Automatic Electric Company in Northlake was looking for people. The message was very broad; they were trying to fill all kinds of jobs. I phoned their employment office and lined up an interview. A nice lady explained to me that the Northlake facility was the manufacturing arm of General Telephone and Electronics. She sent me home with a copywriting test, which I completed and mailed back. A few days later she phoned and invited me to talk to Bert Hansen in Automatic Electric's advertising department.

Hansen was a slight, middle-aged gent whose skin was shrink-wrapped to his skull and face. His thinning hair had a reddish cast and he wore wire-rimmed glasses. I thanked him when he said I'd done well on the copywriting test. He described the job he was trying to fill and showed me a few ads his department had produced for telephone trade journals. Wow! Their bold graphics and sharp headlines knocked me for a loop. "I'd love to make ads like that!" I blurted. Hansen mentioned the salary, which I thought was fine – it was more that I'd been making at Sears. He offered me a job. I accepted gladly. My first day of work was Christmas Eve.

It's for you

Automatic Electric made telephones, consoles and central office switchgear for the General System, that "other" telephone company serving much of rural America. The first thing I learned at AE was that telephony uses a trainload of railroad terms, like *trunk, route* and *line*. This borrowed terminology dates back to Almon Strowger, a telephony pioneer who worked in railroading before entering the telephone business. He found that railroad lingo adapted perfectly to his new field of endeavor. Strowger invented a system using rotary switches at the central office that allowed customers to dial their own calls instead of going through an operator. This remarkable assembly of shafts, contacts, springs and electromagnets was called "the automatic telephone exchange." It revolutionized the telephone industry.

The advertising department at AE operated under the steady guidance of Howard Bersted. He was a tall, likeable man who wore his white hair in a crew cut and believed in management by walking around. You never knew when Mr. B might pop into your cubby for a brief chat. He liked taking pictures and knew that I was into photography as well. Once in a while he'd stop by to show me some candid shots he'd taken at the Randhurst Shopping Center near his house. Bersted's folksy manner was combined with a paternal attitude toward the people under him. Viewing us as a family, he liked to see us eating lunch together in the company cafeteria. One day when I left the AE campus to dine at a local restaurant Bersted seemed offended. He asked me why I hadn't joined the group for lunch.

Writing for Godot

I reported to Bert Hansen, the man who hired me. An assistant ad manager, Hansen had worked at Automatic Electric for decades. He rejected most of my ad concepts, judging them to be too far out for telephone trade journals. Bert always stayed in his office, but never seemed to be terribly busy. So when I submitted something to him, he often asked me to have a seat while he looked at it. Even if it were a brief sales letter, I'd be sitting in front of Bert's desk for an hour. He'd start reading, but a word or phrase would remind him of an article he'd read in the morning paper or something his neighbor had mentioned to him over the back fence. From there our conversation would drift far and wide, until we were talking about strawberries or repairs on the Outer Drive. And that was just stage one. Getting final approval from Hansen involved several rewrites. When the wording was finally getting close to what he liked, he'd say, "It's just a half a note off." At this point I was only a couple of versions away from getting his okay.

Following Bert's blessing the copy was routed for approval to a lengthy list of folks that included numerous management and product folks – a process that took weeks. When all the comments came back, I incorporated them into the text and checked them with Hansen. The copy was then set in type and we received a preliminary proof. Text and graphics were combined on the proof, showing the ad as it would appear when published. One final routing ensured that no detail had been overlooked. Then the necessary elements were sent to the industry trade magazines: *Telephony* and *Telephone Engineer and Management*.

Hansen must have served in the Navy or Coast Guard, because his speech was salted generously with nautical terms: "The big boys are sure to deep six this idea" or "Whoa! Let's throw a dye marker over the side" or "I hope they don't torpedo this whole project." Bert didn't talk much about his family; he referred to his kids as "the boy" and "the girl." He drove a cheap car, which he turned in at 40,000 miles for a new cheap car. One day we drove separately to a meeting at a distant building on the AE campus. With ample parking available, I swung my new Javelin into a space in front of the building. Hansen pulled up right next to me and kicked his door open, denting my passenger door and knocking off a chunk of paint. *You asshole!* He exited his car completely oblivious to what he had done. The blood in my brain boiled; I felt like strangling the klutz but didn't say a word.

"Just keep it!"

If a project required a photo shoot in Chicago I might get to attend in an advisory capacity. This was a welcome break from Northlake. And occasionally I had to have a telephone or office switching console pulled from stock for advertising purposes. The procedure involved filling out a requisition slip, getting it approved and driving over to the warehouse to pick up the needed item. Once, when I borrowed a desk phone for a shoot, it rode around in the trunk of my car for months afterward. Finally, I remembered to return it to the warehouse. The guy I talked to was very annoyed, not because of my tardiness, but because of all the red tape involved in returning an item to stock. "Do you know how hard it is to put something like this back into stock?" he asked. "Do you know all the bullshit paperwork I have to go through? Why don't you just keep it? Take it home. You'll have a nice extra phone."

A little night music

After writing about telephones all day, I still had enough youthful vigor to take music lessons after work. One night a week I'd drive from Northlake all the way downtown for classical guitar lessons. My destination was the Chicago School of Music in the South Loop. I was always early, so I'd kill time by stopping for a drink or to grab some supper. Sometimes I'd eat cheap at Tad's Steak House, a greasy cafeteria on South Wabash under the El tracks. A meal there consisted of a tiny charbroiled steak that was mostly gristle, some shredded lettuce in a small plastic bowl and an enormous baked potato. Tad's had the biggest potatoes I've ever seen – bigger than some melons at the farmers' market.

I liked a place called the Pinch Penny Pub; it was small and dark with walls of natural brick. I'd sit there imagining that some stunning young babe would appear at the bar and want to hear my life story. Unfortunately, nothing like that ever happened. One cold winter night I ordered a martini and then decided to have another, trying to delay the frigid three-block hike to my lesson. When I finally got there, my young teacher, Paul Riley, was waiting. He took a deep breath before sitting down to start the lesson. Used to disappointing sessions with me week after week, he looked tense and apprehensive. On this occasion I gave him plenty to frown about. My fingers fumbled over the frets and I plucked the wrong strings. It was awful – chickens walking on the strings would have made better music. At the end Paul was speechless; he seemed to be in shock. I felt liked I'd killed him.

Mercifully for this terrific teacher, my lessons only lasted for a year or so. At that point, my classical sessions were making me late for the flamenco guitar lessons I was taking in Old Town. When my lesson with Riley was over, the trek back to my car was downright scary. The South Loop was the poor end of downtown; the streets were dimly lit at night and few businesses were open. The lack of people on Van Buren Street was creepy, and El trains thundering overhead made me shudder. I imagined that all that noise would mask the sound of gunshots or pleas for help from the victim of some horrible crime.

Friday night flights

One of my co-writers at Automatic Electric was Lou Hallenstein, an aging bachelor who lived downtown on Chicago's lakefront. He had an apartment in Lake Point Tower, right next to Navy Pier. Lou was always in tune with the newest trends in the Near North area, giving me regular reports on the Rush Street scene. His descriptions were full of words like "boffo" and "campy." Once in a while I'd tag along with Lou on a Friday night when he visited a few nightspots in his neck of the woods. Leaving work at 5 p.m., I'd follow Lou's Buick Skylark south to the Eisenhower Expressway and take it all the way downtown. I might pass him two or three times on the way but somehow he was always in the lead as we entered the Loop.

I'd follow Lou as he drove to some trendy place he said I just had to see. We'd hit spots like The Backroom on Rush to hear jazz piano or The Acorn on Oak to hear Buddy Charles tickle the ivories at the piano bar. Our trip to the Gas Light Club was a night of raucous, unforgettable fun. On another outing we stopped at Punchinello's Bar on Rush Street, where Zsa Zsa and Eva Gabor were sitting at the bar unwrapping presents – little Mark Eden bust-developer dumbbells – gag gifts from some friends. "But I have such good boobs dahling," Zsa Zsa said, giggling, "What would I want these for?" The oddest place Lou introduced me to was Figaro's, a dumpy little bar on Division Street. Protruding from the ceiling over the bar was the leg of a female mannequin sporting a black net stocking and a spike-heeled pump. I enjoyed the colorful locals at the bar, especially Ray Watkins, who sat on a stool playing flamenco guitar. Figaro's was always packed, even though nobody ever cleaned the men's john. It was always filthy – scummier than the worst gas station washroom I'd ever seen.

When music had class

And as much as he was taken with the latest trends, Lou had an abiding love for the big bands of the thirties and forties. Determined to educate me on this magical era, he introduced me to the music of Bennie Goodman, Glenn Miller, Guy Lombardo, Kay Kaiser and Sammy Kaye. And after I'd gained an appreciation of their music, he added more bands: Anson Weeks, Count Basie, Duke Ellington, Cab Calloway, Stan Kenton, Paul Whiteman … Lou kept them coming. Just to make sure I was paying attention, he'd stop into my cubicle and question me. A typical pop quiz would go something like this:

1. Who was "The Idol of the Airwaves?"
2. Whose band featured the Kollege of Musical Knowledge?
3. Who was the Waltz King?
4. Swing and sway with ...
5. What was Count Basie's theme song?
6. Who played "the sweetest music this side of Heaven"?
7. What bandleader led "The Herd"?
8. What was the theme song of Glenn Miller's Band?
9. Name Duke Ellington's most famous song.
10. Which bandleader asked, "Is everybody happy?"

Answers: 1) Jan Garber 2) Kay Kaiser 3) Wayne King 4) Sammy Kay 5) "One O'clock Jump" 6) Guy Lombardo 7) Woody Herman 8) "Moonlight Serenade" 9) "It Don't Mean a Thing If It Ain't Got That Swing" 10) Ted Lewis

Taking the easy route

The needle was on EMPTY. Time once again to slake my car's unquenchable thirst. That Javelin was a cool car but it guzzled gas like a Sherman tank. And the trip from home to my job in Northlake and back put 50 miles on my odometer every day. After a year at Automatic Electric I thought I might be better off with a job in downtown Chicago. I could take a train to work and leave my car at home. I thought I'd gained enough experience to move on, so I checked the Empoyment section of the Sunday *Tribune*. Answering a tiny, two-line ad for a copywriter, I landed a job at Kiver Publications in the West Loop. This outfit churned out trade journals targeting different areas of the electronics field and promoting industry trade shows.

FIFTEEN

SOMEWHERE WEST OF WIEBOLDT'S

"Illegitimi non carborundum!"
("Don't let the bastards grind you down!")
WWII British military slogan

IT WAS FUN TO BE working downtown even if my job at Kiver was pretty dull; I wrote cheap fliers hustling magazine subscriptions and trade show attendance. The senior writer was Hank Foskos, a pleasant, middle-aged man with many years of experience. Hank could crank out the work, taking everything that Kiver threw at him in stride. I learned a lot from him in the brief time we worked together. In midafternoon we'd take an elevator to the lobby and have a Coke at the drugstore. That was the highlight of my day. And a cute little secretary in the office made me look forward to life after 5 p.m. We'd been dating throughout the summer – enjoying movies, plays and eateries in the Loop.

Our boss was a loud-mouthed hack who I'll call Mort. I checked my work with Hank, who liked what I was doing. Then it went to Mort, who never had an encouraging word for me. In spite of this I was turning out good work, picking up speed and getting the hang of my job. Right about then Mort hired a third writer. I could see right away that this young guy had no writing experience whatsoever. He only lasted a few weeks before getting axed. With the goal of replacing him, Mort had run a blind ad for a writer. Unfortunately, our new co-worker made the mistake of responding to it, and was fired straightaway. He had answered a blind ad for his own job. What a cruel twist of fate.

Meanwhile, a flood of fliers, posters and sales letters kept me cranking hard all day. But this intense period ended abruptly at quitting time on a Friday afternoon. Mort told me to push my chair into his office. I was expecting to sit there for a while, but that's not what happened. Mort told me that he was letting me go. I was unable to work under pressure, he said. I disagreed, telling him that the writing coming out of his department was schlock. That was the best retort I could muster at the moment. I knew the real reason I was getting fired, and it had nothing to do with my job performance. But that's another story.

Don't hold your breath

Being axed was a shock, but I didn't waste any time launching a job hunt. I sent out résumés and checked the Employment section of the Sunday paper, looking for something in the writing field. This led to a couple of interviews in the Chicago area: one at the Tuthill Pump Company and the other at the Kendal Company. With my limited experience I had no clue as to what employers like these would expect from me. I signed up for unemployment benefits on the South Side and every week I had to check back with the unemployment office in person and wait in line to report in. It was humiliating and time-consuming. I maintained a job search, dropping off and mailing résumés to local employers.

Week after week rolled by but no unemployment checks came my way. After a month of this, I met with a benefit coordinator who said sarcastically, "It might seem to you that the system is set up to discourage you from collecting benefits." "It sure does, asshole," I wanted to spit back at him. A month later I arranged a hearing at which I presented my case before two aging, gray-eyed gentlemen. They wanted to see evidence that I was conducting a job search. I opened my briefcase and lifted out a stack of 40 or 50 rejection letters from potential employers. The men were astonished. One of them said he'd never seen so much evidence of a job hunt. It seemed that both of these evaluators were on my side, but when the meeting was over I still wasn't sure if I'd receive any benefits. In fact, I did get a check for eight weeks' worth of unemployment benefits, but by that time I was already back to work at a new job.

As luck would have it

After sitting on the beach for two months I spotted a small-space ad for a scriptwriter. The brief job description specified that experience was required. That type of writing was foreign to me, but I clipped the ad from the paper anyway. On my next trip downtown I spent the day dropping off résumés in tall buildings. By late afternoon my aching feet were begging me to head for the train station. I was ready to give in, but I still hadn't followed up on that little ad in my shirt pocket. The outfit seeking a scriptwriter was Coronet Instructional Films on South Water Street. I knew it was just north of the Loop, so when I reached Lake Street I asked a lady on the sidewalk if South Water was nearby. Pointing north, she said I was close, adding, "It's only a block long, so it's easy to miss." Minutes later I found South Water and the Coronet Building. It was 4:30 p.m. On the 20th floor, letters painted neatly on a glass-paned door read Coronet Instructional Films. I entered a small, dimly lit waiting room. It looked artless and dated, like an aging display at the Museum of Science and Industry. A shelf on the wall held a few trophy-like awards that needed dusting.

I rapped my knuckle against the frosted-glass reception window. It slid open. A middle-aged lady asked if she could help me. I said I was responding to an ad for scriptwriter. She asked me if I had any scriptwriting experience. "Yes I do!" I lied. Taking my résumé, she asked me to wait. A few minutes later she reappeared, telling me that Mr. Riha would see me. I followed her down a gray linoleum aisle to his office, where I shook hands with Tom Riha. He was a tall, husky gent who wore a gray moustache, glasses and a slightly distracted expression. Scanning my résumé, he seemed a bit perplexed. "I don't see any scriptwriting experience listed here," he said, looking up at me. "Do you have any actual experience in writing scripts?" "No," I answered. "I told the reception lady that I did so I could get in here and talk to you." Leaning forward and smiling faintly, he said, "Well, at least you were smart enough to lie."

Riha described the position he was trying to fill. It involved writing classroom films about subjects ranging from basic grammar to geography to library skills. I told him it sounded like a fun job and a great opportunity. He invited me to look at a finished script and handed one to me. It had a rigid audio/video format: the left-hand side gave detailed video instructions; the right-hand side held the typed narration for a voice-over announcer. Riha said that with no experience I'd need training and wouldn't be worth much to the company for at least a year. I assured him that I was a fast learner. He offered me a job starting at $90 a week. The terrible salary was a punch in the gut, but I accepted the offer and went to work at Coronet the following Monday.

Looking the part

It was October of 1970 when I started at Coronet. All the scriptwriters were male, and they all wore cowboy boots and Apache scarves. At first glance this getup struck me as having a certain panache, but before long I saw it as a uniform and opted to stick with clothes I felt comfortable wearing. Besides, I thought boots were for cowboys and Apache scarves were for hairdressers. To help me look like one of the guys, Mel Waskin, the head writer, gave me a handsome scarf he'd crafted with his own hands. I thanked him for it, but never wore it. My sister Marg thought the scarf was pretty, so I gave it to her.

Having just broken up with my girlfriend, my early days at Coronet were tinged with loneliness. In no hurry to get home after work, I sometimes viewed films from the Coronet archives after quitting time. One night I screened an old black-and-white flick recreating scenes from *The Pickwick Papers*. What a gem; the actors did a superb job of portraying the colorful characters. Of course, it's hard to go wrong with Charles Dickens. I also enjoyed movies about famous authors, and one that focused on the work of philosopher Bertrand Russell. Those archives were worth looking into.

An elite corps

We writers came from varied backgrounds that gave each of us a different take on things. Mel Waskin's writing was clear and direct, reflecting his systematic approach to things. He enjoyed lively lunchtime conversations, but always got back to work within the allotted hour. On the other hand, Larry Pont never let schedules get in the way of a good time. The brief profiles below give more details about these two and the rest of Coronet's writing force.

Mel, who was in his mid-forties, had encyclopedic knowledge gained from decades of writing about every possible school subject. He was a calm, even-keeled man, very comfortable in his own skin. His writing was upbeat and lucid. Mel had an answer to any question I ever asked him. He was very smart, but beyond that, he was wise and caring; he took time to listen my troubles and gave me thoughtful advice. Mel had a deep, soothing voice and a vast vocabulary, which he tried not to flaunt. He once told me that if he encountered an unfamiliar word, it didn't bother him. "If I don't know it by now," he said, "it's probably not worth knowing."

Larry was a talented writer in his early thirties who fought the Coronet system at every turn. I admired him for this. His stubbornness resulted in films that were better than anything the other writers were churning out. I thought it odd that rebellious Larry hung out with Steady Eddy Mel. Pont's gray metal desk lined up squarely with the door to his office. Passers-by could look him right in the face. And the front of his desk bore the official seal of the President of the United States. He liked to impress young gals from the office and elsewhere, which made his life interesting, if not happy.

Tom Ascher (aka Mr. Science) resided one door north of me. Tall, pushing forty and balding, he was adept at conjuring up science demonstrations. In fact, Coronet let him direct and shoot some of the films he'd scripted. When Tom returned from lunch each day he closed his door and took a nap on the floor, using the seat cushion from his chair as a pillow.

Some lucky people are naturally upbeat and fun. Don Abel was one of them. He was in control of things in a happy, relaxed manner. On some mornings he seemed absolutely buoyant. I envied him for his ability to deliver one good script after another and keep all of them within Coronet's miserable budgets. Don was two or three years younger than me, but more worldly-wise and mature. I enjoyed lengthy, after-work chats with him at Bob Elman's deli on State Street, or at the Orange Julius across the street. We'd sit and talk about the great things we intended to accomplish in life.

Rick Hawthorn threaded and ran the projector at our weekly screenings. This was not a special honor; it was a job delegated to "new boy," the last writer hired. Rick started two weeks after I did, so I only had to run the projector twice before Rick inherited the task, which he was stuck with for two years. Rick was a high school teacher who wanted to create curriculum instead of teaching it in the classroom. An ardent gear head, he often had his nose in *Hot Rod* or some other automotive magazine. Rick had a peculiar way of organizing his thoughts: he'd start scribbling in the center of a page and work his way outward in a spiraling pattern. His notes looked like little hurricanes.

Every morning at 10:30, all the writers and some of the production folks went next door to a little cafeteria for a morning break. These sessions were dominated by conversations between Mel and Larry. Tom injected a few words on occasion, but they were largely ignored. For my first few months at Coronet I felt frustrated sitting there watching *The Mel and Larry Show*, afraid to cut in on their heady persiflage. Once, when Mel and Larry were discussing religion, Ascher offered the brilliant insight that "Catholicism is based on cannibalism." His comment made my blood boil but I just kept my mouth shut. It didn't seem to bother anyone else at the table. One underwhelming moment that came each week was the delivery of my $90 paycheck from Esquire in New York. It was oversized, like a stock certificate, and the contrast between its grand dimensions and its paltry worth was laughable. However, one nice perk we Coronet employees enjoyed was a complimentary copy of *Esquire* magazine each month.

Deadline? What deadline?

Work at Coronet moved at a snail's pace. Ideally, each of us writers was supposed to churn out one script per month, but only Mel and Don met this quota. Hard deadlines were nonexistent. And the pathetic salaries Coronet paid did not inspire productivity. Rick Hawthorne and I, the new boys, wrote scripts for basic geography films, like *The Middle Atlantic States* and *Canada: The Prairie Provinces.* Writing these scripts wasn't a ton of fun, and it demanded a lot of fact-checking. But it was better than working on bizarre little films like *Are You Popular?, More Dates for Kay, How to Think* or *Making the Most of Your Face.* Rick got stuck writing *How Billy Keeps Clean,* so I was thrilled when Riha assigned *Basic Tumbling Skills* to me. What an unexpected breath of fresh air.

Another surprising event at Coronet was a visit from a smallish, elderly gent from Esquire Inc., our parent company and publisher of *Esquire* magazine. His large office was right next to my small one, and no one ever occupied that huge space except him. I remember the first time I spotted this little man at Coronet. He walked by my office wearing an overcoat with a fur collar and toting an umbrella. On his occasional visits from New York he'd use a key to enter his office and close the door behind him. He was visiting one night when I had to work late, and I saw light streaming from beneath his door as I left for home. That little fellow was in there doing something, but what? I wondered how long he'd stay – a few hours? All night?

When I came in to start work the next morning the curious visitor was gone; his door was closed and locked. He'd be likely to return in another few months. Nobody I asked knew who he was or what he did. I peeked inside his office once when a secretary was delivering a chromed water bottle. The walls were blonde wood paneling and the floor was carpeted in red. I entertained the thought that he was a time traveler – a visitor from years past – probably the thirties or forties.

Then I learned about "Esky," a gentleman mascot created by Esquire back in 1934. This little, three-dimensional character was featured on every cover – dining, dancing and cavorting with glamorous women – until 1961. When I started working for Coronet in 1970, only his face remained on the cover – dotting the "i" in the Esquire logo. Maybe this little fellow from New York was Esky come to life.

Lucky day on the CTA

On a steamy July morning in 1971 I took a seat on the El at 95th Street, the end of the line on the Dan Ryan CTA route. The car was nearly empty as a young lady in a purple midi seated herself a few rows in front of me. I promptly transplanted myself next to her. It looked as if she was headed downtown to work, just like me. She was carrying only a purse, so I tried to break the ice with, "Don't you take your lunch?" I introduced myself as Joe and she said her name was Mary as the train pulled out of the station. We struggled through some awkward conversation on the way to the Loop and exited at the same elevated stop. As we walked north together on Wabash she looked at me with an expression that seemed to ask, *Are you still here?* We soon reached South Water Street where I had to head east.

I turned right at the corner. She did the same. Fifty feet later we both entered the Coronet building. In the lobby I assured Mary that I hadn't been following her. "I work on the 20th floor," I said. We caught an elevator where I managed to get her last name. When we stopped at the eighth floor, I asked where she lived. "Around 101st and California," she admitted, stepping off the car. That night I looked up her last name and found an address in the general area she gave me. I dialed the listed number and asked for Mary. Seconds later she was on the line. After we talked a bit I asked for a date. She agreed to meet me for lunch the next day at Bob Elfman's Deli on State Street. I got the impression that this would be a trial date to see if I'd qualify for a real, full-fledged one.

Milking The Goat

A favorite lunch spot for Coronet folks was the Billy Goat Tavern on Lower Wacker Drive, just a couple of blocks from South Water Street. Half a dozen of us would walk north on Michigan Avenue and cross the bridge over the Chicago River toward the Wrigley Building. As we neared that famous structure the scent of grilling onions emanated from a hole in the sidewalk. Here we descended a staircase to The Billy Goat Tavern, commonly known as "The Goat." Larry Pont fondly referred to it as "Sir William's." Whenever a bunch of us headed for that establishment I had a feeling that anything could happen. Getting back to work was rarely a priority. Depending on the day or hour, you could find some colorful folks dining or drinking at the Goat. You might see pressmen from the *Tribune* sitting at the bar wearing little square hats folded out of newspaper. I guessed that their hand-made headgear shielded them from the grease and grime of those giant printing presses they operated. Once in a while you could spot Mike Royko or Studs Terkel sitting at the bar.

Our Coronet group liked to sit in the VIP room, off to one side and smaller than the main dining area. We would pull two small tables together to accommodate all of us. Arriving at 11:45 a.m., we might stay an hour or several hours. After a round of cheeseburgers and beer, the possibilities were limitless. Conversation drifted from philosophy to foreign filmmakers, from double-a dragsters to bolting from Chicago for parts unknown. Draft beer and Greek Roditis wine were cheap, so that's what we drank. Returning to my office I'd sometimes find a bright red, white and blue box on my desktop from the nearby Little Corporal Restaurant. Inside was one of their delectable pastries, a gift from Mary, that girl I met on the train and was now dating.

During one of our longer sessions at the Goat we ran out of money twice and sent runners back to the office to fetch more cash. On that occasion we closed the place after 13 hours of drinking. Luckily, I had enough change for carfare home on the CTA. A few years later the Billy Goat was featured in some great comedy sketches on *Saturday Night Live*. John Belushi played Sam the owner taking orders: "Cheezboogah, Cheezboogah, Cheezboogah … Coke? No Coke – Petsi!"

Checking out the competition

Once a week we writers reviewed educational films made by Coronet's competitors. After lunch we'd congregate in the viewing room to critique one or two of them. They were usually one-reelers (about 14 minutes long). There was always plenty to poke fun at, like bad writing, poor lighting and choppy editing. While one of these films played, smart-mouth comments and loud guffaws cut through the darkness. Sometimes Tom Riha, who was pretty straight-laced, would sit in on these viewings. The profanity that flavored our comments rubbed him the wrong way. When the show was over and the room lights were on, we followed up on the spontaneous comments made during the screening.

As a rule, the films were not very good. Like the ones Coronet made, they were usually stilted, didactic and made on the cheap. A straight-arrow, voice-over announcer carried the narration. A bit of stock music here and there helped enliven the droning educational message. One afternoon we were reviewing a film about shop safety that was so bad we were all laughing our asses off. Mel asked Rick to turn off the projector, and while he was rewinding the film, someone got an idea. "How about we run that film without sound and listen to the audio track to a kids' filmstrip?" The ridiculous audio-visual mismatch gave us all some welcome comic relief.

Once in a while we'd view a really filmic film – one that didn't try too hard to be educational. What a refreshing treat! I enjoyed one about a young boy who played in a tree house in a big oak that was slated for removal by a land developer. On the day it was to be cleared away the kid holed up in his little house while below him sat a bulldozer with its motor running. The driver was waiting for the boy to come down to earth. That standoff ended the film. Another terrific film showed the structure of Haiku poems with serene music under the visuals. And I liked a film about batik that simply showed the dying process and the beautiful results. There was no narration, just visuals and flowing music.

Banned in Yokohama

The first script I wrote at Coronet was for a geography film entitled *Japan: The Land and the People.* I worked from an educational outline prepared by a nice, older lady who researched background materials and organized salient points into one or two typed sheets that read like a list. Using her outline as a guide I banged out a treatment that described, in paragraph form, the script I intended to write. After Tom Riha gave the treatment his blessing, I prepared a detailed script that listed all the shots on the left-hand side, including camera angles, camera moves, cuts, dissolves, etc. The right-hand side held the narration and indicated where music and sound effects should be used. All the information was conveyed via "voice-over" narration; there were no people talking on camera in most Coronet films. After a year-and a-half I finally got to write a "talkie," with folks actually speaking to each other. Below is a scene from *Fun With Speech Sounds,* a primary-level film written in fairy-tale form. It shows the detail involved crafting a script at Coronet.

CLOSE, 3/4 SHOT, SLIGHT
LOW ANGLE looking up at
Throne – KING and PRINCESS.
KING is seated on THRONE and
PRINCESS STANDS next to him.

KING LOOKS toward SOUND TESTER and SPEAKS	KING (TO SOUND TESTER)
KING turns his head slightly and	Well, Sound Tester, give him the test.
SPEAKS to TOM.	
	KING (TO TOM)
	Good luck boy, do your best!*

Years after leaving Coronet I learned that the detailed scripts I'd written there were actually shot sheets. They were intended to simplify the work of the cameraman, who was often shooting in some distant locale. (Coronet farmed out many of its films to independent shooters.) In contrast to this method, scripts for major motion pictures are far less specific, leaving the shot selection, camera angles and such, up to the director.

Tom wins the hand of the princess in Fun with Speech Sounds.

The handwriting on the screen

Smart, "with it" kid shows on TV, like *Sesame Street* and *The Electric Company*, plus the advent of videotape, foreshadowed the death of Coronet Films. Savvy competitors were producing educational videos on VHS tape cassettes that were cheaper to make and priced lower than films. They also held up better because they didn't take the beating that films get as they pass through the metal sprockets of a projector. Mel Waskin, who had been writing Coronet films for decades, said he'd churned out several hundred scripts, covering every subject area and level – from kindergarten through grade twelve and beyond. When we were joking around one day he called Coronet "a living fossil." Having been part of the scene for so long, Mel knew where the company was coming from and could see where it was going.

Fun on the run

I'd met Mary in July and we embarked on a whirlwind dating campaign that would kill us today. Our adventures took us to the beach in Indiana, live, outdoor theater at University of Chicago, Beethoven beneath the stars in Grant Park and sketch comedy in Old Town at The Second City. Right across the street we heard great folk music at the Earl of Old Town. In New Town, just a short ride north, we caught Steve Goodman and Kris Kristofferson on the same night. Further north, near Mary's apartment, we found more folk music at the No Exit Café. We munched pizza at Papa Milano's and gobbled subway sandwiches at Little King's underneath the El tracks.

Mary finds a dry route across Sugar Creek at Turkey Run State Park, Marshall Indiana, 1971.

Month after month, I kept asking Mary to marry me until (hallelujah) she finally gave in. We tied the knot in May of '72 and honeymooned in Mexico City and Mazatlan. Returning late on a Sunday night, we rose early the next morning, scrounged beneath the couch cushions for carfare and headed off to work. At this point I'd put in two years at Coronet and was still earning next to nothing. So in October I told Tom Riha that I needed twelve grand a year. He looked shocked and promised me that there was no way I could get a raise that big. His response was just what I expected. Fed up, I gave two week's notice and left without having the slightest prospect of another job. Not the smartest way to leave one's position, but it felt great to cut the cord.

I was free to make a full-time hunt for a job that could pay me a living wage. After a few weeks on the street I got a call from Dan McConnell, the young Coronet director who was assigned to my fairy tale film. He said he'd be shooting it the next day at Jack Lieb Studios and invited me to drop by. The film featured beautiful sets and characters in colorful costumes. It would be exciting to watch everything come to life in front of the camera. "I'll be there," I promised.

When I walked onto the set the next day Dan pointed to me and shouted "Author! Author!" All the actors stood and applauded. *Wow! They're clapping for me!* What a thrill! It was the most satisfying feeling I ever got from Coronet and it came after I'd quit. The King and Royal Sound Tester actors told me what a rare treat it was to be involved in something so much fun. After watching McConnell direct a scene or two, I hoofed it over to State and Lake and took the El to Oak Park, where Mary and I were renting an apartment. Flipping through the new Coronet catalog a few months later, I came across a photo of Tom and the princess from my little film about speech sounds. I clipped it out and framed it. That picture is still hanging on the wall of my office at home.

Retro Downtown Chicago Matching Column

A. Grant Park	____ Had its own zip code
B. Wrigley Bldg.	____ Lower Wacker pub
C. Billy Goat	____ Deep-dish decadence
D. Picasso sculpture	____ Free classical concerts
E. Conrad Hilton	____ Dipped into Subway
F. Water Tower	____ Pre-Playboy beacon
G. El	____ Bright white at night
H. Palmolive Bldg.	____ Survived Great Chicago Fire
I. Merchandise Mart	____ 3000 rooms
J. Uno & Due	____ Civic Center Plaza

Answers top to bottom: I, C, J, A, G, H, B, F, E, D

SIXTEEN

JUST LIKE DOWNTOWN

*"It's easier to get into medical school
than to land a writing spot in a good agency."*
– Interviewer, Chicago ad agency

SOON AFTER LEAVING CORONET I found a writing job at an actual ad agency, thanks to some help from a family friend with connections on Michigan Avenue. I was thrilled to start work at Vollbrecht Advertising, a small outfit downtown on East Erie Street. John Vollbrecht, who ran the place, was an old pro who had been a creative director at some big Chicago shops in his day. His agency handled a few industrial accounts, a floral association and a musical instrument company. Working with John I got lots of practice in dreaming up ad concepts. He was a great teacher who made my day when he said, "You're a good ad maker, Murph!" John once confided in me saying, "In this business you've got to lie a little!" Business was shaky when I started at Vollbrecht and it didn't improve over the few months I worked there. Then one morning John called me into his office and told me matter-of-factly, "Joe, I'm making some staff changes and you're one of them." He let me use my office and phone to hunt down a new job. Fortunately, I landed one within a week or two. Mary and I flew out to California for a week between jobs. When we got back I started at CNA Insurance at the south end of the Loop.

Smooth operation

On my first day at CNA I reported to a modern red building at Wabash and Van Buren. I worked under Jim Schmid, a creative director who gave his people a good measure of freedom. Jim ran the advertising department like an ad agency. On most projects a writer was teamed up with an art director. This dynamic duo started a project by sitting down together to noodle out a plan of attack. Then, returning to their separate offices, each would go to work – the art director at the drawing table and the wordsmith at the typewriter. In a day or two they'd get back together to see how well the art director's ideas matched up with the writer's headlines and copy. My job provided a good deal of variety – everything from posters and brochures to ads and slide shows. On most projects my partner was Pat McCoy, a big young guy who laughed a lot. Once in a while we'd have a beer together after work and talk about off-the-wall projects – things we might do just for the fun of it. We actually started working on a board game called Heaven and Hell.

While we worked quietly on the 22nd floor, CTA trains below us screeched around the elevated tracks at the southeast corner of the Loop. Downtown elevated tracks encircled a one-square-mile chunk of turf considered to be the heart of downtown Chicago. In the seventies that area was home to major department stores (Marshall Field's, Carson's, Weiboldt's), thriving movie houses (Lake, United Artists, Woods) and great restaurants (Blackhawk, Fritzel's and Berghoff, among others). Then, as now, trains heading east from Wells Street, ran along Van Buren to Wabash, where they turned north and continued up to Lake Street. There they turned west, rolling straight to Wells. And here they turned south, making their way back to Van Buren and completing the "Loop."

CTA El tracks encircle the Loop

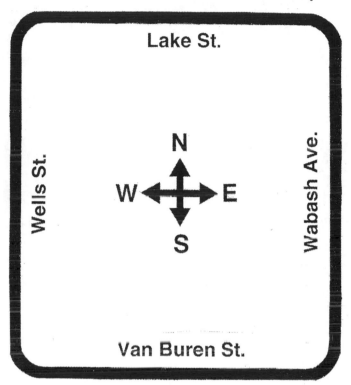

Blessed event

At CNA I had more to think about than my job. Mary was pregnant; her due date drew closer with each October day. Everything was going well, so there was nothing to worry about. On Halloween we went to a lively costume party. We were having a ball, but after an hour, Mary wanted to leave. So we drove home to our Oak Park apartment and turned in. About two a.m. Mary woke me up. It was time to head for the hospital, she said. Without delay we drove east to the University of Chicago Hospital. Mary was dressed in a hospital gown and helped into bed. So far, so good, but she would be in for a long, uncomfortable labor. Our blessed bundle didn't arrive until about ten a.m., but it was worth the wait. Mom delivered a healthy daughter weighing seven pounds, two ounces. She came out with her arms swinging like a little prizefighter. We had already decided on the name Bridget if the baby were a girl. The nurse swaddled the new arrival and handed her to Mary. She smiled sweetly and started nursing Bridget without delay.

It was time to tell the family. I dashed off to find a phone. At a nearby diner I had a cup of coffee and got plenty of change to use in their pay phone. I called my parents' house. Nobody answered, so I called my sister Joan. No luck there either. Next I rang up Aunt Martha, she was sure to be home. Uh-uh. I tried calling Mary's folks without any luck. *Where the hell is everybody?* I fretted. Then it hit me: it was November first, All Saints Day, a holy day of obligation for Catholics. They were all at church attending mass. Back at the hospital I swore to Mary that I had dialed my fingers to the bone trying to spread our good news, but my nativity notice had to wait till after lunch.

Baby, it's cold outside!

The winter of '74 started with nearly two feet of snow and unrelenting, subzero temperatures. Getting downtown from Oak Park on the CTA was no joyride. There were long delays along the Lake Street elevated line. When a train finally pulled up to the platform and the doors opened, I could hardly wedge my body into the car. The motorman tried over and over to shut the shuddering doors as riders attempted to back away from them. On one jam-packed morning I couldn't find anything to hang onto but there was no danger of falling. Passengers packed in tighter than sardines kept me vertical all the way downtown. I really wanted to get to CNA because it was a payday. As I stepped off the elevator, a secretary handed me my paycheck and told me to go home.

On bitterly cold days I was glad that CNA was right across the street from Lyon & Healy, the big music store. It was fun to stop in and browse their guitar selection. My favorite instrument was a guitar that looked like a lute. I'd tune up that gourd-shaped beauty and strum the chords to "Greensleeves," imagining that I was making music for a scene from

Shakespeare. When warm spring days arrived, a group of art directors would often walk north on Michigan Avenue at noon to watch some short, "artsy" films at the Art Institute. Out of curiosity I went along with the group one day. The films were quirky and entertaining, so I went back to see more of them a week later. This time a really dark film made me depressed; I was happy to get back outside into the summer sun. The following week I left CNA at noon with the moviegoers, but reaching Michigan Avenue, an irresistible urge made me turn and walk south. After a few blocks, vast green Grant Park appeared on my left. I stopped at the Fine Arts Building, took a peek at the elegant lobby and ate lunch next door at the Artist's Café.

The dartboard disaster

Leaving work one night I overheard a couple of men on the elevator talking about playing darts at a neighborhood tavern. This struck a chord with me because I had a great dartboard and a new set of darts at home collecting dust in a closet. The next morning I brought the dartboard to work and hung it on the partition separating my cubicle from my neighbor's. Within twenty minutes, art directors were in my space tossing darts at the target. Dumping the darts into my desk drawer, I told them they'd have to wait until lunchtime to play. Pat McCoy loved to sling my darts as far as he could. At six foot three he could easily see my dartboard from his cubby. He would back way up to the window and hurl darts over his cube's partition at the target hanging in my cubby.

I returned from lunch one afternoon to discover that my dartboard was gone. Ellen, one of the writers, informed me that the department head (our boss's boss), had marched into my cube, ripped it off my partition and stormed out with it. "But why?" I asked. She told me that a dart tossed by Pat McCoy had sailed over my partition. Someone screamed. When a group ran to investigate, they found a young man lying on the floor. Pat's dart had penetrated his shoe and was stuck in his foot. It turned out that the wounded fellow had just finished a job interview and was heading for the elevator. McCoy was scared as hell, and for good reason. It was no fun losing my board, but under the circumstances I didn't think it wise to ask for it back. Trying to envision the episode on my way home that night, I nearly laughed out loud. I never learned the name of the dart victim or if he was taken to the emergency room or if he got hired or what. I thought he might want to take CNA to court, knowing that the company was well insured. McCoy laid low after the dartboard incident. In fact, it wasn't long before he left CNA. Pat and his wife moved to Colorado to raise chickens.

Things were going well at CNA when I saw an ad from Impact International, an outfit that promoted trade shows. They were looking for an advertising manager. I had interviewed at Impact two years earlier without any luck. But now, armed with more experience and bolstered by more confidence, I decided to take another crack at the job.

A brief endeavor

I lined up an interview with Impact and talked with Jay Luyre, the company's founder. This time I was able to get myself hired as Impact's advertising manager, working directly under Luyre. He was a pioneer in event marketing who focused on association conventions. His business approach was to build attendance through marketing partnerships. I started at Impact thinking that most of my job would involve coming up with clever promotions for conventions and trade shows. No such luck. I spent most of my time working on bulky broadside mailers that featured dozens of convention speakers. These supersized creations unfolded like maps and could cover a desktop. I spent a lot of time on the phone with the speakers gleaning background info from them. Then I scrunched their lofty credentials into two or three lines of condensed type about an inch wide that appeared below their postage-stamp sized photos.

Lurye used a handful of stock promotions again and again. One of his favorites showed an infant clutching a clothesline, hanging on for dear life. Printed below it was the line, **Hang in there baby, help is on the way!** Graphic elements like the baby were stored in horizontal flat files with wide, shallow drawers that slid open on rollers. They were packed with a bewildering mishmash of photos and negatives thrown together like dirty laundry. Labels on the drawers didn't jibe with the contents. Nothing was kept in envelopes or folders. Trying to find something took forever; it was like digging through a garbage dump. After a week of this I conscripted Mary to come downtown on Saturday and help me organize that colossal mess. After working from noon till 5 p.m. we figured it would take another Saturday session to put things in order.

My second week at Impact was even more chaotic than the first. The routine was aggravated by Jay Luyre's antique, off-brand copy machine that made dark, muddy copies about as legible as carpet padding. I marveled that he had the chutzpa to send such horrible copies to clients. On Monday morning of my third week Jay called me into his office where he and one of his cut-rate suppliers were going over a paste-up for a broadside mailer. This huge art board was covered with itty-bitty photos and tiny copy blocks whose corners were curling up like flakes of peeling paint. In an angry tone Jay pointed out several "glaring errors" that I'd committed. Walking back to my office I wondered, *What the hell am I doing in this dump?* On my desk I found a box of 100 brand-new business cards with **Joe Murphy Advertising Manager** printed on them. I read my official title aloud. Pretty impressive! I got back to work, editing tiny biography blurbs to make them even tinier – squeezing the very life out of them. At noon I put on my jacket, chucked my business cards into the trash, and headed for the elevator. Eight years later I was downtown waiting to cross the street when a bald, middle-aged man approached me and asked, "Are you Joe Murphy?" "Yeah," I answered. "I'll never forget you," he said. "You're the guy who went to lunch and never came back!"

The quick brush

After leaving Impact International I pounded the pavement for a few weeks before hooking up with a marketing outfit in the Civic Opera Building on Wacker Drive. *A first-class place to work*, I thought, but from day one I had no place to sit. I set up shop at the empty desk du jour, depending on who was out that day. Bob, the frenetic little man who hired me, wrote small jobs for a collection of clients scattered far and wide. He liked to brag about how much he'd just billed somebody for a small-space ad that took him 20 minutes to dash off. Then he'd disappear for a couple of days and breeze back for an afternoon before blasting off to who knew where. Bob's frantic flitting back and forth made me want to smack him with a fly swatter. I needed him to look at what I was writing and give me something new to keep me busy. After a week or two Bob drove me up to Michigan to meet his big boss, who told him (I later learned),"Don't ever bring that guy back here again!"

Then it happened. One Monday morning I couldn't find an empty desk to save my soul. Where the hell was I going to sit? Then the CEO's secretary told me that he was on vacation till Monday. Hallelujah! I could sit in one spot for an entire week. Even better, I could sink my buns into to a posh leather chair. I set my typewriter on top of a massive oak desk and started writing a brochure about vacuum cleaners with "cyclonic suction." A few minutes later who bounced in but Bob? Taking a seat opposite me, he reported that all the feedback he was getting about me was negative. "I've got to let you go," he said in an urgent voice. Poor Bob. It sounded as if everyone was holding a collective gun to his head. I departed the Opera Building without a single printed sample to show for my efforts. Being banished so suddenly left a bad taste in my mouth, but I wouldn't miss that flaky, touch-and-go job or my frenetic, absentee boss. And hey, how many folks can say they were canned while sitting behind the CEO's desk? So I was back on the street again, but I had the consolation of going home to an understanding, sympathetic wife.

What next?

After moving from Coronet to a string of short-term jobs, my résumé looked like a train wreck, but there was a method to my messiness. After a certain length of time on a job – usually a year or two – I felt that I'd learned as much from that job as I was I ever going to learn. I figured that my real pay was the experience I was getting by doing so many different kinds of writing. So I stuck to my loose plan, hoping it would lead to a job writing TV commercials at a big agency. In retrospect, I'm surprised that anyone viewing my rag-tag employment history wanted to hire me. Maybe not asking for too much money worked in my favor. And now, with half a dozen jobs under my belt, I saw myself as a real creative bargain.

SEVENTEEN

THE HOME FRONT

"You haven't really been anywhere until you've got back home."
– Terry Pratchett

WHEN MARY AND I GOT married I was living in the attic apartment of a bungalow near 43rd & Pulaski on Chicago's South Side. Soon after moving in, a friend referred me to a carpet installer who had some rolls left over from a huge job. He gave me an estimate for the installation that was too good to refuse. So my living room and hall were upgraded with wall-to-wall, muted green carpeting accented by big yellowish blobs that looked like unshelled peanuts. I soon added an old green recliner purchased from a lady at work. In a resale store I found a bed, sofa and cocktail table. This sudden acquisition of material wealth made me feel like a millionaire. The apartment was a cozy space, but a large, square kitchen took up half of it. My friend John Kerrigan came over one night and helped me paint the kitchen yellow. Then we painted the refrigerator orange to match the orange chairs in the cheap dinette set I'd purchased at a discount store. All this happened right before I met Mary, so I was never sure if she liked the eclectic décor. Nevertheless, she made the most of it, adding some curtains to the kitchen windows and avocado paint to the door and window trim.

No kids allowed

I'd lived in my attic apartment for about a year before getting married. The tenant's entrance was in the rear. I opened the door to an enclosed stairway and climbed to the second floor. As a bachelor I often got home after 8 p.m. during the week. I'd be tired and hungry, but I didn't like to cook. And the aroma of boiled cabbage that often escaped from the first floor didn't help my appetite. If I were really hungry, I'd throw something together like frozen vegetables cooked in a pot with canned Franco American beef gravy. This diet changed drastically once I got married. Mary made well-balanced meals that tasted good and fit our budget. I can't remember that we ever had leftovers. Being a new homemaker, there were things Mary had to learn. The first time she cooked a turkey she slid it into the oven without removing the gizzard, liver and neck. And once, when her parents were coming over for dinner, she pre-sliced a whole ham before baking it; all the slices cooked up as crisp as potato chips.

When I bought a new, 19-inch, black-and-white Admiral TV I thought my life was complete. That cheap TV was an entertainment gold mine. Like a lot of folks back then, Mary and I wouldn't think of going out on Saturday night without first watching Mary Tyler Moore and Bob Newhart, whose sitcoms aired back to back on CBS. We didn't have much money to go out, anyway. We felt safe and snug in our cozy little nook. In case of a fire we could escape using a clever device mounted next to the kitchen window. Basically it was a coiled-up cord with a handle you grabbed hold of before jumping out the window. The spring-tensioned cord would supposedly deliver you safely to the ground and then recoil back to the second floor to pick up the next escapee. Being young and naïve we trusted this Rube Goldberg contraption.

Our happy situation changed abruptly when Mary learned that a little one was on the way. I got home from work first one night while she was delayed by a doctor appointment. I heard her coming up the back stairs and opened the door. "Hi, pops," she said, stepping into the kitchen. We were going to be a family. I'm not sure how the landlord downstairs found out about Mary's condition, but he told us we'd have to move out before the baby arrived. Uh-oh. We'd miss the place and the cheap rent, but it wouldn't have been a great place for a toddler to run around in. We were forced to make a quick exit, but at least it wasn't through the kitchen window.

A place of our own

Location, location, location. I'd been told repeatedly that those are the three most important things to consider when buying a home. Mary and I took this advice to heart and bought our first house in Downers Grove, a charming old suburb west of Chicago. And here we were, moving in. Our tiny clapboard house looked like a cottage compared to the substantial, well-kept homes surrounding it. We had scrimped to scrape together a down payment for this shack. It was nobody's dream house, but it was a home. A start.

Unloading the U-Haul trailer on that hot June afternoon, I tried to keep my spirits up. I wondered how long it would take me to land a job. Two weeks earlier I'd been let go from my writing post at that frenetic marketing outfit in the Civic Opera Building. With a wife and baby girl to support, unemployment had a dark new meaning for me. I had to bring home the bacon and pay the mortgage. My worried state of mind magnified the drawbacks of our little place. The rooms were small and dingy; the walls were covered with cheap paneling that had been painted over; the carpeting was a weird rust color darkened by years of wear. Beyond that, the two-car the garage out back was so packed with junk, we couldn't fit the one car we owned into it. Well, we could look into those matters after a good night's sleep.

Sweet dreams

Mary and I located all the parts to our bed, put them together and turned in early. Loud scuffling, scratching sounds awakened me. I was standing scratching my head when Mary woke up. "What's that sound?" she asked anxiously. I told said it had to be some kind of animal. "Is it on the roof?" she asked. I told her it was up in the attic. She shook her head resignedly, shrugged her shoulders and went back to sleep. We had an emergency on our hands, and the next day was Sunday. I phoned the exterminator and left a message. Then we drove down to Ogden Avenue and ate a hefty breakfast at Mark's Big Boy. Back home we sized up the eclectic jumble of crap in the garage. Sheets of warped plywood leaned against one wall. Adjacent walls were lined with tomato cages, milk crates, cinder blocks and boxes of asphalt shingles. We found more debris on the floor – rotted two by fours, rusty pipes, copper tubing and curtain rods. Resting on the rafters overhead were a couple of doors, a rickety old ladder, bamboo fishing rods, arrows without any feathers, a deflated kids' swimming pool, a moldy pup tent and a badminton net.

We spotted two old bikes leaning against the back wall – a boy's model missing its seat and chain and a girl's model, which seemed to have all its parts. I found a bicycle pump and filled the tires. An hour later the rear one was still holding air, so I patched the front one and pumped it full. Good. We had an extra set of wheels. Mary and I spent the rest of the day hauling junk from the garage to the front curb: long lengths of rusty pipes, bed frames, wooden crates, lengths of cable and chains, broken garden tools, old newspapers and bushel baskets filled with busted toys. This routine continued each weekend for a month.

On Monday I rode the girl's bike downtown to the Downers Grove Library and checked through a directory of Chicago ad agencies, scribbling a few notes before heading home. That night I typed letters, added résumés to them and stuffed envelopes addressed to prospective employers. I mailed them in the morning on my way to the train. The Burlington took me to Chicago's Union Station, where I disembarked and hit the sidewalk, schlepping my trusty portfolio. I checked out big buildings, looking at their lobby directories for the names of possible employers. If one of them looked promising I took the elevator up and left a sheet with the receptionist. This exercise was largely a waste of time, but it made me feel like I was doing something.

Meanwhile, back in Downers Grove, a man from the pest control outfit checked out our roof. He told Mary that our rooftop invaders were raccoons – a whole family of them. They had pawed their way through a soggy spot in the roof and taken up residence in our attic. One of our oak tree's big limbs had been resting on the roof and keeping the rain from draining off. For years water had been seeping in through the shingles and into the wooden roof underneath, turning it to mush. Resourceful raccoons had pawed their way through that soggy barrier into our attic where they romped among the rafters. The exterminator rousted the raccoons and called in a roofer who put a patch over the hole. When I got home from job-hunting that day, a worker on the roof was hammering a sheet of plywood in place. He told me to get the tree limb removed and gave me a number to call in case I wanted a whole new roof. Luckily, I found a job a few weeks later at Weber Cohn and Riley. My first check covered the roof patch and the mortgage.

Mission impossible

Another girl! Mary delivered a seven-pound, eight-ounce baby girl on September 13th, 1975. What a doll! She looked like a red-haired version of her sister Bridget, born two years earlier. A few days later I was scheduled to pick up mother and child at Hinsdale Hospital and drive them home. I took the train downtown and walked to my office at Weber Cohn & Riley that morning, intending to leave at noon in order to reach the hospital by 2 p.m. But there was a hitch. The account exec on a new real estate account was out sick. What to do? The agency biggies recruited me to drive out to Cary, Illinois and present a newspaper ad to their eccentric client. It was all pasted up and ready to run; we just needed an approval before placing it in the *Tribune*. I took off on my mission, riding the Burlington back to Downers Grove and walking a mile to my house. There I jumped into my car and I drove 20 plus miles northwest to Cary.

I found the development and located the sales office, where I shook hands with the client. He was dressed in a nicely tailored, solid-red suit, almost Santa Claus red. But this character was not the jolly old elf. Not by a long shot. He was old, skinny, wrinkled and ugly; his basic expression was a snarl. When I presented the new ad he took it from my hands and examined it, turning it one way and another, as if he couldn't make heads or tails of it. Really pissed, he said the ad just didn't look right. It should be slicker, he insisted. I started to make a suggestion when he cut me off. "You'll print it on a goddam brown paper bag if I want it that way!" From that point on he did all the talking while I took notes. *I wish you'd hurry, asshole*, I thought. *This bullshit is really screwing things up!* I wasn't going to make it to the hospital on time.

When this creep had fully vented his spleen, I darted to my car and took off, pedal to the metal. I'd only gone a few miles when the flashing MARS lights of a police car appeared in my rearview mirror. The cop pulled me over and told me I was doing 15 over the limit. I tried to explain the reason for my rush. "You see, officer...." "Tell it to the judge!" he barked, handing me a hefty ticket. I proceeded cautiously for a few miles before stomping on the accelerator. When I got to the hospital, Mary was standing on the sidewalk holding her new bundle of joy. I felt like a heel for showing up late. And I was pissed at my employer for sending me on such a kamakazi mission. The next day I called in sick and stayed home with my newly expanded family.

A chilling lesson

One frigid weeknight in January Mary and I were relaxing after supper when she found something of interest in the local paper. Downers Grove High School was offering swim lessons for infants. She talked me into taking four-month-old Bridget to the pool for lesson one. So I strapped little B into our bone-chilling Corvair and drove to the high school, hoping to see her take to the water like a tadpole. I couldn't imagine a *grownup* going for a swim on a night like that, so it seemed to me that an infant would like it even less. Four or five other parents showed up to subject their little ones to this ordeal. With Bridget in my arms, I slipped off the side of the pool into the water. *Brrrr!* My body went into shivering spasms. I couldn't believe water could remain in a liquid state at that temperature.

Our lady instructor explained that we were going to completely immerse our babies into the water and quickly pull them out. But first we had to blow into their faces to make them stop breathing. One, two, three – blow! We dunked our clueless infants and quickly pulled them up. When I lifted Bridget from the water she shrieked and punched me squarely in the nose. I was embarrassed in front of the other parents and amazed that their infants popped up out of the icy water totally calm and unfazed. My nose was smarting, but I could see Bridget's point. I took her to the locker room, dried her off and bundled her up for the ride home. True to form, the Corvair failed to produce a breath of warm air all the way back to our house.

Bridget gets even

"Why did she wait till age three to start sucking her thumb?" I asked. Mary didn't seem overly concerned about Bridget's new habit, but I was perplexed. We talked things over and decided to coat her thumb with a foul-tasting product concocted to discourage thumb sucking. After she was asleep one night I brushed the liquid onto her right thumb, thinking she'd get a taste of it in the morning. But in the middle of the night B tugged on my shoulder, waking me up. "My thumb tastes terrible," she said. "Is it magic?" "I don't know," I mumbled, getting out of bed. I picked her up and carried her back to her crib. The next morning, when she complained to Mary about how bad her thumb tasted, Mary played dumb.

That night I waited till Bridget was asleep and recoated her thumb. About 2 a.m. she woke Mary, complaining about how awful her thumb tasted. Offering some quick explanation, Mary put B back in her bed. A similar scenario ensued for a couple more nights. Then one morning I began brushing my teeth, and ugh, what a disgusting taste. I darted into the kitchen and asked Mary, "What's in this toothpaste? It tastes horrible!" "It's not the toothpaste," she replied. "It's Bridget." "What?" I gagged. "She found the thumb medicine and put it on your toothbrush. She did the same thing to mine." I was dumbfounded. Bridget had figured out our little game and decided to give us a taste of our own medicine. I looked at Mary and we both started laughing. What a clever little girl we had. She could outfox Mom and Dad.

After supper that evening, Mary and I were relaxing in the living room while Bridget was playing on the floor. "Come over here," I said to her. When she walked up to my recliner I gave her a good swat on the butt. She straightened up and looked daggers at me. "You know why I did that?" I asked. "Because you're a mean stupid dummy!" she replied angrily. "Why did you put that stuff on our toothbrushes?" I asked. "How do you like it?" she barked back at me. Mary and I could hardly keep from laughing. We put Bridget to bed that night without painting her thumb. After she was asleep we discussed our daughter's revenge plot. Figuring out just what to do, she had climbed onto the bathroom sink, opened the medicine chest, identified the thumb goop and applied it to our toothbrushes. Wow! It looked like B intended to keep sucking her thumb for a while. But what precocious ingenuity! I thought maybe she'd grow up to be a detective.

Painting the house

When the spring of 1975 arrived I sized up the house's exterior. Its yellow clapboards were looking dingy and peeling badly. Our little shack was the sorriest looking place around. Thinking it would boost my spirits, I tried to spot a nearby house that was in worse shape than ours. In fact, I took different routes on my walk to the train station each morning, hoping to locate such a disaster. No luck. The situation ate at me through the fall and winter, so by spring, I was ready to slap a fresh coat of paint on our humble abode. Of course, it wouldn't be that simple. The peeling paint, many coats and colors thick, had to be removed, and regular scraping wouldn't get the job done. That crispy curling crud would have to be softened by a blowtorch before it could be scraped away. Then I'd have to disc sand the clapboards to grind off the crust that was still clinging to them. But wait, there was more: cracks and voids aplenty had to be caulked, and then the whole place needed a coat of primer before I could apply the first drop of paint.

In April I started in on the clapboards with a propane torch and a putty knife, inching my way along the narrow slats. The blistering paint stunk and nasty smoke made my eyes water. After a weekend of this folly I figured there had to be a better way, so I took a trip to my favorite hardware store. Here I found an electric grid on a handle that looked like it would cover twice as much area as my torch. I also picked up a few tubes of acrylic caulk. Back home I plugged the electric gizmo into an extension cord and got back to scraping. Now I was working twice as fast.

I scraped for months, then disc sanded, burning out the electric drill I'd borrowed from Dad. Blowtorching the soffits and scraping the paint off them was no fun. I'd be standing near the top of the ladder with my neck bent all the way back. The paint came off in sizzling hot strips like poisonous bacon and fell straight into my face. I bought a clear protective mask that wrapped around my forehead. It looked like something from Buck Rogers, but did a good job of shielding me from the hot, sticky crud. Torching the old paint made a lot of acrid smoke that stung my eyes. In fact, it left them bloodshot for months. Folks at work asked me if I was getting enough sleep. While I was scraping on Saturday afternoons, Mary would seat baby Eileen in a little wind-up swing in the living room. She looked like a little dab of toothpaste curled up in the canvas seat. Before I went outside to scrape I turned the key that wound up the swing and nudged it gently to set it in motion. Then, every half hour or so, I went back inside and wound it up again. My brother-in-law called our little swing "the neglectomatic."

Me (left) and brother Jim (right) take a breather after
burning and scraping paint off my house, 1976.

Our front porch in Downers Grove, July 4th, 1976.
Mary's holding Bridget, I'm holding Eileen.

Back to Oak Park

In June of '78, Mary and I, now with two little girls, returned to the Chicago area after a two-year pursuit of distant career opportunities. We bought an old house in Oak Park with a long side yard that ran from the front sidewalk to the garage in back. There was room aplenty for kids to romp and play, but first we had to cut down a forest of weeds. The house was a modest story-and-a-half frame job with clapboard siding and a steep roof. In back a concrete parking slab three cars wide sat next to the garage. Our across-the-alley neighbors were an Amoco station and a hardware store. We bought the house from the hardware store owner, who had been renting it for years and using the garage as a stockroom. He wanted to keep his storage space, so at the closing I suggested that we rent it to him. We settled on a 36-month period, so Mary and I parked our Toyota wagon outside on the concrete slab for three years.

On the first morning in our new home we found a new Cadillac stretched across our slab on a forty-five degree angle. Its owner was getting free parking and ding-free doors while stealing all the space from my family and me. I stuck a sign under the windshield wiper explaining that I owned the property and didn't want anyone parking on it. When this didn't work I stuffed a fistful of weeds under his wiper. He came back the next day. Finally, two bushels full on his hood did the job. Meanwhile, Mary was sizing up the inside of our place. Astonished that former occupants had painted over the oak woodwork, she began to strip the many layers of latex and enamel from the wood trim on the first floor. Unfortunately, the rising fumes seeped through the ceiling into the bedrooms upstairs, giving the kids headaches. So Mary had to limit her paint removal to daytime hours. On weekends I stripped paint from the bathroom woodwork, a project that dragged on week after week. When Bridget's kindergarten teacher asked her class what their fathers did for a living, Bridget answered, "My daddy works on the bathroom." I finished that project after a few months, but Mary's downstairs paint-stripping campaign stretched on for a couple of years.

Cool mornings on Wabash

Throughout the dozen years we lived in Oak Park it was easy to get to work on the CTA. The street-level rapid transit station was a five-minute walk from home and the Congress El ran straight east to Chicago's Loop. Finding an empty seat, I could read, doodle or sleep on the way downtown. It took about 30 minutes to reach my stop. Then it was a short walk to my office on Michigan Avenue. Door to door, the commute was about 45 minutes. Mary and I agreed that we should both get more exercise, so I started exiting the train at Jackson and hiking a few extra blocks to reach work. I could feel my body absorbing the Loop's abundant energy as I walked east to State Street, then north to the Palmer House. I often cut through that classy hotel over to Wabash Avenue. It was a fun shortcut that added a touch of warmth to cold winter mornings. The broad passageway was lined on both sides by exclusive shops, whose windows showcased luxurious goods like Gucci handbags, exotic perfumes from Paris and designer 14-karat gold jewelry – all of it light years out of my league. Exiting onto Wabash, I hiked north beneath the El tracks. The thunder of overhead trains shook loose any morning cobwebs nesting in my brain. That stretch of tracks along Wabash defined the east border of the Loop.

Angel killer!

Very few things have made me feel as bad as destroying my little girl's Christmas costume. Mary had crafted an angel costume from sheer white curtain material for Eileen, hoping she'd win the prize for best costume at her first-grade Christmas party. I had cut a pair wings out of Styrofoam, painted them light pink and glued them on an angle to a flat base so they flared out a bit. Then I fashioned a halo of stiff wire, allowing for a straight length that I bent and rooted into the base. Gold paint and glitter made it look heavenly.

When Mary showed me the sheer white costume she'd made, I decided to secure the wings to it with screws. Cutting slits in the back,

I pushed the wings through them. I thought drilling pilot holes for the screws would help, so I aimed my electric drill at a spot between the wings and slowly squeezed the trigger. *WHIPWHIPWHIPWHIPWHIP!* The entire costume wrapped itself around my drill like a ball of cotton candy. *Oh God, I've wrecked the thing!* I thought. *Mary will murder me!* I went upstairs holding the balled-up mess and sheepishly confessed to my crime. Mary was near tears; she said there was no way she could make another outfit before school started. I left for work feeling like a heel, and the feeling stuck with me all day. When I got home, Mary greeted me with a smile. She reported that Eileen had won first place for her angel costume. "How did you pull off that miracle?" I asked. Resourceful Mary had scrounged up some more old curtains and sewn a new costume in record time. She used a white sash to attach the wings to it bandolier style. Eileen had skipped off to school without even being tardy.

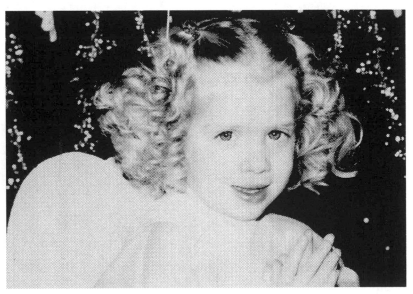

Eileen smiles angelically, Christmas, 1980.

Lessons unlimited

Mary made sure the kids stayed active. She was determined to make sure that all of their talents had a chance to blossom. Bridget and Eileen took music lessons, gymnastic lessons, ice-skating lessons, swimming lessons…. They loved Gina Orlando, their piano teacher at Ascension, our neighborhood Catholic grammar school. Gina had B playing in competitions at age six. Eileen starred in gymnastics, traveling to tumbling meets throughout the Midwest. I can't forget a special trip to Central Illinois. On a dark, freezing Sunday afternoon E and I drove south to a meet in a small town I'd never heard of. The competition lasted several hours, and Eileen won first in her age group.

We left the gym savoring our victory and found our Toyota wagon in the parking lot clad with a thick coat of ice; it looked like a huge glazed dumpling. I used the ignition key to chip away the ice covering the keyhole and unlocked the door. Luckily the engine fired right up. The tires ripped away from the icy asphalt with a loud crunch. We crept slowly over the slippery main drag to the edge of town, only to find that we were headed in the wrong direction. So we backtracked to the other end of town and headed into the inky blackness beyond. Eileen was soon asleep. The treacherous pavement made for slow going. After an hour or so Eileen woke up, checked the map and looked out her window. "Dad, you missed a turn way back there," she announced. I pulled over, and she showed me where I'd gone astray.

After we turned back, E stayed awake until we hooked up with I-57, which took us back to Oak Park. The road was slick and skittish all the way. It was 3 a.m. when we got home. Mary sent Eileen straight to bed. Then she gave me some news she'd received about the van carrying most of E's gymnast teammates: it had gone off the road into an icy ditch. No one was hurt, but everyone on board spent the night in a motel. Mary let our gymnastics champ sleep late and sent her to school in the afternoon. After supper that night I'd just settled into my easy chair when I overheard Eileen in the kitchen describing our trip to Mom: "Dad doesn't know how to read a map. He keeps getting lost all the time."

Do you wanna dance?

This should be fun, I imagined, walking up Oak Park Avenue on a summer evening. I was headed for the field house at Fox Park for a group tap dancing lesson. About 30 students of all ages were standing on the floor when I entered. A pleasant young fellow up front described tap as a fun form of dance that provided great aerobic exercise. He told us to relax our ankles. Having relaxed ankles, he said, is the secret of tap. We should make a conscious effort to keep them loose and keep their movement minimal. This sounded easy enough.

Then he picked up the pace, throwing a lot at us in a hurry. We should lean forward so our center of gravity stays in the middle … hold most of our weight forward … balance on the balls of our feet … make sure we keep in time to the music. *Maybe this won't be all that simple*, I feared. We learned the toe tap and the heel tap. Not too hard. But then we had to combine them and move around the room in a circle toeing and heeling. My feet seemed to be drunk; they were way out of step with this simple exercise. Then came more steps: the brush and drag, the shuffle-hop step, the pull back. My muscles refused to obey the signals from my brain. As things got worse my embarrassment became complete.

Then the tap guru explained a few "simple" combinations and transitions. The class tapped its way around the room again, integrating these new maneuvers. When I reached the corner near the door, I shuffled my way out of the building and walked home, thinking that I might give square dance lessons a shot.

Video pioneers

Cablevision of Chicago had come to Oak Park and opened their offices a few blocks from my house. They were offering classes in TV production for folks interested in public access TV. Mary spotted their announcement in our local paper, *The Oak Leaves,* and said that maybe I'd want to I check it out. I signed up for the course without delay and was soon standing behind a camera in the studio. Along with other public access trainees I learned about white balance, bloom and other video phenomena. A few weeks later, with a bare-bones knowledge of video, I submitted an idea for a series of public service clips showing familiar locations around Oak Park. The working title was "Hysterical Landmarks." The director of the program, who called us "video pioneers," liked the idea. The following weekend I was out shooting my first video. A girl at work named Cathy, who wanted to get some experience producing video, agreed to help me with my project. We made a deal that she would help me now if I would help her with a future project she had in mind. I wrote some silly sketches in which I stood in a familiar Oak Park location and absentmindedly explained what it wasn't. Near the end of my spiel a line superimposed on the screen spelled out the real name and address of the place.

In one of the "Landmarks" I talked about the giant hockey pucks at the outdoor Oak Park mall. In reality they were a group of round, low profile stone seats. The temperature was around zero on that Saturday morning. Cathy and I were freezing and the camera batteries were not delivering full power. We retreated to a corner restaurant, where we had a cup of coffee while the batteries warmed up. After half an hour we went back outside and finished the shoot. On Monday I returned the colorful Chicago Black Hawks jersey that the equipment manager had loaned me for the project.

We shot other sketches at locales that included City Hall, the Oak Park Library and the Oak Park Conservatory. My Hysterical Landmarks were not all that hysterical, just mildly humorous (and pretty corny). But the title of my public access project caught the attention of a young reporter for the *Chicago Tribune*. She interviewed me and included my project in a story about public access TV. Darned if it didn't appear in the Sunday paper. Lots of people read the article, including the president of the ad agency where I was working. He visited my office Monday morning looking a bit concerned. "You're not getting paid to do that stuff, are you?" he asked. I assured him that I was not.

Cathy and I shot seven or eight sketches before burning out on the series. We were getting on each other's nerves, and Cathy said she wanted to work on something "fun," which rubbed me the wrong way. We didn't talk to each other for quite a while, and I never did help her with her video project. The way I handled that situation still bothers me. The Hysterical Landmarks aired for several months on the public access channel, prompting family members and friends to call and comment on them. But all too soon they were gone. I recalled a quote from my high school Latin book, "Omnis gloria fluxa" (All glory is fleeting).

Don't touch that dial

While working downtown at Campbell-Mithun Advertising I taught a night class at Columbia College in the South Loop. My boss, Al Parker, who headed up the school's radio department, was a station announcer at ABC TV with offices downtown on State Street. I came to him with an idea for a class in comedy writing for radio, bringing with me a tape of humorous sketches and radio spots. I played it for Parker, who laughed out loud more than once. He asked me to write up a proposal outlining what I wanted my course to include. A week or so later I got back to him with a prospectus. Parker was impressed; he gave my course his official seal of approval. We decided to call it *Fun With Comedy Radio*. Hallelujah! Now all I had to do was teach it.

The first night of class was chaotic; people talked without raising their hands and chatted with each other at full volume. *Unbelievable!* I decided to start each class with a written quiz, figuring that routine would quiet everybody down. It worked, so that's the way I started every class from that point on. I'd play a cassette recording of a funny radio sketch or a clip from an old-time radio show. My students had to listen carefully if they wanted to get a good grade. The quiz put them into a thoughtful mood; it really helped to get each class started in the right direction. The mix of students was quite varied – most of them were college-aged kids, but there were a few people who looked 30ish as well as a couple of middle-aged folks. The older students always did their homework. We spent some time on old-time radio sitcoms, like *Fibber McGee and Molly* and *Amos 'n' Andy*. Then we covered humorous radio sketches by comics like Bob and Ray and Stan Freeberg. For good measure, I tossed in a few episodes of Dick Orkin's *Chickenman* series that aired on Chicago radio in the early sixties.

The homework assignments were to write funny scripts, which we read aloud in class. Writing was more popular than reading, but I could count on a few extroverts to read their own material or anybody else's. One kid, who attended class regularly, was not on my class roll. I kept telling him that he wasn't enrolled and he kept swearing that he'd signed up late for the class and that was why his name wasn't on my list. He turned in all his assignments, got an A on every quiz and was a terrific script reader. He even took the final exam, and aced it. When I turned in the final grades, I checked with the office one last time to see if this super student had ever signed up for my class. They assured me that he had not. It was strange, but I was flattered that he liked the course so much. And there was one young man who was very outspoken in class, but he just couldn't read. Not even small, one-syllable words. Unfortunately, he wanted to become a disc jockey. I wondered how he got the okay to take my class. But at that time the open-enrollment policy at Columbia College was pretty lenient.

Keep 'em laughing

For several months I wrote jokes and short blurbs for a Chicago disc jockey named Doug James. He was the morning man at US99, a country-and-western station broadcasting from the John Hancock Building downtown. I dreamed up imaginary lists of top ten country songs, fictional news clips and silly fairy tales with surprise endings. On several occasions Doug asked me if I'd heard him read the newest lines I'd written for his morning broadcast. I had to say "no" because he was going off the air when I was getting out of bed. "I gave you a credit man," he'd remind me. "Here's something from my friend Joe Murphy in Oak Park!" I enjoyed this quirky writing stint for the first couple of months, but it was taking up a lot of my time.

One morning I got up early to finish writing my weekly batch of humor but couldn't think of a funny line to save my soul. *Just keep going,* I urged myself as the clock ticked away. By the time I'd finished writing it was almost noon. *What the hell*, I thought. *I've got a regular job to take care of!* It was the middle of the day and I still had to deliver the material to the John Hancock Building before heading to my regular job. I was ready to tell Doug that I had to stop writing lines for him when he phoned me at my office. He said he was leaving US99 to focus on doing voice work for radio and TV commercials. Before long he was appearing on-camera as a spokesman for national TV advertisers. Way to go, Doug.

Summer of the 13 sparrows

"Not another one!" I shouted, finding a dead sparrow on my office couch. The situation had gotten out of hand. We'd been living in our Oak Park home for five years and all of a sudden sparrows were piling up in our basement. Sometimes, while working down there in my office, I'd suddenly hear chirping or the rustling of feathers. Looking up I'd see a sparrow flying into a windowpane, going nowhere, falling out of view and coming back to try again. I'd prop open the window to help, but the terrified bird would fly deep into the basement, eventually to find its way back to the open portal and make its escape. This was on a good day. On other days a sparrow would opt to hide underneath the couch, making rescue a time-consuming pain in the ass. And that was just the day shift. Some birds arrived by night.

Heading downstairs one morning to finish a writing job, I found my notes decorated with sparrow poop. That afternoon I discovered a dead bird on top of my filing cabinet. The next day I found another one in the laundry tub. Where the hell were they coming from? Mary figured they must have come flying down the chimney. Sure, maybe, but why so many and why all of a sudden? I opened the furnace door; there to greet me was a dead sparrow. My clever wife was right. I wondered why all thirteen of our winged visitors were little brown sparrows. Not a single robin or finch or warbler had flown down our chimney to brighten things up. Well, maybe sparrows are more curious than their feathered friends. Or maybe just dumber. We called a chimney sweep, who discovered that a critter-blocking steel mesh covering our chimney had rusted through, allowing access for the birds. Then he reported that our chimney was full of soot and in need of cleaning. So we killed two birds with one stone, as the saying goes, and got both problems taken care of. Still, it took two or three months before we found the last sparrow, nestled behind a couch pillow.

Cleared for takeoff

One spring we dared to crap out on the Midwest and spend Easter in Florida. Mary and the kids were upstairs packing; I was in the basement finishing up a writing project. Suddenly I heard a throaty, slushy sound coming from the side yard next to our house. Then there was a loud scream from Bridget. I ran upstairs to find her in the dining room looking very upset. "Oh Daddy!" she sobbed. "A car just drove right through our yard!" Everyone ran outside to investigate. There was no vehicle in sight, but even in the dark we could see plenty of property damage. Someone had indeed driven from the front to the back of our property. "He should be executed!" Bridget screeched. Veering off the street, the car had torn through the yard and rear parking area, taking out our chain-link fence before turning up the alley. We found the gas tank resting on top of some flattened bushes, so we knew its owner couldn't be too far away. The police found him and his Buick LeSabre in the alley half a block north of our house.

We refused to let this mishap kill our vacation plans. Before turning in I called the insurance company and left message on their voice recorder. We arose early the next morning to get a better fix on the damage. Our front parkway and sidewalk had not escaped the wrath of that big Buick. Tire marks running through the yard showed that it had missed our house by inches. I went inside and called a cab. Then our insurance agent phoned; I gave him a quick rundown on the scene before our cab arrived. Having to contend with this last-minute crisis, I felt that we Murphys deserved a vacation.

We spent a week in Clearwater, Florida visiting Mary's parents, who were renting a condo for the winter. At the beach Mary and I walked the clean white sands while the kids splashed in the surf. I'd heard that Clearwater Beach had a great reputation, and after seeing throngs of bikini-clad ladies strolling the shore I could see why. On the promise of viewing a spectacular sunrise, Mary and I got up in the dark one morning and drove ten miles to a prime viewing spot. It was well worth the drive. Back at the condo our kids were content to sleep till noon. We all enjoyed a week of 80-degree temperatures and cooling ocean breezes while folks in Chicago endured a week of freezing sleet and hail. Arriving home, we all felt refreshed and optimistic that sunny days would be coming soon. Our insurance agent informed us that a well-oiled young man from Cicero was behind the wheel of the car that had chewed up our property.

While Mary and I were discussing our predicament, Eileen reminded us that the previous spring she and her next-door friend, Ann Wohleschleager, had slept overnight in the side yard in a pup tent – right in the path of that bulldozing Buick. I decided to build a barrier that would stop anything on wheels from tearing through our yard. Using landscaping timbers, I hammered together a deep, extra wide flower box and filled it with a foot of dirt. Stretching across the front of our yard, it looked great summer after summer, sporting flowers grown from plantings from the Oak Park Farmers Market.

Christmas scenes

"Why do you keep moving every ornament I hang?" Mary asked in an irritated voice. I told her I wanted to make the tree look balanced. Then I tried to move few lights around. "It's too late for that," she assured me. "You're knocking the ornaments off." I was really annoying her, and things got worse when I started hanging tinsel a few strands at a time. "You're really taking the fun out of this," she remarked. It was

December 1972, the first Christmas season of our married life. We were home in our attic apartment trimming the scrawny, moisture-starved evergreen we'd bought at a local gas station. Here at this joyous time of year I'd managed to start our first argument. Luckily, it didn't last long. I flopped into my recliner while Mary wrapped a colorful plastic skirt beneath the tree.

I kicked back and started reading the paper ... tick, tick, tick, tick.... Uh-oh, needles were falling from our dehydrated tree, hitting the skirt beneath it one after another: tick, tick, tick, tick .... Mary poured water into the stand and headed off to bed. I went back to my reading but the steady ticking of dry needles against plastic was getting to me. Determined to finish the paper, I turned the page and noticed a handsome ad for Christmas trees from a nearby nursery. The headline read: FRESHEST TREES IN TOWN! Tick, tick, tick, tick.... *That's where we should've gone,* I thought. *Well, maybe next year.* The needles kept falling, like the drip, drip, drip of the dreaded Chinese water torture on a victim's forehead. I finally got up and hit the sack. In the morning we found a festive green donut of needles surrounding the base of our tree. Mary poured more water into the stand before we left together and caught the Archer Express bus to our jobs downtown.

All throughout the holidays Mary swept up needles and put them into a can. When we finally took the tree down, a couple of good shakes dislodged most of the needles still clinging to the branches. Mary scooped them up and added them to her stash. "Why are you saving those needles?" I asked. "So I can burn them," she said. That's just what she did. For the first week of the New Year, she lit up a handful of needles each night. They made our apartment smell more Christmassy than ever. And they burned with a gentle crackle, much easier on the nerves than that maddening tick, tick, tick, tick....

Summer in December

It was a Christmas miracle! I got up and looked out the window to a bright, clear morning. And what the hell, a young man with no shirt on was pedaling past the house on his bike. Even weirder, he was an account exec I worked with at my job downtown. I had wished him a happy holiday as I left work the night before. Was this Christmas or April Fools' Day? To check my sanity, I woke up Mary and asked her to take a gander out the window. She said it looked like a beautiful day, but she couldn't believe my report about that shirtless biker. I went downstairs and opened the front door. It felt like Florida. This was one helluva Christmas present. I gave Mary a joyous weather report before she got the kids up. Our gift-opening ritual was accelerated by our collective wish to get outside and romp in the balmy weather. We took a bike ride over to nearby Rheem Park, where I shot photos of the kids climbing the monkey bars – not an exercise that would become a Christmas tradition. Back at work the next day I told the account man that I'd spotted him riding shirtless on Christmas morning. It turned out that he lived just a few blocks from our house. Small world.

We'll be home for Christmas

Year after year, Mary and I took the kids for Christmas Day visits to both sets of grandparents. On Christmas 1976, when Bridget was three and Eileen was one, we buckled them into the back seat of a used VW Beetle that I'd bought few weeks earlier. Our ride got off to a chilly start as we drove south from Downers Grove, and it didn't get any warmer. The heater was out to lunch. Our first scheduled stop was my folks' house in Mount Greenwood at the very south end of Chicago. "Daddy, I'm freezing!" Eileen complained as we entered the Tri-State Tollway. "Yeah, why aren't we getting any heat?" Mary asked. I didn't have an answer, so I focused on driving, glad that I'd remembered to bring my gloves. My whole family sat frozen solid all the way to Mom and Dad's place. We were all thrilled to get there and hustle into their toasty foyer.

After unwrapping gifts, eating Christmas dinner and singing carols, Mary and I bundled up the kids and packed them back into the freezing Beetle. We trundled a few blocks east to visit Mary's folks, where we exchanged gifts, ate more turkey and sang more carols. Blankets borrowed from both Mary's folks and mine added a bit of warmth to our icy ride back home. We all caught colds from that holiday trek. As it turned out, the tiny heater box in our VW was frozen shut, keeping any warm air from reaching us. Mary and I dreamed of the day when we could buy a new car, hoping that day would come before the holidays rolled around again. *Better Christmases are sure to come,* I thought. And they did. The most comfortable ones were warmed by the security of a full-time job that included health insurance and a nice Christmas bonus. That extra cash paid for gifts, poinsettias, spirited liquors and other seasonal trappings. It felt great to know that everyone was healthy, happy, warm and secure. The kids played on the floor with their toys while Mary and I listened to Christmas carols playing on our reel-to-reel tape deck. I reclined in my Barcalounger while a turkey roasted in the oven. All was right with the world, at least for the moment.

Making McMerry

When the kids were a bit older we started Christmas day by attending morning mass at Holy Name Cathedral downtown. Although Mary and I were not regular churchgoers, we wanted to give the kids some positive exposure to the Church. So while B and E endured the long service, they got to look around at the majestic cathedral, decked out for the season with red and white poinsettias. The service attracted many well-heeled Chicagoans, some of whom I recognized as they returned to their pews after receiving communion.

As a reward for sitting through the lengthy service one Christmas, Mary and I took the kids to a McDonald's on Chicago Avenue, just a stone's throw from the cathedral. On the sidewalk in front of the door, a homeless man asked us if we could spare some change, but we didn't respond. Inside, the kids asked me why I didn't give that poor man anything. I told them he'd probably spend it on booze, which wouldn't do him any good. Mary suggested that we buy him some food instead, so before we enjoyed our McBreakfast, the kids went outside and handed the guy a cheeseburger and coffee.

Urgent Christmas

It was always great to see Mom, Dad and my siblings on Christmas. Exchanging presents reminded me of many Yules of yore, except that as grownups, our gift giving was simplified to a grab bag, so each of us had to buy only one present. There were lots of laughs, especially when two of us got the same gift. Everyone enjoyed a sumptuous turkey dinner prepared by Mom and Dad. I remember one Christmas when my brother Tom was washing the dishes and I was drying. Suddenly he let out a loud yelp and yanked his hand from the dishwater. It was gushing blood. We put it under running water and found a long, deep cut. The cause of Tom's injury was a sharp carving knife that had been lurking in the murky dishwater. "Who'd be dumb enough to drop that knife in with the dishes?" he growled as we sped to the emergency room at Little Company of Mary Hospital.

When we got there the waiting room was packed. There were several little boys with their parents. Victims of new toys with sharp edges and moving parts, I imagined. We waited for an hour before a young doctor examined Tom's hand. "You're going to need a few stitches," he said in a sympathetic voice. The procedure took only a few minutes. Tom and I were soon back home reveling in the holiday festivities. Mom sat at the piano and played a few carols from a little book resembling a kid's Golden Book. She'd played from it on every Christmas that I could bring to mind. The family huddled around her little Baldwin spinet and sang, "Deck the Halls" and "Oh Little Town of Bethlehem." Later we played the home version of Jeopardy; it was fun, lively and loud. My brothers put on quite a show: Jim had amazing general knowledge and Dan was unbeatable when it came to history. We used little clickers to signal that we knew the answer. It was hard to tell who was the quickest clicker, but Dan kept screaming that he clicked first. His constant complaints were comical to a point, but on this Christmas the game got him so pissed that he dropped out. Dan always had a hard time losing.

EIGHTEEN

HELL ON WHEELS

"Little GTO, you're really lookin' fine
Three deuces and a four-speed and a 389..."
– *"GTO,"* Ronny and the Daytonas, 1964

MY VERY FIRST DRIVING LESSON was from Dad. It was August 1961 and our family was on a weekend getaway to Turkey Run State Park in Indiana. I was relaxing in the lodge, beating the heat when Dad decided to teach me to drive a "stick." We walked to the parking lot, where his black '54 Buick sat baking in the sun. Shimmering heat waves rising from the asphalt put my sweat glands into overdrive. We got in the car and rolled down the windows. Dad headed for a shady corner of the lot and we switched seats, so I was behind the wheel and he was riding shotgun. Before I turned on the ignition, he explained the pedals: gas, brake, clutch. "Make sure you let up on the clutch nice and slow so the car won't jerk," he told me. I followed his instructions; the car started to roll. "You're going too fast," he shouted. "Stop!" I slammed on the brakes without pushing in the clutch and killed the engine. "No, no, don't ever do that!" he yelled. My second attempt got us off to a bucking, bouncing start. "Now shift!" I put the car into second; the ride smoothed out. "Good, now turn!" I swung the wheel too hard; the tires squealed. "Slow down!" I came down too hard on the brake pedal. "Clutch in!" Oops, too late – I'd killed the engine again. Frustrated, pissed and soaking in sweat, I told Dad I'd had enough for one day. He was happy to get behind the wheel; I was eager to get off the hot seat and back to the air-conditioned lodge.

After driving the Buick for a few years, Dad sold it and bought a used, four-door 1960 Mercury Marquis. That rolling behemoth proved to be the best family hauler he ever owned. Weighing in at a full two tons, it was nearly18 feet long and six-and-a-half feet wide. The exterior was black and the interior was loud red vinyl. That Merc was a poor man's limousine, furnishing vast reaches of inner space. I could lie across the back seat without tilting my head. Seven family members rode in comfort on weekend getaways and fall trips to Notre Dame. But for everyday use around town it handled like an aircraft carrier. Dad kept backing it into parked cars, guardrails, telephone poles and garbage cans like he was driving a carnival bumper car.

Into the woods

A week or two after I'd started college my cousin Mike phoned me with big news. His brother-in-law had given him a '37 Chevy. Suddenly he had his very own set of wheels "Does it run?" I asked. "Sure it runs!" he promised. Mike said he'd drive over to my house after supper and take me for a spin. When the doorbell rang about seven Mike was at the door. I walked out to the curb with him to look at his car. The old buggy was in remarkable shape – very little rust and just a few small dents. With Mike at the wheel we drove south. Knowing that I didn't yet have my license, he asked me if I wanted to practice my driving. "Why not?" I answered nervously, thinking that he'd pull over so we could switch seats. Instead, he drove south to Dan Ryan Woods, a county forest preserve, where I would have a vast empty parking lot to drive around in.

Darkness swallowed us as we entered the preserve from 87th Street. Mike came to a stop in the middle of nowhere. He went over the gear pattern, showing me how to shift from first to second to third. The shift knob was attached to a long steel rod that ran forward a couple of feet before turning sharply into the gearbox. Then Mike reviewed the gas, brake and clutch pedals with me before we switched seats. The headlights drilled two bright tunnels of light into the blackness before us. I pushed the clutch pedal down, put the car into first and started to ease up on the clutch. "Down on the gas, up on the clutch," Mike coached me. "Slowly." *Gas down, clutch up, slow!* I told myself. Here we go. The car slipped into gear – we were rolling. "Okay, now slow down!" I hit the brakes and the car shuddered to a stop. I hadn't pushed the clutch in far enough. "Let's try it again," Mike said. Time to concentrate: *Gas down, clutch up, slow...clutch in deep, then brake.* I pressed the starter button. The engine sputtered to life. *Gas down, clutch up slow.* The old Chevy rolled forward. Suddenly I saw trees in front of me. "Stop!" But it was too late. A thick steel cable brought us to an abrupt halt. We got out and surveyed the damage. That cable had dented the grille and scrunched the pod-like headlights, so they were looking toward each other cross-eyed with their beams intersecting a few yards in front of the car. "Lets get out of here," Mike suggested in a remarkably calm voice. He took the wheel and drove me back home. If he was angry he didn't show it. His calm demeanor really surprised me.

A jarring event

On a cold, gray Sunday afternoon in November of '62, my brother Jim took me with him to an international folk festival at Navy Pier. He drove his black '52 Buick, which was sporting a huge dent in the front passenger-side door, compliments of my last driving lesson. We parked on a downtown street and walked six blocks east to the pier. Once inside its long building we visited one colorful exhibit after another. It was great fun listening to ethnic music, watching folk dances and sampling tasty tidbits from Greece, Hungary, Italy, France and other countries. Jim was especially keen on the Hungarian venue because of his fixation on that country, which had started back in high school. So we revisited the Hungarians, savoring second tastings of goulash before heading home.

It was dark when we reached the car carrying bags stuffed with little flags, buttons, patches and pamphlets. Driving south toward home we took a route that ran parallel to the Dan Ryan Expressway, which was still under construction. Suddenly it occurred to Jim that certain stretches of the Ryan were already open. I couldn't recall reading or hearing anything about this, but Jim, the adventurer, was convinced that we could find an open stretch to drive on. As we approached the ramp at 63rd Street, I noticed that the wooden horses intended to block the entrance had been pulled aside. It looked like the work of some neighborhood kids.

Jim headed down the ramp with glee. Looking ahead, I couldn't see a thing. "Slow down!" I pleaded. "No, you have to accelerate!" he insisted, stepping on the gas. The darkness loomed deeper and blacker as we picked up speed. I saw a massive pile of construction clay dead ahead of us. Jim slammed on the brakes! *Scriiitch* … we skidded across a film of sand and pebbles. *Thunk!* The car plowed into the solid mound. The hood flew off. Jim and I pitched forward. My nose melted into the steel dashboard. I was bleeding profusely. My brother exited the driver's door in pretty good shape. I opened my door, stood and started to scream. "Help! Help!" I cried for all I was worth. Some folks looking down from the bridge above us shouted that an ambulance was on the way. Jim didn't seem to be the least bit hurt physically, but he felt very guilty and demanded immediate punishment. "Hit me! Hit me!" he begged at the top of his lungs. I waved him off and covered my face with my hands. The police arrived in minutes. An officer was writing Jim a ticket when a fire department ambulance pulled up.

I was taken to the emergency room at St. Bernard's Hospital, where a young doctor stuffed my flattened schnoz full of gauze. He advised me to talk to Dr. Scaramella about getting my nose fixed. Small world: Scaramella and I had met a year and a half earlier when I was laid up at St. George's Hospital. He was visiting a kid in my ward and stopped at my bed. "You should let me fix that lump on your cheek," he said. While we chatted I told him I'd be entering the pre-med program at Loyola University in a few weeks. He shook my hand sincerely and wished me good luck. I was recalling this scenario when who should walk into the ER but the very same Dr. Scaramella.

Haven't we met before?

The good doctor approached and asked me what had happened. I gave him the details, and mentioned that we'd met at St. George's Hospital. "Ah, you're the fellow in pre-med," he said. "I remember that lump on your cheek" I was more concerned about my crushed nose at the moment. Smiling, he promised to make it look like new. And since I was a pre-med student, he thought I'd appreciate watching the operation. "It would be a good experience for you. We'll set up a big round mirror so you can see the whole thing." *Are you joking?* I wondered.

As luck would have it, my surgery was scheduled on the same day as the intramural football championship game at Loyola. It was the biggest touch football contest of the year and I wouldn't be playing in it. The independent team I was on, the "Huns," would be playing the Tau Kappa Elipson fraternity boys (the Tekes). I knew the Huns would win handily with or without me, and they did. But I still wish I could have played. I took the El to the 63rd & Harvard stop, walked around the corner and entered St. Bernard's Hospital. In my room, I put on one of those strange one-sided garments that tie in back. An hour or so later I was wheeled into an antiseptic, tiled room and transferred to the operating table. A masked nurse wheeled a huge, round mirror (like those at the rear of supermarkets) close to the table so I could view the procedure. I stared at the bright lights above me for a moment before Scaramella entered my field of vision, wearing a cap and surgical mask. "All set, Joseph?" he asked. His voice, with its Italian accent, sounded robust and optimistic.

The operation started with some pain-killing shots administered through my nostrils into my nasal passages. Then the real fun started as Doctor S reached even farther into my nasal recesses with long, sharp instruments. He poked, prodded, twisted and snipped. I looked at the mirror trying to watch but my eyes teared up. I felt sick to my stomach. The doctor made a few brief comments as he pushed my nose from side to side, bringing it into alignment. He packed it with gauze, took a couple of stitches on the bridge and taped a metal splint over it. Wow! I'd suffered throughout the whole ordeal without screaming or passing out. Scaramella seemed impressed with my performance. "See you soon," he said before I was wheeled back to my room. Even though I didn't "go under" for the operation I had to stay overnight in the hospital. In the morning Scaramella stopped by and asked me if I'd found viewing the operation worthwhile. Lying, I told him that it had been a great experience. "You should let me remove that growth on your cheek," he reminded me. With my nose still aching I didn't favor him with an answer.

Home from the hospital that afternoon, I still felt a bit woozy from the pain meds I had taken in the morning. My sister Marg commented on the splint and white tape covering my reconstructed beak. Just for fun she tapped the end of it with her finger. "Owww!!" I screamed. The pain was spectacular. The next week was suffocating; the gauze stuffed into my nose kept me from breathing normally. When it was removed I inhaled great lungsful of crisp, December air – ahhh.... Back on campus, one of my football teammates told me that a photographer had snapped a picture of the victorious team for the yearbook. *Damn!* I felt that I'd missed my chance to become a part of Loyola history. A few days later I bumped into Pete Bruska, the starting Huns quarterback, on campus. He told me that every player on the Huns got a trophy and he had been saving mine for me. I arranged to pick it up the next day at the dorm. Knocking on Pete's door, a muffled voice told me to come in. I let myself in but didn't see anybody. Again, the muffled voice: "Is that you Murph?" "Yeah," I answered. "I'm on the crapper – your trophy's on the bed!" I picked up my award, a little gilded man running with a football, and started for the door. "Thanks, Pete!" I shouted before exiting. Bruska was a senior, so there was little chance of seeing him in any classes during the spring semester. Truth is, I never saw him (or any of the other Huns) again, except for Hugh Bell, a big redheaded guy who was in my Spanish class.

The Huns, 1962 Loyola Intramural Touch Football Champts. <u>Standing</u>: Tom Lanigan, Bill Blyth, Terry Muler, Jack McWalters, Pete Brusca. <u>Kneeling</u>: Bob Lappin, Emmett Gantz, Tom Hallett, Jim Vlazny, Hugh Bell, Mike Daley. <u>Absent</u>: Joe Murphy (pictured at left). Main photo courtesy of Loyola University Chicago Archives and Special Collections.

Fast-forward to June, and my first car

"A NEW CAR? ARE YOU JOKING?" I asked in amazement. Out of the blue, Dad had suggested that I buy myself a car. It wasn't like he was tired of my borrowing his Buick; I'd never once asked to use it. But now that he'd broached the subject, the idea of owning a brand new set of wheels was exciting. And luckily, money was not a problem. I'd just been awarded a hefty Workmen's Compensation check for injuries I'd received from my bicycle accident in '61. Dad argued that I could use a car and might as well buy a new one. He recommended a Rambler. It was a reliable vehicle that didn't cost a fortune, he assured me.

Dad was a lot more excited about Ramblers than I was. My taste in autos leaned toward low-slung European sports cars. And strangely enough, it was Dad who introduced me to the realm of exotic vehicles. A decade earlier he had taken me to the big General Motors Motorama in Chicago. What a spectacular car show! I was dazzled by all the shapely "concept cars" slowly rotating on glitzy turntables. And the shapely female models leaning against them added a strange kind of excitement that I didn't know what to make of. Now, in July of 1963, I was heading into my junior year of college. I'd taken public transportation to school for two years, traveling from one end of the city to the other. The Chicago Transit Authority was a cheap ride but far from first class. Carrying an armload of books and transferring between buses and trains was hard travel. Commuting in my own car would be much faster and easier, I thought.

Let's roll.

Before the week was out Dad and I took a ride to Rambler City, a thriving American Motors dealership near Midway Airport. After supper we drove west along 79th Street to Cicero Avenue and then turned north. After a few blocks I recognized the big Ford plant where B-24 bombers were built during World War II. A few years later the much-hyped Tucker Torpedo automobile was made there. Too bad only fifty cars rolled off the line before the company folded.

As we continued north, Dad assured me that buying a new Rambler was the right thing to do. If I bought a used car, he said, I could get hit with a sudden repair bill that would cost me more than I'd paid for the car. A new Rambler was not a sexy convertible or an exotic import. It wasn't even a new Ford or Chevy, but it wouldn't break the bank. Thoughts of pricier wheels would have to stay garaged until after college when I had a job. Still, hunting for a new car, even a modest one, was exciting.

The farther north on Cicero we traveled, the more industrialized things looked. I knew we were close to our destination when a haze of red light caught my eye. It emanated from huge neon signs fronting the Johnson & Johnson building and the neighboring Cracker Jack plant. As we passed by, I turned around to catch a view of them glowing through the rear window. Up ahead on the right we spotted Rambler

City, wrapped in more neon than a Vegas casino. The massive curved window bulging from its side seemed to cut right into Cicero Avenue.

We parked beside the showroom and walked in. Three salesmen converged on us as if we were their first customers of the week. One of them nearly broke into a run and got to us first. Smiling, he shook my father's hand. Before Dad could utter a word, this eager beaver was talking up the Ambassador, Rambler's deluxe model. His toothy grin slowly receded as Dad explained that we were looking for a basic vehicle with a manual transmission – a car for driving back and forth between home and school. Recalling the salesman's face, the name Al just seems to fit, so I'll call him Al. He started walking and beckoned for us to follow. He kept Dad distracted as we passed the boxy little Rambler American sitting in the corner. Al didn't want to sell us the cheapest car on the floor. The stubby two-door American looked as if a giant cleaver had chopped off its front and rear ends. We stopped at a colorful floor display touting the '63 Rambler Classic as Motor Trend magazine's "Car of the Year." Picking up a brochure, Al thumbed through the pages noting the performance and safety features highlighted in bold type: beefed-up unibody construction, rustproofed frame, dual brake cylinders, reclining front seats…. "And how about these curved door windows?" he asked. "Is this a great-looking car or what?"

Pedal to the metal

Dad seemed impressed by the data on the four-door Classic, and he liked its size. "How about this red one?" Al asked, gesturing toward the vehicle sitting just a few steps away. Before I could answer, Dad was seated behind the steering wheel. When I approached, he slid over and let me have the driver's seat. "Whattaya think? You like it?" he asked as I gripped the wheel. "Er … yeah … it's …it's …" "Good!" Dad responded. *Are we done already?* I wondered. *Did we just pick out a car in five minutes flat?* Dad told Al that we'd be paying cash; all that was left was the paperwork.

As I followed our salesman to his cramped cube of an office, a patch of bright blue caught my eye. Turning, I spotted another truncated Rambler American, but this one was a convertible. Wow! Sporting a ragtop, the car's boxy shape looked downright cute. But at just over $3,100, it was out of my price range. Besides, the tiny rear seat was a joke – I thought it might hold two bags of groceries or maybe a couple of toddlers. And Dad would surely frown on a car that couldn't haul a few family members.

At his desk Al took us through the required forms. With what I took for sincerity, he said, "Ya know, there's just something about a red car – it really gets noticed!" His comment quickened my pulse. Finally, he went over some charges not reflected on the sticker price. My father didn't buy the $30 charge for removing a protective coating on the car, so that fee was dropped. All told, my new Rambler cost just over $2,000. "You're getting a helluva deal!" Al assured us. I was happy that Dad and I had found such a nice guy of a salesman. We had to wait a day for the service department to prep the car. Then Dad and I drove over to Rambler City again, this time to pick up my new car. As I followed his Buick back to our home turf, I enjoyed the feel of the three-speed manual transmission and the brand-new smell of my car's interior.

It was dark when I turned onto Peoria Street; I didn't see the welcoming committee waiting in front of the house until I pulled up. Before I could open the door, my brothers and some neighborhood kids herded up to the car. "How 'bout a ride?" "Yeah, Joe – let's go for a spin!" I took two or three of the kids for a brief jaunt and returned to pick up a second bunch waiting at the curb. The next morning, Uncle Lee dropped Aunt Martha off at our house for a visit with Mom. After they'd sipped some tea and caught up on things, Mom asked me if I'd treat Martha to a ride home. "Sure," I answered, flattered to be chauffeuring my first grownup passenger. "Let Martha sit up front," Mom insisted. I helped my mother into the rear seat, closed the door and walked around to open the front passenger door for my aunt. I gripped the handle and pulled it right off the door. *What the hell?* I pondered, staring at the hunk of chrome in my hand. *This is Motor Trend's "Car of the Year?"* I hoped that episode wouldn't be an omen of things to come down the road.

My sister Marg poses with my new Rambler, 1963.

Pimping my ride

I wasn't crazy about the upholstery in my Rambler. It was a loud, black-and-white check pattern that looked like a used car salesman's jacket. I drove over to a seat cover outfit in the Evergreen Shopping Plaza on South Western Avenue and picked out some vinyl covers that tried hard to look like black leather. A girl at the front counter wrote up my order and said the installation would take about 45 minutes. She exited to take my paperwork to the installers and returned shortly to help other customers.

I took a seat in the waiting area and started reading a magazine. As more folks came, the girl at the counter got very busy and made several trips to the shop floor. After an hour I asked her how my installation was going. She said it was taking a bit longer than usual. After twenty minutes I asked her for an update. She made a call and reported that my car was almost ready.

Fifteen minutes later I heard angry voices coming from behind the waiting area. Sensing that something was amiss, I asked the helpful girl what was happening. She went to check and came right back looking a bit flushed. "I hate to tell you this," she confessed, "but they put your seat covers on the wrong car." "What?" I shouted. "It was a new red Rambler just like yours!" To complicate this mess even more, another team was busily installing that *other* Rambler's seat covers into *my car.*

Hold everything! It was time to put the right seat covers on the right damned seats. I heard more cussing as the workers started uninstalling the covers and switching them from one car to the other.

Half an hour later my car was ready. *Hallelujah!* I opened the door, anxious to be on my way. But shit, the stitching on the split-back front seats didn't match. The driver-side cover was on the passenger side and vice-versa. *Unbelievable!* The dyslexic installers shook their heads dejectedly. Enough fun for one day! I made an appointment for a make-good session later in the week.

A work in progress

I enjoyed keeping my new vehicle clean and shiny. Washing and waxing it was fun, but even all shined up it needed more curb appeal. I tried to imagine it sporting a slight forward rake and a set of mirror-like "moon" hubcaps instead of the little bottle caps it came equipped with. I walked over to Major Motors a couple of blocks west of my house and bought a "spinner" for the steering wheel, thinking that it would make turning easier and show passengers what a hot driver I was. I attached this plastic knob to the wheel, drove to the corner and whipped the steering wheel right. Fun! Coming out of the turn, the wheel snapped back. OWWW! The spinner slammed into my left hand. It hurt so much that I pulled over. Waiting for the pain to subside, I watched as the base of my thumb swelled up. *Nice going, hot shot.* I tried to be careful with that nasty little knob, but after a few more smacks in the hand I took it off the steering wheel and chucked it onto the garbage.

After a few months I concluded that trying to jazz up my Rambler was like trying to pose Betty Crocker in a bikini; the subject just didn't lend itself to sexy adornments. Still, I couldn't resist the urge to add some custom touches, starting with a set of rear speakers. At Star Electronics on Halsted I bought a couple of six-inch speakers and a row of control buttons that would let me select front or rear sound. I installed the speakers, covering them with black metal mesh and silver rims. Running wires under the carpet up to the dashboard, I cut a hole and installed the pushbuttons. I clicked on the radio and tried the buttons. They worked! Time to try out my new my sound system on a few select passengers. Unfortunately, they were not thrilled with it. "Way too loud!" and "Turn it down!" were the main comments. With their ears just inches from the speakers my riders couldn't handle the volume: "Lower … A little lower … Just a tad lower … Okay, that's good." Great, but by then I couldn't hear a damned thing!

I was happy enough with my car's simple three-speed transmission. At the time I didn't know squat about four-on-the-floor, synchromesh, downshifting or double clutching. I drove with passion, ramming the shift lever from gear to gear with all the force I could muster. Wasn't this the way a cool young dude should spur his steed? While taking a spin with Jim Bradley one night, I had trouble getting into second gear. I told him that it had been sticking like that for weeks. "No wonder!" he shot back at me, "You ram those gears in like a stupid maniac!" I asked Jim how he'd feel about walking home.

Horn of plenty

I loved my Rambler despite all the pesky little things that went wrong with it. The horn could be really annoying. It looked so simple: just a chrome cap sitting atop the steering column. There was no extra ring to press like on fancier cars. I just pushed down on that oversized chrome button. It worked fine most of the time, but if I used too much force it would stick, and the horn would keep on blaring. The only way to silence it was to yank the whole button right off the column. After a couple of embarrassing episodes, I found that if I pushed down really hard and turned it clockwise, the button would bounce off into my hand. Boing! The beeping would stop but I'd be left without a horn.

My sticking horn got me into some tight spots. If someone cut me off I instinctively leaned on it. When I tried to let up, it kept on blaring. One summer night my brother Dan and I were heading north on the Outer Drive toward downtown when a car cut in front of us. I slammed on the brakes and blasted my horn. I eased up but it kept blaring. Trying to loosen the cap, I pushed it in with all my strength and tried to rotate it. "That's enough," Dan screamed into my ear, "Stop it!" He tried to pull my hand off the horn while I kept pressing it. The car swerved to the right. "Let go!" I yelled. Dan thought I'd flipped and kept pulling on my hand. It was infuriating. The car swerved to the left, and as I swung it back the horn stopped. The chrome button came off in my hand. I tossed it into Dan's lap, telling him that I hadn't been trying to blast the horn all that time. We made it downtown without much conversation. The shouting was over, but neither of us was in the mood for small talk.

Northwestern fantasy

One spring day between classes at Loyola I drove up to Northwestern University in Evanston, just a few miles north on Route 41. That fabled institution had a strong fantasy appeal for me. Over the years, several major movie stars had taken classes there: Charleton Heston, Warren Beatty, Ann-Margaret and Jennifer Jones, just to name a few. The road to the sprawling NU campus was curvy, with Lake Michigan on the right. A clear sky rendered its waters a deep, vibrant blue. It felt great to take that drive in my Rambler, imagining that it was an open-top roadster and I had my right arm around a cute blonde coed. I thought of Northwestern as a dream college where beautiful people met. Kids who went there didn't worry about quizzes or final exams. They were too busy rehearsing for a big musical.

On reaching the campus I enjoyed looking at the venerable ivy-clad buildings and Dyche Stadium, where the Wildcats played other Big Ten schools. I'd been to the stadium a few years earlier with my brother Dan. We took the El up to NU in the summer to watch the college all-stars (best of the country's college footballers) practice for the annual All-Star game, coached by football legend, Otto Graham. In August the team would face the reigning NFL champs at Chicago's Soldier Field. And although they rarely won, Dan and I rooted for Graham's boys every summer. Next to Notre Dame, Northwestern was my favorite college football team, maybe because of its rousing fight song: "Go U

Northwestern…." Its power to raise goose bumps was right up there with "Cheer, cheer for Old Notre Dame!" The Northwestern Wildcats were trying hard to win without coach Parseghian, who had left to lead the Fighting Irish to a national championship in '66.

Metamorphosis

After driving the Rambler for a few years I sold it to my brother Jim and bought a '61 Ford Falcon from a college friend. Why, I don't know. Maybe it was temporary insanity. The Falcon was bad news right from the start. Its sluggish acceleration was a drag and electrical problems made it impossible to start on moist mornings. No mechanic I consulted could fix it. Besides, its dull, green paint refused to take a shine. After a year with that that pathetic heap it was time to scrap it and buy myself a real car. On a frosty Saturday morn I drove to a nearby Chrysler dealer. As I entered the showroom an eager young salesman darted toward me. I told him I wanted to trade in my car for something newer. "Newer?" he asked, "You mean new don't you?" "No, just newer!" I insisted. "What's newer than new? You want new!" We went back and forth on "new" and "newer" until I convinced him that it was a used car I wanted.

Outside the building I showed him my moldy little Falcon. Its paint was dull and the front end was sporting a huge dent from a recent driving lesson I'd given my brother Dan. "You're driving that piece of shit?" he shouted. "Man, you want something hot – what you want is a cunt wagon!" It was hard keeping up with this character as he strode through the lot. He stopped at a '65 Plymouth Fury – big, red and shinier than glass. "C'mon, lets take this beauty for a ride," he urged. I got behind the wheel; he slipped in beside me. Wow! I'd never seen so much chrome on the inside of a car! The instrument panel gleamed like a row of toasters in the noonday sun. I pulled out of the lot and headed west on 111th Street. "This thing can really scoot!" I remarked. "There's 383 cubes under that hood!" my passenger boasted. The car's power and acceleration roused my sleeping soul as we as we passed Mount Olivet and Holy Sepulchre cemeteries.

Heading back to the dealership, my itch to own that car grew into an obsession. Temporary insanity prevailed. The finance man prepared all the paperwork at warp speed. Inside half an hour I was seated in my big Fury, ready for takeoff. I turned the ignition key; the monster engine roared to life. Pulling out of the lot, I caught a final glimpse of my forlorn Falcon in the rear view mirror. What a buoyant ride – it was like driving a cloud. I clicked on the radio and tuned into a country and western station. The clean, honest music came at me from all directions. *This is class*, I thought. *What babe in her right mind wouldn't crave a ride in this buggy?* Things soon took a turn for the better. Not having to date girls in a dingy, dinged-up heap, I started going out more often. That big Plymouth made me feel like a millionaire except when I pulled up to the gas pump, which was way too often.

Muscle cars

From the mid '60s to early '70s, "muscle cars" were blistering the asphalt from coast to coast. This unforgettable era started with cars like the Pontiac GTO, which even had a song named after it. Ford unleashed their Mustang, a galloping success right from the get-go. GM added their Chevy Camaro and Pontiac Firebird to the herd. Not to be outdone, Chrysler gripped the strip with the Plymouth Barracuda and Dodge Charger. The new breed of overpowered vehicles boasted massive engines with four-barrel carburetors, four-on-the-floor manual trannies and paint jobs louder than Jimi Hendrix. Not to be outdone, gutsy little American Motors came out with their great-looking Javelin and its muscle-bound cousin, the AMX. My brother Dan and I got swept up in this madness and bought muscle mobiles. Dan pulled up to the house in a sharp-looking, blue Camero. A few weeks later, I fell in love with AMC's Javelin. To my eye, it had the best-looking front end of all the ponies in the muscle car stable.

I checked at two or three American Motors dealerships on the South

Side, trying to get the best price. At a place on South Cicero Avenue, I spotted a cherry-red Javelin with a black vinyl top. It had a husky, 343 cubic-inch engine with a four-barrel carburetor and the same four-speed manual gearbox found in the Chevy Corvette. A young salesman backed the car out of the showroom and took me for a blast across 63rd Street that pinned my ears back. I was smitten. After securing a loan through Sears Bank a few days later, I roared home in my muscle machine, making sure to use all four gears. Throughout the summer I washed and waxed that car faithfully, figuring the shinier it was, the more young females it would attract. I dated a few girls from Sears who were more impressed with the car than they were with me.

Watching me change my own oil inspired my brother to do likewise. He made the effort on a warm Saturday night when he was home visiting our folks. While I was dressing up for a date, he crawled under his Camero and started feeling around for the plug. Exiting the house, I spotted Dan in the driveway beneath his car. He wiggled his way out and flagged me. "Hey, I wanna make sure I do this right. Is this the plug?" He reached under the car. I followed his arm with my fingers until we were both touching the same spot. "Yep, that's the plug," I assured him. Then I took off to pick up my date. On Monday morning Mom called me at work. "Dan just phoned me," she said. "He wants to kill you!" "What? Why?" I asked. She explained that after changing his oil, Dan was driving home on Dan Ryan Expressway when his car started chugging and smoking. He pulled off and drove to a gas station, where a mechanic put his car on the lift. After a few minutes he told my brother that he had no transmission fluid, but there were ten quarts of oil in his engine.

NINETEEN

RIDING THE RAILS

"There's something about the sound of a train that's very romantic and nostalgic and hopeful."
— Paul Simon

GOING TO COLLEGE MADE ME a serious train traveler. I commuted between the South Side and Loyola's Lake Shore campus via the Chicago Transit Authority. Boarding a bus at the CTA pocket near 80th & Halsted, I rode north to the El station at 63rd. Here I transferred to a Howard A train that took me twenty miles up to school. As it rolled north of Englewood the neighborhoods looked shabbier and shabbier. Gazing out the window I saw alleys littered with glass shards from broken booze bottles and garage roofs strewn with liquor bottles of all kinds. Most of them were flat brown bottles that might have held pints or fifths of whiskey. Quart-sized beer bottles, brown and round, had been filled with Blatz, Meister Brau, Hamm's or Drewrys. Other bottles were clear or green. Those with fancy shapes might have held wine or pricey liquors. Bottles, bottles, so many bottles. Looking down on them in their decrepit, shattered state, it was hard to imagine that their contents had ever held a good time for anyone.

The train veered east, over the Dan Ryan Expressway, still under construction. After that the terrain was downright depressing for quite a stretch. At the 35th street station a big sign read, COMISKEY PARK. In summer, droves of South Siders exited here to see the White Sox play. Rolling north, the train crawled through a landscape of old brick buildings, coming within a few feet of some. Many brick structures still wore traces of advertising signs painted onto them decades earlier. My favorite was MAN-ZAN FOR PILES. When I looked into the history of this remedy I learned that Man-Zan ointment sold well for decades – until 1966. At that point the Federal Trade Commission ordered its makers to stop claiming that it would "shrink, heal, cure or remove hemorrhoids or do anything beyond bringing temporary relief."

Just north of the Chinatown stop at 22nd Street the train burrowed into the subway, stopping at busy Loop stations – Jackson, Monroe, Washington – and then careened through a long sweep of curved track that made the wheels scream bloody murder. If a few windows were open the sound was deafening. I finger-plugged my ears to cut the noise. Soon the train was elevated again and approaching the Fullerton station on the North Side. At Belmont, two stops later, I was reminded of Riverview, the big amusement park two miles west, where I had such great times as a kid. The next stop was Addison, where Cubs fans exited for Wrigley Field in the summer. A little farther north the train slowed for a curve skirting an old cemetery. On a gray morning the view reminded me of a spooky Gothic novel. When I mentioned this place to my history-savvy brother Dan, he told me that I'd passed Graceland Cemetery, final resting place of many legendary Chicagoans. The moss-tinted gravestones and mausoleums were crafted in elaborate Victorian detail for local luminaries like merchants Potter Palmer and Marshall Field. Daniel Burnham, master designer of the Columbian Exposition, is buried there, along with George Pullman, inventor of the railroad sleeping car and Alan Pinkerton, founder of the famous detective agency. It's ironic that the word, "Graceland," is more likely to make Chicagoans think of Elvis Presley's home in Memphis than the storied cemetery in their own home town. After a few weeks the novelty of riding up to 6500 North Sheridan wore off. And although that long commute could be boring, it wasn't uncomfortable. Occasional delays, however, could be nerve-wracking. An untimely interruption in service might make me late for a class or a big test.

Co-commuters

Occasionally I'd bump into former classmates from Leo High School on the train. Like me, they were commuting to Loyola. It was always fun to joke around with John Kerrigan, Jim Hay or Phil Carollo. John had a quick wit that always made me laugh. Jim, who stayed abreast of the news, would comment on some amazing story he'd read in the morning paper. And Phil had a refreshing optimism that was contagious. On occasion, I'd see Jack McWalter, who played on the Huns intramural football team with me. And once in a while I'd run into Ed Murphy (no relation) from my neighborhood. He was a bright kid majoring in chemistry. Ed lamented that there was never enough time to get all his studying done. His mom was a sweet lady who had worked with me at Frank's, our neighborhood department store, when I was in high school.

That blurry bullet train

As a freshman heading home from school, I waited on the Loyola El platform for a Howard A train to take me back to Auburn Gresham on the South Side. Tracks for north-and-southbound trains flanked both sides of the platform. And running parallel to the CTA tracks were tracks owned by a different passenger line. One afternoon I saw a short, blue-green train streak by in a blur. *What the hell was that?* I noticed that the front and rear cars were rounded, like bullets. Very cool! Before long I learned that the streamlined little train was the North Shore (officially the North Shore and Milwaukee Railroad), which ran between downtown Chicago and Milwaukee, making stops at north suburban towns like Evanston, Winnetka, Lake Forest and Waukegan on its way.

*Restored Chicago North Shore and Milwaukee Electroliner at
Illinois Railway Museum, Union Ill. Photo by Robert Banke.*

Doing a bit of research, I learned that the North Shore Line had
been operating since 1891. Over the decades it had earned a reputation
as America's fastest interurban railroad. Unfortunately for me, this
remarkable commuter line was near the end of its lifetime. In fact,
operations ceased in January 1963. Two decades later, while working at
a Chicago ad agency, I was teamed up with Bill Hurtle, an art director
who had taken the North Shore downtown from Lake Bluff every
day for years. He reminisced about the cozy bar car where he sipped a
leisurely cocktail as the train tore along at 80 mph. Bill's description of
the North Shore made me feel that I'd missed out on something special.
Bummed that I'd never taken that train even once, I wondered what I'd
been doing on the day of its final run. The North Shore Line was a piece
of the past that had passed me by. Fortunately, some of its engines and
cars are preserved at the Illinois Railway Museum in Union, Illinois.

Better pay attention

Anything could happen on the CTA. Scrambling up the stairs at the Loyola El stop, I reached the platform too late – my train was pulling away. Damn! Wait a sec! The rear door of the last car opened and two grinning teenage boys tossed something huge onto the tracks. It was a passenger seat – the cushion, the legs, the whole shebang! Luckily for me, it tumbled onto the northbound tracks. It wouldn't affect my trip home, but it was bound to play havoc with El trains headed north.

On another occasion a Loyola student toting an armload of books was running to catch his train. On his way through the doorway he bumped his elbow, dislodging one of his textbooks. It fell through the gap between the train and the platform onto the track bed. He looked down, shrugged his shoulders and darted into the car. I couldn't help laughing. Then I imagined myself in the same situation. I would have waited till the train pulled away, climbed down from the platform and retrieved the book.

Sentimental journey

On a warm spring evening in my sophomore year I enjoyed an enchanting El ride home. It was nine p.m. and most of the windows were open, ushering in a stream of cooling air. Gazing out the window put me into a mellow mood; the lights on the streets below seemed to float by. At the Bryn Mawr stop I read the marquee on the Bryn Mawr Theater. *Lord of the Flies* was playing. The rush hour was long past; folks entering the car were unhurried. On some of the sharp curves the train slowed down and rolled eerily close to old apartment buildings. As it approached one of them, I looked into an open window at the silhouette of a young woman. Seated in a chair against a background of yellow incandescent light, she seemed to be rocking with laughter. It looked like she was laughing at nothing. I guessed that she was watching something funny on TV. *Get Smart? I Dream of Genie? My Favorite Martian?* In retrospect, riding the El during off hours was not the smartest way to go. I came across some pretty crispy critters. Luckily I never got robbed or beat up.

Don't make me late again!

Delays on the CTA could make life interesting. Bad weather, equipment failure and miscellaneous quirks of fate could really slow me down in the morning. Shit happened. A lot of kids like me were taking public transportation from one end of Chicago to the other to reach Loyola. School was no half-a-block cakewalk from the dorm. And commuters who drove to school had to brave the blizzard-blasted Outer Drive in winter. Walking into class late could really rile some teachers. I didn't *want* to be late. I didn't *try* to be late. But sometimes I couldn't help it. After driving to Loyola on some winter mornings I felt like I'd completed a successful combat mission by getting my passengers there safely. At times I thought that we commuters, who made long, arduous treks day after day to get our education, deserved a little recognition for our efforts. Maybe bright shoulder patches with COMMUTER CORPS embroidered on them might have boosted our status a bit.

Winding down

On the way home after a tough test at the Lewis Towers campus, I sometimes rewarded myself with a ham on rye at a corner restaurant on Chicago Avenue. Seated at the counter, I'd relax while the facts, names and dates I'd crammed into my cranium the night before evaporated. Then I'd head straight for the subway unless some distraction slowed me down. It was hard to pass Standard Photo without stopping in to browse. They sold film, cameras, and photo gear, like tripods and enlargers. A vinegarish smell emanated from the processing lab at the rear of the store. When I got home my mind was fuzzy from lack of sleep. To relax I grabbed my bongo drums and put an album on the phonograph in my sister Marg's room. I loved to play along to my *Bongo, Bongo, Bongo* album by Preston Epps and an album of throbbing, "jungle exotica" music by Don Ralke's orchestra. With the door shut I pounded away until someone complained about noise. Then I might head for the den and take a nap on the couch.

DANGER HIGH VOLTAGE!

I was getting soaked waiting in the rain for my A train while other folks were piling into a nice, dry B train. And though it was headed in the right general direction, that B train wouldn't take me where I wanted to go. But just to get out of the rain I boarded the B, reminding myself to transfer to an A at 51st Street or go miles out of my way. I took a seat, nodded off … and woke up at the end of the line in Jackson Park, worlds away from my home turf. The rain was still coming down and darkness had fallen. I needed to get to the opposite platform to catch a train headed back to my transfer point, where I could board an A train. Standing on the wet platform, I searched my pockets for a quarter. No luck, not even a penny. What now? I could go downstairs to the booth and explain my plight to the ticket agent. With any luck I'd be allowed to slip through the turnstile for a free ride back to 51st Street. That would have been the sensible thing to do. So why didn't I do that?

Instead, with a pile of books under my left arm, I lowered myself from the platform and scrambled across two sets of tracks, each with a high-voltage third rail that rose above the regular rails. When I climbed onto the opposite platform, an elderly black man approached me, looking as if he'd seen a ghost. He shook his finger at me shouting, "Don't you EVER do that again! If you hit that third rail it'd bust you wide open!" Whenever I recall that stunt I shudder and wonder if the events of my life prior to that day had given me a death wish. Riding through the subway one morning I felt the cold finger of death as the train approached Washington. It slowed and stopped just short of the station and sat there for forty minutes. We passengers squirmed in our seats, cussed and tried to imagine what was causing the long delay. At last the train rolled slowly into the station. When the doors opened I heard snippets of chatter from folks entering the car: "Jumped in front of the train … pretty young gal … suicide!"

Subway surprises

After a tough history test at Loyola's downtown campus, I stood on the subway platform at Chicago Avenue waiting for my train home. Drained from the test and from cramming until 3 a.m. the night before, I stared blankly at the dirty tracks below me. A mouse scurried out from between two ties and disappeared between two others. It was the first time I'd ever noticed a subway rodent. Too pooped to even blink, I stayed focused on that section of track. A minute later another mouse skittered from one black recess into another. I decided to keep my eyes locked onto that scene to see what else would develop. Soon a third mouse appeared, and then another. *There must be a million of them down there*, I concluded. The dank subway tunnel smelled like a basement storeroom. There was little down there to comfort a person, except for a couple of lonely vending machines sitting atop red posts that were bolted to the concrete platform. One of them dispensed square pieces of Wrigley's gum for a penny; the other sold penny slugs of Hershey chocolate. Those sturdy little machines were more reliable than the CTA's worn-out transfer-stamping machines or their trains, for that matter.

CTA all the way

Here I was working for the Chicago Transit Authority after riding their buses and trains to school for three years. I'd landed a summer job as a ticket agent, taking fares at stations along the elevated and subway lines. This was a unique job that mixed long stretches of boredom with sudden bursts of intense rush-hour chaos. I usually wound up working the first or third shift. Both were quirky in their own ways. It was 1964, and the adult CTA fare was a quarter – a real silver quarter (before today's mystery metal coins went into circulation). A transfer cost a nickel.

Along with taking fares, we ticket agents punched transfers and answered questions from travelers in need of directions. But before being assigned to a ticket booth we got a week of training. On my first day of on-the-job practice I showed up for the morning shift at 7 a.m. at the Jackson/Van Buren subway station. The agent on duty said she'd just arrived and assured me that she was in the right place at the right time. Uh-oh. I phoned my instructor at CTA headquarters, who told me that there were *two* Jack/Van booths – one in the State Street subway and another in the Dearborn Street subway. "Get your butt over to Dearborn," he grumbled good-naturedly. I ran east one block through a long, dimly lit tunnel clad in antiseptic white tiles. The agent at the State Street booth was waiting with his coat on. He told me I was late and then bolted.

One fun part of the CTA job was relieving other ticket agents at stations along the South Side elevated lines (the Howard A line to Englewood or the B line to Jackson Park). I rode the train from stop to stop, giving agents 15-or-20-minute breaks. The stations all had newspaper stands with magazines, snacks, candy and cigarettes. Still, every station had its own special character and aroma. Stepping off an evening elevated train in Jackson Park, the intoxicating scent of barbecue permeated the air. It was like arriving at some exotic island destination. When I finished my relief shift I headed back to the 63rd & Halsted station and bought a glazed Huck Finn donut before transferring to a bus that took me south to 79th & Halsted.

My CTA job was full of surprises. Coming off the night shift at a South Side El stop, I found a broken pair of women's glasses and a single high-heeled pump on the platform. *What the hell happened here?* A few feet away sat a huge wooden box with SAND stenciled on its side. It was plenty big enough to hold a person. And after what I'd just found on the platform, I decided to lift its heavy, hinged lid and peek inside. Only sand, to my great relief. I went downstairs to the ticket booth and made out an incident report before catching a train back to Englewood.

Where's the @&#%§ key?

My work schedule with the CTA was a ragtag mix of different shifts on different days, including weekends. Once I worked the night shift at 63rd & Dorchester on the Southeast Side. The booth, which was right on the platform, had three windows. The main one in the center was flanked by smaller ones, each set at a 45° angle, making the booth look like a big bay window. Manning the main window throughout the night, I managed to stay awake with help from a thermos of coffee and a book of crossword puzzles. I was happy to see another agent arrive at 7 a.m. to take over for me. But first I had to stick around for the morning rush hour. We were supposed to move to the side windows to catch commuters coming from two directions. There was a key that opened those windows, but where was it? My co-agent said he'd worked the station before. A key was always hanging on a nail to the right of the middle window, he assured me. But it was missing that morning.

We searched frantically, checking drawers, nooks, crannies and corners with no luck. Meanwhile, a relentless throng of El riders converged on my window, slapping down quarters, asking for transfers or wanting their transfers punched. The melee lasted an hour or so. When it was over, my helpless helper congratulated me on handling all that traffic by myself. Remarkably, when I tallied up all the fares, things balanced out exactly right, except for a British shilling that someone had slipped me in place of a quarter.

The stakeout

The station at 43rd Street on the Englewood Line was held up more often than any other spot along the CTA tracks. I knew this when I arrived there to work the night shift. As I approached the ticket booth, a young gent in a suit stepped out of the men's room. He introduced himself as a CTA cop and said he'd be sitting in the washroom all night peeking through a small hole in the door, which had an OUT OF ORDER sign posted below it. He told me what to do if someone tried to stick me up: "Just stay calm and go along. Hand over the money. When he steps away from your booth I'll shoot him." What? I couldn't believe my ears. About three in the morning the peeping cop exited the john, stretched his legs and went back in. At daybreak he emerged, told me to have a nice day, and split. I was relieved that nobody had tried to rob me and happy that I didn't have to watch someone get wasted.

Two-bit interlude

It was about two a.m. at the Roosevelt Road subway stop. I was engrossed in a Mickey Spillane novel, when a small, middle-aged man in a tattered suit stopped in front of my booth. He said he didn't have a quarter and asked me if I'd let him pass through the turnstile. When I told him I couldn't do that he looked disappointed. The guy said it was important that he get through. I stood firm, refusing to let him pass. "How do you know this isn't an emergency – a matter of life and death?" I stuck to my guns, insisting that I couldn't let him through. Then he talked about the Christian virtue of charity and told me about St. Christopher, who risked his life to help travelers cross a raging river. What would he think of a guy like me? At this point I was ready to give him a pass, just to reward him for perking up my dull shift. I glanced down at Mickey Spillane for moment. When I looked up the little man was gone – he'd disappeared. After I'd read anther chapter or two he reappeared in front of my booth. "Me again!" he said, vaulting the turnstile. "Hey!" I shouted. Smiling, he stopped, leaned back toward my window and slapped down a quarter in front of me.

The haunting beauty of a late-night subway.
Courtesy of the Chicago Transit Authority.

Under attack

Another exciting episode in my CTA summer occurred when I worked the midnight shift at 51st Street. Two black male teens jumped my turnstile. When I yelled after them, they came back, leaping the turnstile again just for the hell of it. They started giving me grief. One of them shook the bars in front of my face while the other ran behind the booth and climbed through a large window that was right behind me and about seven feet up. His head and torso were in my booth – he was actually hanging upside down. Grabbing my thermos, I warned him that I'd crack his skull if he didn't back off. He didn't seem to hear me, so I made an urgent call the CTA dispatcher and reported my situation.

Both troublemakers bolted seconds before two CTA policemen arrived. One ran upstairs to check the platform while the other one made a fast phone call from my booth. He hung up and told me that the kids had been nabbed at the next station. Seconds later he informed his partner, who'd returned from the platform. The CTA gave me a date to identify these kids in court but it conflicted with my plans to drive to Quebec with my brothers.

On a lighter note...

Some experiences in Chicago's subway system were pure fun. Working downtown during the seventies and eighties, I enjoyed some great entertainment in the Dearborn Street subway. The broad platform flanked by tracks on each side was filled with riders heading west and northwest. Often there was a singer with a guitar who could really perform. Folk artists sang everything from Woody Guthrie to Bob Dylan to Joni Mitchell. Appreciative commuters tossed coins or singles into the instrument cases lying open on the concrete. One night at rush hour a young man with a sax was playing such an enchanting rendition of "Harlem Nocturne" that I could hardly tear myself away to board the train.

On another occasion I heard chamber music in the subway. *Is that classical music coming from a boom box?* I wondered while making my way through the throng of commuters. The volume increased as I pushed ahead. Then the crowd parted, revealing a trio of youthful musicians seated on folding chairs; they all appeared to be in their early twenties. There were two girls, one with a violin, the other with a viola; a young man played a cello. "This is class!" I joked to a woman standing next to me. She laughed and tossed a few coins into the cello case that lay open on the platform. "Thank you, thank you," said the musicians, smiling and nodding. The roar of an approaching train drowned out their classical strains. The music makers paused as the train stopped, discharged passengers and picked up others. After it pulled away, the group resumed their performance – until another train screeched into the station. *This one is mine*, I reminded myself. Tossing a quarter into the cello case, I turned and boarded the Congress A train bound for Oak Park.

On yet another occasion, two young performers were imitating the Everly Brothers, singing, "Wake up little Susie, wake up!" They even handled their guitars like Phil and Don, slamming the same percussive chord progressions. *These guys are great, and they even* look *like the Everly boys*, I said to myself. Between songs I asked them if they ever played at parties. "All the time" they assured me. One of them handed me a card as my train arrived. I was dead sure that I'd call them for some kind of an event. But at home I put their card in nice safe place and never saw it again. The most memorable subway performance I witnessed really knocked me for a loop. A young black man was dancing to swing music blasting from his boom box. Dressed in a tux and black patent leather shoes with white spats, he tapped his way all over the place – at first between commuters, then in broad circles as folks backed up to give him more room. It was spectacular. Too bad I didn't have a dollar or even a quarter on me to leave as a tip.

A brutal battle

Unbelievable! The Bears had made it to the 1963 NFL championship game against the New York Giants staged at Wrigley Field. And even more remarkable, my brother Jim had somehow procured two tickets. He was just a kid, two years older than me, but he could afford tickets to the biggest pro football game of the year. Those were simpler, more affordable days for sure. The NFL had yet to absorb the AFL and the championship game had not yet morphed into the hyperbolic, commercial-crammed Super Bowl. There was no daylong marathon of pre-game hype like we have now. Pro football had not yet exploded into the multi-billion-dollar industry that it is today. In 1963 the average NFL player earned $30,000 a year. The highest paid ones made less than $60,000. Advertisers paid a pittance to hawk their wares compared to what they shell out today. In 1963 it cost $2,000 to run a 30-second commercial during the championship game. Four years later, in the first Super Bowl, the cost to air a 30-second spot was $42,000 – chump change compared to the five million bucks plus an advertiser forked over to broadcast a single 30-second commercial in the 2017 Super Bowl.

After a season fraught with injuries and close contests, the banged-up Bears emerged as the NFC champs. They had home-field advantage for the big game. Well, sort of. Although the game was played in Chicago, it took place at Wrigley Field, home of the Chicago Cubs. It was a much different scene than Soldier Field, where the Bears played their home games. Coach George Halas arranged for this odd venue, despite arguments from NFL Commissioner Pete Rozelle that Soldier Field would hold more fans. Halas was adamant about Wrigley Field, figuring it would give the Bears an advantage: the Giants would be battling in completely unfamiliar surroundings.

Jim and I took the El to the Addison stop, and walked a couple of blocks to Wrigley Field. The ten-degree temperature stung our ears. We were almost there when I paid Jim for my ticket. "You're three bucks short," he complained. I reminded him that I had picked up his loafers at the shoemaker's the day before and paid for them. He argued that I still owed him half a buck or something like that. Here we were at the world championship game arguing over nothing. I had two bucks in my wallet for coffee and train fare home and I wasn't going to give it to Jim.

Our tickets landed us in two strange seats flanking a big, thick post. In order to see anything we had to bend to one side. Jim leaned left. I leaned right. Watching that contest really worked our abs. Giants quarterback Y.A. Tittle hit Frank Gifford for a first quarter touchdown. But he was soon intercepted by linebacker Larry Morris, who ran the ball back to the Giants' six-yard line. Two plays later, Bears QB Bill Wade scored on a quarterback sneak. A second quarter field goal by the Giants put them ahead 10-7 at halftime.

Really hurting in the third quarter, Tittle tossed more

---

*   Syracuse.com ftw.usatoday.com

interceptions – one to the Bears' Ed O'Bradovich, who ran it back deep into Giants territory, setting up a one-yard Bears TD. Making the extra point, Chicago led 14–10. Then a fourth quarter pick by the Bears iced the game. Richie Petitbone intercepted in the end zone with ten seconds left on the clock. The Bears were the world champs. I was happy about that, but I felt sorry for Tittle, who was hit hard in early going and played hurt for most of the game.

TWENTY

IVORY TOWER TALES

"As far as I know, here I am."

– Fred Sherwood,
Copywriter, Weber Cohn & Riley

IT WAS LATE AFTERNOON ON a sultry July day in 1974. I stopped at the Billy Goat Tavern after dropping off résumés along Michigan Avenue all day. The Goat was cheap, friendly and located right underneath the Wrigley Building. A stairway in the sidewalk outside that fabled structure led me to the dark underworld of Lower Wacker Drive, home of the Goat. I walked in, found a pay phone near the bar and called Mary. She said somebody named Bernie Bahr had called from Weber Cohn & Riley Advertising. He'd looked at the sheet I'd dropped off and wanted to see my stuff. *A live one*! I phoned Bahr in a flash. He asked me if I could drop off my portfolio. I told him I was at the Billy Goat and had my book with me. Minutes later at Weber Cohn I told the receptionist I was leaving my portfolio for Bernie Bahr. She told me to wait while she called him. A few moments later he came up front and shook my hand. "Come on back," he said. In his office Bernie flipped through my book without making a single comment. But he asked me to leave it so he could show it to Ron Cohn, the creative director.

The next night I returned home from my job hunt to learn that Bahr had phoned again. I called him back and got some promising news: Cohn had reviewed my portfolio and wanted to see me the following day at 3 p.m. The next morning I shined my shoes and slipped into my only suit. Pumped as I was about the afternoon interview, I tried to put the a. m. hours to good use by dropping résumés in tall downtown buildings. By 2:30 I was tired and hungry. I stopped at the Goat where I washed my face and combed my hair. On the way out I paused at their huge condiment counter, and loaded a paper napkin with tomato and pickle slices. I wolfed them down on my way upstairs to street level.

At Weber Cohn the reception girl showed me to Ron Cohn's office. It was large with an oak parquet floor. Cohn was sitting with a phone in one hand and a cigar in the other. He gestured for me to sit down. After a few minutes he hung up and leaned over his desk toward me. We shook hands. He said that he'd looked at my book and liked some of the promo pieces I'd written at CNA Insurance. He thought I might be a good fit for a few of the agency's real estate accounts. Anxious to have a job and determined to put food on the table at home, I asked for just a little more money than I'd been making on my last job. He agreed and we shook hands again. It was a done deal; I would start the following Monday.

Riding the elevator to the lobby I could feel myself shedding the weight of some heavy worries. I called Mary from a pay phone in the lobby and gave her the good news. She was delighted, of course. And I felt good knowing that she would now have less to worry about. If I'd had a few bucks on me I would have celebrated in the Wrigley bar with one of their generous martinis. I thought working in the prestigious Wrigley Building was going to be fun. The entrances to both towers were dressed out handsomely in ornate brass. White marble lobbies led to gleaming brass elevators tended by uniformed elevator starters. Everything was strictly first class and beautifully maintained. And that TLC has continued over the years. Today, the Wrigley looks as good as ever. Its white terracotta exterior makes it stand out handsomely on North Michigan Avenue. And after dark, banks of lights illuminating both towers create a unique Chicago image.

Hit the track running

On my first day at Weber Cohn I was delighted to find myself in a large, well-lit office with a window that gave me views of Michigan Avenue and the Chicago River. The agency put me right to work. Ron Cohn came in and gave me a few facts about a new condominium client. He told me to come up with as many promotional lines as I could ASAP. I shut the door, turned to my typewriter and pounded away. An account exec (who I wasn't yet introduced to) stopped by every twenty minutes or so to pick up the lines I'd typed. Ron Cohn was in a meeting, but somehow this account man was feeding my stuff to him. Cohn was choosing the lines he would use for an afternoon presentation. I kept cranking away, wondering which ones, if any, would be picked. I could see that the agency was up against it to pull things together. *If this is a typical day here I'm not going to last long*, I told myself. Unfortunately, I wasn't part of the big show that afternoon, but at the end of the day Cohn stopped by my office and said that things had gone well. As I was leaving for home, I peeked into the conference room. Wow! There were a couple of my lines blown up to mega size for all to see. I departed with a feeling that I'd accomplished something on my first day.

So many ads, so little time

For the most part, my job at Weber Cohn was writing ads for low-budget real estate accounts. My art director, Bruce Kramer, used crisp line illustrations that really got attention. Bruce worked fast; he could assemble an ad's visual elements before I had time to write the copy. In fact, he often handed me a photostatic copy of a layout that included all the artwork but no headline or copy. "Just fill in the blanks," he'd shout, running off to put out a fire somewhere. At first I found this method pretty constraining, but it forced me to keep my copy short. Bruce and I turned out a ton of good-looking ads using his shorthand system. With tight deadlines to meet, I sometimes stayed late waiting for an ad to be assembled. All the elements – artwork, headlines and copy – were glued down (aka pasted up) on a piece of illustration board. On my way home I'd walk the finished product across the street to the *Chicago Tribune* before heading for Union Station.

Riding a late westbound train I'd sometimes see a young, redheaded gal who got off at Downers Grove. Walking home from the station one night we found ourselves chatting. It turned out that her reason for running late was the same as mine; her job at a Michigan Avenue ad agency kept her working overtime. Her name was Sarah. She was a keen observer of office politics – who was fooling around and who was getting canned. Sarah liked to mimic the corporate mumbo jumbo she overheard – little blurbs like, *This is a game-changer – a definite paradigm shift; going forward we'll have to massage our methodology* or *Is this the whole ball of wax? Let me eyeball it before the meeting tomorrow* or *We can't cherry-pick our clients at this juncture; for now, we'll just have to aim for the low-hanging fruit.* She belched out these lines in a deep voice and giggled like a little girl. One night Sarah remarked that her boyfriend had an authentic speedboat that needed a home for the winter. I mentioned my two-car garage that was holding only one car. She talked to her boyfriend; I checked with Mary. We made arrangements to house the boat, a purebred racer – jet black, sleek and super shiny. I think we charged ten bucks a month – not much, but back then every little bit helped.

Jim Riley

Jim Riley was the best-dressed man I ever saw. His suits fit him impeccably and were completely wrinkle-free. He cut an impressive figure with his well-groomed white hair and mustache. Outgoing Riley had personal charisma and truly liked people. He often greeted me in the hallway with a hearty "How are ya, pal?" Jim was away from his office quite a bit. His role at the agency was meeting folks and keeping them entertained with the goal of developing new business. I remember one morning when he came in looking really spent. Admitting that he was wasted, he confessed, "I was out all night with the King of Sweden."

Riley wasn't easy to contact even when he was in his office. The door was often closed as he conferred with real estate clients.

Jim cavorted with political bigwigs in Chicago. He was a member of the Irish Fellowship Club of Chicago, whose membership included many local politicians – alderman, judges, even Hizzoner, Richard J. Daley. While I worked at WCR, Riley was made the president of the club, a twelve-month honor bestowed on a different member from year to year. I enjoyed meeting some of the colorful folks in the club and writing the Irish Fellowship newsletter. It was a crisp-looking six-pager printed on heavy white stock and accented by bright green leprechauns, shamrocks and other Gaelic embellishments.

The annual banquet

As a reward for working on the Fellowship account, I got to attend the banquet with my wife Mary. We dined on corned beef and cabbage while enjoying the Cabaret Show from Jurys Hotel in Dublin. The troupe was flown to Chicago just to perform at the dinner. A colorful blend of song, dance and Irish wit, the show made for a night of spirited entertainment. The first year Mary and I attended the banquet we were seated near a set of big double doors that opened to the kitchen. Waitresses breezed by our table, scurrying to and fro. It was fun to watch, but we were not being served. It seemed that we were sitting in a blind spot. The servers were looking right over us at tables in the distance. Folks were chomping on their corned beef, but nobody had yet taken our orders. Finally, I stopped a waitress and told her, "We didn't even get our salads yet!" She apologized and dashed into the kitchen, returning with plates piled with lettuce. I was eager to dig in, but I noticed something odd – smoke was curling up from underneath the lettuce! Lifting a leaf, I uncovered a lit cigarette! In the interest of time I didn't complain. When the main course arrived, I figured that the cabbage with my corned beef would cover my veggie quota.

Stat machine saga

Back in the seventies a device known as a "stat machine" was an ad agency workhorse. A combination camera and printer, it turned out crisp, black-and-white copies for the art department from morn to night. A stat machine produced a very high quality copy – same-size, bigger or smaller. You just placed a document or piece of artwork in front of the camera, focused and pushed a button. The machine developed the image and delivered a sharp, photostatic copy in minutes. It was a Xerox from heaven, printed on thick photographic paper. The stat machine at Weber Cohn was housed in a little room across the hall from my office. I learned how to operate it one afternoon from a technician who was fixing it. Overhearing his conversation with one of the art directors, I grew curious and walked over to see what was up. As he made test copies, I asked him a few questions. He wound up taking me through all the steps involved in making a stat; it was amazingly simple.

Word spread fast that Joe Murphy knew how to make stats. A few days after acquiring this skill a young art trainee asked me if I'd make her a stat of some artwork. "Just this once, please" she pleaded. Under the camera's canvas shroud I brought the image into focus. "Wanna take a look?" I asked. Emerging from under the hood I was surprised to find Ron Cohn staring me in the face. "What the hell are you doing making stats?" he barked. "I was just helping this lady," I answered. Cohn looked at the frightened girl and yelled, "This guy is a writer! We're not paying him to make stats!" He turned to leave, but stopped and looked back at us. "Wait here!" he commanded before marching off. A minute later Cohn returned with Bernie Bahr and another art director. "Just so all of you know," he announced, "Joe Murphy is employed here as a copywriter. He does not make stats for you people!"

A week or two later I was plodding my way through the afternoon, cranking out small space real estate ads, when Cohn walked into my office. Looking frazzled, he said, "Joe, I'm in a jam. I need a stat right now." "No problem" I answered, getting up from my desk. Ron needed a small map blown up for a client meeting. I set it up on the camera and got under the hood. While focusing the image I heard voices above me. Bernie Bahr was conferring with Cohn about something. I snapped the picture and came out from under the shroud. Bernie looked surprised and then grinned. As the finished enlargement squeaked its way out of the machine, I picked it up and handed it to my boss. A little embarrassed, Cohn smiled and said, "Murph makes a nice stat, doesn't he?" I went back to my office, closed the door and laughed out loud.

Daley TV campaign

Jim Riley had political connections in Chicago that helped him attract political-candidate clients. The agency had put together successful campaigns for Richard Elrod for Sheriff of Cook County and Mike Howlett for Illinois Secretary of State. I contributed lines for these campaigns but don't recall if any of them were used. Based on the successful work the agency had done, we got a shot at Mayor Daley's re-election campaign in 1976. Daley was a shoe-in, which took much of the heat off us. I thought this was wonderful; we couldn't go wrong no matter what we came up with. It was quite a thrill when Cohn and Riley asked me to come with them for an input session at City Hall. Cohn, Riley, Fred Sherwood and I jumped into a cab and shot across the Loop to the big gray structure known as City Hall.

We exited the elevator and stepped into a small conference room where we met with Frank Sullivan, the mayor's press secretary. Frank was very frank; he said the mayor was a busy man, but he'd agreed to let us follow him around with a camera for a day as he went about his business. Sullivan suggested that this would give us enough footage for two or three 30-second TV spots. A voice-over announcer would furnish the audio portion. It sounded like a done deal – we'd follow Hizzoner's guidelines and try to make the finished spots look as slick as possible. Sullivan gave us two or three weeks to put something together for him to look at. Everything seemed pretty cut and dried. The cab ride back to the agency was strangely silent. Sullivan's brusqueness left our group a bit nonplussed. The next morning Cohn called Fred and me into his office. He thought that the creative parameters set by the mayor's press secretary were too narrow. We had to show more creativity, he insisted. First off, we needed a line. I came up with "Daley has made the difference," which didn't knock anybody's socks off, but we used it as a working theme.

Then Cohn said we needed some music; he asked Sherwood and me to write a jingle about Daley and Chicago. This approach was light-years away the from the press secretary's guidelines. Fred and I collaborated on some lyrics that were pretty forgettable, but I remember that they started with: "Look at yourself Chicago, you're beautiful...." Cohn got Marty Rubenstein, a well-respected composer with a classical background, to write the music. He laid down a preliminary music track that was peppy and upbeat. I liked it. Fred brought a tape if it over to my house on a frosty Saturday morning for a work session, but the first order of business was breakfast. Mary served puffy apple pancakes, always a surefire hit. We ate and talked, washing down the pancakes with hot coffee. Mary sat with us, holding four-month old Eileen. Bridget toddled into the dining room. Looking at Fred, she pointed at the bundle in Mary's lap. "Baby!" she babbled. "Bridget has really gotten cute," our guest commented affectionately.

I racked up Fred's tape onto my reel-to-reel recorder and pushed PLAY. Reading the words from a typed script, Fred and I sang: "Look at yourself Chicago, you're beautiful...." To our delight, those words and the ones that followed fit perfectly. Back at the agency on Monday, we reported to Cohn that things were shaping up well. We only had a few days left to pull things together for our presentation at City Hall. Rubenstein was working on the finished music track. I got the tweaked lyrics typed and took them over to Marty at Sonart Studios. He said he had someone in mind to sing the words to our mayoral jingle. At the end of the day we hadn't yet heard from the maestro. Cohn contacted him the next morning, learning that the studio session joining the music with the singer's voice would have to wait till the next day. *What?* I wondered. *That's the day we're due at City Hall to play the finished tape for Sullivan.*

Bridget cuddles her lovable hobo, 1975.

Congestion session

What could we do but sit on our hands and hope that things would go well? I still didn't know who the mystery singer was. The next day our whole team – Riley, Cohn, Fred and I – prepared ourselves for battle. Everything hinged on the Dick Daley song, which was not yet put together. Right after lunch we cabbed it to Sonart to record the singer and marry his voice to the music track. Riley stuffed some cash into the cabbie's hand and told him to wait for us. Inside, Rubenstein introduced us to a young black vocalist who couldn't stop sneezing and coughing. He tried to apologize about his cold, but a barrage of coughing and sneezing kept him from finishing a sentence. Our engineer played the music-only track; it sounded great. The singer coughed and got behind the microphone. Someone handed him a glass of water.

The engineer voice-slated our first attempt, "Daley campaign jingle, take one." The tape rolled. The singer sang, "Look at yourself Chicago, you're caughahaggh! I'm sorry, let me clear my throat." He gulped some water and signaled that he was ready. "Daley jingle, take two," the engineer droned. The tape rolled. "Look at yourself Chicago, you're beautiful. You're cuogaghacoughouag! Sorry, just give me a second to caggoughagaugh …" *Holy shit. This guy should be in the hospital,* I thought. Riley and Cohn looked at each other gravely. Our voice talent tried again to get through the song. His voice cleared a bit, but it was straining on the high notes. Shrieking might be a better description.

The clock was ticking. It was 2:15 and we were due at City Hall at 3:00. The singer gulped more water and we kept going. After a few more takes he made it to the end of the song. We called the session, figuring we could cut parts of different takes together to make one decent track. Mr. Voice left, apologizing on his way out. Our engineer sliced and spliced furiously, then played the resulting track for us. Not wonderful but not horrible. We told him to add the music and play the combined track. Definitely not horrible. Riley took the tape and bolted for the door with the rest of our group in hot pursuit. Outside, our steadfast cabbie was waiting behind the wheel. Riley stuffed more cash into his hand "Wow, thanks," he yelled. "Well, you waited for us, pal!" Riley said thankfully.

Ten minutes later our team was sitting in a conference room at City Hall waiting to see Frank Sullivan. He entered at 3 p.m. sharp, seated himself at the table facing us and asked what we had to show him. Cohn gave a brief spiel while Riley walked to a nearby table and tried to rack up our demo tape on a small player. He switched it on. Nothing happened. Cohn rewound the tape and rethreaded it. He switched it on. Out came our Daley song loud and clear: "Look at yourself Chicago, you're beautiful…." Sullivan sat stone faced as he listened. At the end he looked straight at Cohn. "You want to sell Mayor Daley with a jingle?" he asked in disbelief. Cohn started explaining how the music would blend magically with the right video. "I see the mayor's face rising like the sun over Lake Michigan!" The press secretary looked at our creative leader in disbelief. Not much more was said. Sullivan thanked us, rose from his chair and left the room. A minute later Cohn, Riley, Sherwood and I were standing in the hall waiting for an elevator to take us back to earth.

Dot pattern discord

I was on my way out the door one night when Bruce Kramer stopped me in the hall and asked me to look at an ad that was pasted up on an illustration board and ready for press. Sounding urgent, he said it had to run in the *Tribune* the next morning. "Can you hang around a few minutes and look at it?" I reluctantly said "Okay" and went back to my office. (Like many of the ads for new homes we cranked out, this one included an illustration of the floor plan.) Five minutes later I heard a loud voice coming from a nearby office. I walked over to find Ron Cohn expressing his concern about the floor plan illustration. The bathroom floor didn't look right, he said. Like the floors in all the other rooms, it was shaded by tiny dots, but Cohn noticed that the dots on the bathroom floor were bigger than those on the floors in other rooms. To me it looked like something the paste-up artist could fix in a flash.

Jim Riley walked in; Cohn brought the problem to his attention. Now they were both upset about the dots. *This is nuts,* I thought. They started rummaging through proofs of old ads, trying to find a floor with the magic number of dots per square inch that could be pasted into the bathroom. I wondered what the hell possessed them to become absorbed in such minutiae. Before long they had recruited others to join in their search. It seemed that some kind of bizarre mob mentality had taken over. Everyone was comparing proofs and dots in search of the right floor. I decided to stay out of it and left for home. The next morning, Rob Halpin, one of the young account execs, told me that Riley was really pissed that I'd bailed on the dot quest the night before. Eventually, someone had located an ad proof with a floor containing the magic configuration of dots, and it was patched into the ad. Rob told me that as he and Riley left the building that night, they witnessed an accident right in front of them on Michigan Avenue. A pedestrian had been hit by a taxi and was lying hurt on the street. "That's gonna be Murphy tomorrow!" Riley grumbled.

Up in smoke

Sometimes I used the stat machine after hours to tweak samples for my portfolio. There might be a clever ad that would look better without some ugly logo or disclaimer that had been crammed into it. I would remove the unsightly junk and then take a photo of the cleaned-up ad with the stat camera. After hours one night I set a real estate ad in front of the camera and switched on the lights. Vertical stacks of bulbs on both sides of the camera burned bright and hot. I got under the hood and brought everything into sharp focus. Suddenly I smelled smoke and lifted my head. Holy shit! A plume of orange flames was shooting toward the ceiling. Their source was a huge mounted photo that had been leaning against some of the lights. I threw the flaming picture onto the floor and stomped out the fire. The photo turned out to be a glamour shot of a swank new condo development on Lake Shore Drive, the agency's newest client. I'd completely destroyed the image in seconds. *Nice work, Joe.*

I got right to work cleaning up the mess. Not only was the huge picture ruined, there were ashes and black marks on the floor and a big scorch mark on the ceiling. I swept the floor and scrubbed it with wet paper towels. Then, standing on a stool, I wiped the dark spot from the ceiling. Things cleaned up well. But what to do with the charred remains of that photo? *Better destroy the evidence.* I took what was left of the picture into the mount room, used the paper cutter to chop it into small pieces and stuffed them into a trashcan. Running back to the stat machine, I quickly shot the picture I'd set up earlier. I couldn't wait to flee the scene; waiting for the stat to inch its way out of the machine seemed like an eternity. By this time it was nearly 9 p.m. I rolled up the stat, slid it into a mailing tube and stole out of the building with it tucked under my arm.

A few days later all hell broke loose. I was working quietly in my office when I heard desperate voices shouting. The creative director and account exec were searching for that big photo I'd destroyed. "Where the hell is it?" "I don't know! It just f…king disappeared!" They needed the picture for a meeting with the client. I felt guilty as they tore through the agency, ransacking one office after another in their search. But after they left empty-handed I couldn't help smiling.

Eyes on the prize

I kept working on make-believe TV spots at night and keeping my eyes open during the day, checking *Advertising Age* and other trade papers to see what was shaking along Michigan Avenue. Sometimes after work I'd stop at Riccardo's Restaurant, right behind the Wrigley Building. It was a popular lunch spot and a longtime watering hole for ad people. On any weeknight I could join the crowd huddled around the bar. Their talk included scuttlebutt on what accounts were moving from one shop to another, and which agencies were looking for people. Just standing amid the herd nursing a drink you could pick up useful info. The bar itself was shaped like an artist's palette, and encircling it were seven wall-mounted murals depicting the seven lively arts: drama, architecture, music, literature, sculpture, painting and dance. In 1947 "Ric" Riccardo, the original owner, commissioned each of six different WPA artists to paint one of them, and he painted one himself.

I liked lunching at Ric's. The food was good and not overpriced. On spring and summer evenings Ron Cohn and a gang from the agency would often sip cocktails at a sidewalk table. These outings were fun and relaxing, but sitting there, I felt an urge to wander inside and sniff out some job leads. Once in a while at Ric's, I'd bump into someone I'd worked with in the past, someone who might give me a hot tip like, "Burnett just got a juicy new TV account – they might be looking for writers." And sometimes a job lead would come out of left field; my office phone would ring and the caller would be a headhunter from another state asking if I wanted to interview with an agency in

Columbus, Ohio or Jacksonville, Florida. How did folks like this even know I existed?

Homespun commercials

After a year at Weber Cohn none of the accounts I worked on had asked for a single television commercial. I was desperate to put together a reel of TV spots. When I mentioned this to one of the art directors, she told me where I might be able to videotape some "homemade" TV commercials. The College of DuPage near her folks' house had a media lab, she said. Students used its studio to videotape sketches and promos for their classes.

That night I drove out to the campus where I met Ken Krueger, the young engineer who was running the lab. He liked my TV commercial concepts and was eager to help me shoot them. A week later we started taping 30-second spots starring college kids who happened by the open door of the media lab. We asked them if they wanted to be in a TV commercial. Luckily, there was no shortage of willing talent. I could only get into the studio one night a week, but writing scripts and scrounging up props kept me busy on the other nights.

The first spot featured a girl talking into the camera about Oxy5, a zit-zapping lotion that had just come onto the market. As the weeks rolled by we taped spots on Dr. Pepper, Pringles and some products I dreamed up, including waterproof books for bathtub readers. Our spontaneous talent did a terrific job, and before long, friends of theirs started showing up to watch our sessions. Some of them asked if they could help out. At this point we had the luxury of auditioning folks for parts. My ever-helpful brother Pat joined us one night, playing a defective potato chip in a commercial for Pringles.

John Boland, a friend of my brother Dan, heard about my project and dropped by out of curiosity. He helped me set up the shots and keep things organized, and came back week after week – all the way to the last night of shooting. Even better, he really enjoyed himself.

With six TV spots taped I was anxious to show them to creative people who might be able to hire me as a broadcast writer. The first person that viewed my tape was a big-agency pre-screener. Smiling, he said they showed a lot of creativity and initiative. "Yeah, sure!" I said to myself. A week or two later I played the spots for a creative group head at D'Arcy MacManus & Masius, who really liked them. He even fetched a couple of producers, telling them, "You gotta see this. Here's a guy who made his own TV commercials!" As it turned out, I would later go to work for D'Arcy. But that's another story.

A taste of Champaign

On a Monday afternoon in June an out-of-town headhunter called me at work about a job opportunity in downstate Illinois. A small agency wanted to talk to me the very next day. *How crazy can you get?* I wondered. Nonetheless, I agreed to be there at 2 p.m. I took the following day off and caught a train headed south. Tom Froedert, the owner, picked me up at the station, greeting me with a smile and a hearty handshake. He chauffeured me to his agency, which was housed in a handsome, low profile building. Tom and his wife Sarah flipped through my samples and seemed to like what they saw. They showed me some work that their agency had done for a range of clients. The print stuff left me cold, but the TV spots they'd made for a huge utility company were damned good. Another TV client – a grocery account – had them worried. They were under the gun to get a batch of spots finished and on the air. With scheduled airdates approaching fast, they needed a writer yesterday. It seemed that getting hired hinged on my immediate availability. I told them that I owed my current employer two weeks' notice before moving on. "Two weeks?" Tom asked in disbelief. He and his wife looked at me as if I'd left them hanging from the edge of a cliff.

Back in Chicago the next morning I gave Ron Cohn three whole days' notice. He looked very disappointed, which surprised me; I'd always thought his regard for me was so-so at best. He asked angrily why I was giving him a lousy three days' notice. I tried to explain that my new employer was in desperate need of help ASAP. This did not move Cohn to tears. I walked back to my office and started packing.

The next day a young art director told me that he and a few others wanted to take me to the Billy Goat after work on my last day. On Friday I departed Weber Cohn & Riley with four or five junior members of the creative staff. We hoofed it to the Goat, grabbed a table and ordered a pitcher of beer. More people drifted in until there were about a dozen of us. We pulled two tables together and ordered more beer. Wishing me well, the group gave me a couple of novels as a farewell gift. On the way to the train, I stopped at the bar in Marina City for a martini. Looking out at the Chicago River, I wondered if I'd be leaving the Windy City for good. Then, determined to make a first-class exit, I cabbed it over to Union Station and climbed aboard the westbound Burlington.

Saturday morning I backed a 20-foot U-HAUL truck into our narrow driveway. Mary and I started loading our hand-me-down furniture into it when my brother Pat showed up to help with the heavy lifting. We had to get a piano onto the truck. It was just a spinet but it was plenty heavy for two average-sized guys to handle. Mary was still packing while I finished typing an article for the Jaycees that would run in the local paper. Finally, Mary put the kids in the car and I backed the truck out of the driveway. With Mary trailing me in our little Opel, we traveled 150 miles southeast. Arriving in Champaign, we were greeted by Mary's cousin Theresa and her husband, who lived nearby. They had recruited two strong young males, who unloaded the piano and hauled it up a fight of stairs into our new apartment. The crew seemed happy enough when we paid them with pizza and beer. When they left Mary and I took a nap on the floor with the kids.

TWENTY-ONE

ON THE ROAD AGAIN

"If you come to a fork in the road, take it."
–Yogi Berra

My FIRST DAY WITH TOM and Sarah was a beaut. I worked on a big batch of price-and-product (weekly special) TV commercials for a local grocery outfit. The video portion of these spots had already been shot on film. My job was to write some voice-over narration to match wallpaper visuals of shoppers in the store that had been shot earlier. The spots followed a "donut" format with a middle section reserved for showing the weekly special items. Then back to more visuals of happy shoppers to finish the spot. Special items could be anything from steak to cherry pie, but most often they were the delectable duo of frozen pizza and frozen orange juice. I wrote new narration for the sale items each week. The spots ended with voices singing a dreadful, forgettable tag line. Dull as it was to produce these commercials at the local TV station, making them look good was challenging and fun. When we were shooting pumpkin pie for Thanksgiving, the whipped cream on top kept melting under the studio lights, so we used shaving cream instead. It looked great and held up heroically.

The energy client was the agency's biggest account, and their TV campaign aired nationally. My art director and I came up with a spot that showed people playing an energy game – a board game like Monopoly. We had fun designing it and making sure it was bright and colorful. I wrote a 30-second narration that Froedert presented to

232

the client's committee members. Incorporating all their hand-written comments stretched the audio to 90 seconds, the length of three 30-second commercials. I struggled to make the most important fixes and keep the spot from running long. This meant writing the whole thing from scratch and ignoring most of the comments. It would surely insult the committee and create havoc for Tom, but it was the best I could do.

The way things were done at this little agency was baffling. One person produced all the big-budget TV spots *and* the humorous radio spots I wrote. This situation was killing my soul. I thought that the light touch I'd written into my radio scripts would be obvious to anyone, but it escaped the agency producer completely. He could turn a humorous script into a very unfunny commercial. Also, the agency had a young research lady who could have been a big help to me, but she was always buried in some top-secret project. I wound up doing my own research, which could have been fun if I'd had enough time. I was already working late and on weekends to handle the writing part of my job. My solitary research took me to a cavernous University of Illinois library, where I had to park illegally or not at all. My car collected parking tickets aplenty, which I paid myself.

Other things that irked me were lack of privacy and blatant disrespect. Sarah had no qualms about opening my personal mail. And on more than one occasion she sent me out to the parking lot to fix flat tires for female employees. When Tom bought himself a new Cadillac he called on me one afternoon to chauffeur him and a client around town in it. Back in Chicago I'd heard stories about little mom-and-pop agencies in out-of-the way places – how they could be little shops of horror. I wished that I'd been listening more closely. My situation with Sara and Tom deteriorated rapidly.

Working from morn till night on New Year's Day did not get my 1977 off to a happy start. But one bright spot in January was the sale of our house in Downers Grove. Someone made a bid on it, which we accepted in a flash. The interested party was a young industrial arts teacher employed by the local high school to teach building trades. Maybe the fact that our shack needed decades of repairs made it the home of his dreams. Whew! We couldn't have survived another month of making both rent and mortgage payments. Meanwhile, the scene at work was quickly worsening. Fearing that Tom and Sarah might cut me loose any day, I scrambled to launch a job search. In April I answered an ad for *Agency Copywriter* in a trade journal that led to a Saturday interview in North Carolina.

On Friday Tom sent a memo to all that said, "We'll be working tomorrow." *Oh shit!* I caught him in the hallway and explained that I had to attend an important family event on Chicago on Saturday. He let me off the hook. Whew! The next morning I flew to Raleigh, where two biggies from Lewis Advertising met me at the airport. One was Don Williams, a principal in the agency; the other was John Polous, the creative director. Don drove us to the office in Rocky Mount, about 20 miles south. Lewis Advertising handled several TV accounts – Hardee's hamburgers, a grocery store chain and several local banks. Williams and Polous liked my portfolio, and Williams really sparked to my radio spots. He offered me a job for more than I was making, and I accepted.

Arriving back in Champaign, I told Mary that we were moving to North Carolina. She was glad to see me get out of a tight spot, but not at all thrilled about moving again. Monday morning I awakened with plans to give my notice at work, but I couldn't get out of bed. My lower back was killing me. I couldn't sit up. Mary slipped a hot pad under me and I spent the day looking at the ceiling. Tuesday I managed to get into work. On the way to my office a surly secretary told me that Sarah thought I was dogging it the day before. She followed me into my office, elaborating on Sarah's comments. I cut into her report with "Tom should take Sarah out and shoot her!" The secretary gasped, snarled at me and left in a huff.

Ten minutes later Tom paid me a visit. "I understand you don't like the way this place is run," he said calmly. I hesitated a moment and answered, "That's accurate." "When are you leaving?" he asked. "I can give you my notice or I can leave now," I replied. "Why don't you leave now?" he suggested. I took the painting off my wall. (I'd removed the rest of my stuff a week earlier.) In the hall I turned toward the nearest exit. Three or four folks were holding the door open for me. My painting and I made a quick exit.

Carolina, here we come

Freed from the Froederts, I told Lewis Advertising I was ready to go to work. Don Williams suggested that Mary and I come down to Rocky Mount, visit the agency and explore the surroundings. So we left baby Eileen with my mom, packed three-year-old Bridget into our Opel and drove south. On the way the ailment in my back went to my lungs. I couldn't stop coughing. We stopped for the night. Bridget looked at our motel room and complained, "This is not my house!" I inhaled Vicks VapoRub, which didn't help much. By morning Mary was coughing. Her condition worsened as the day wore on. Arriving in Rocky Mount, we headed straight for the hospital, where Mary and I were diagnosed with the flu.

Somehow we dragged ourselves to a Chinese restaurant that night, where we met Gene Lewis, his wife and a bunch of folks from the agency. Mary and I were coughing so much that talking was nearly impossible. Don Williams turned to us and said, "You should both be in the hospital!" It was time we got going, but before we left, a lady across the table told us about a house that was ready to go up for sale. The next morning she phoned us at our motel. We had an appointment to look at that house, she told us. It was small but tidy and had a big back yard bordered by bushes of red roses that were in were in full bloom. Mary fell in love with the place. We put in a bid on it before driving back to Champaign. The realtor in Rocky Mount phoned us with good news: our bid had been accepted. In our apartment we recuperated for a few days. Then, after lunch on Easter Saturday, I said goodbye to my family and headed south once more – this time to start work. Arriving in Rocky Mount on Monday, I was surprised to find that most every business in town was closed. "Easter Monday" was a public holiday in North Carolina at that time. I got a motel, saw a movie and rested up.

Morning mayhem

My first day of work started with a traffic meeting in Gene Lewis' office. It covered the status of every job on the agency roster. At any given time the agency was working on about 30 accounts, so the number of projects to keep track of could be 100. The meeting checked the progress of every job going through the shop. And a hefty stack of new jobs was added to the workload. For me the hardest part of this meeting was spitting out an estimated date for finished copy. Once I nailed a date onto something I was expected to deliver the goods on time. For the first week I worked late every night trying to catch up with the backlog of jobs that had been waiting for the "new writer."

The tsunami of work at Lewis never abated; it scared me at times. How could I do a good job on every project when there was never enough time? The projects kept coming – for restaurant clients, a quick mart outfit, food store chains, local banks, tobacco growers, a truck body manufacturer.... New job folders were added to the pile on my desk every day. Hardee's, the fast food chain, was the agency's biggest account. We produced ads and commercials for one of the company's large franchise operators. Their size gave them the autonomy to make TV and radio spots beyond the Hardee's national ad campaign. They looked to Lewis for broadcast advertising tailored to their special needs. And thanks to the decent budgets they gave us, we were able do a good job for them.

Back in Champaign Mary supervised the movers as they loaded our furniture onto a van. Then she flew down with the kids. We took up residence in our new abode, but, unfortunately, the moving van was delayed. Our beds, tables, chairs and clothes were offloaded into a warehouse, where they sat for several days. Meanwhile, Mary and I and the kids slept on the bedroom floor. We were elated when our furniture finally arrived. It felt good to come home to a bed after working until late at night. Exploring our new neighborhood on the weekend, we found a huge city park nearby with a small lake, nice stretches of grass and lots of tall broadleaf pine trees. The cones that fell from them were as big as footballs. What a place – it even had a huge carousel from an old amusement park that still worked beautifully. There was ample space for walking and letting the kids run free. That refreshing park helped me put work on the back burner, if only for an hour or two on the weekend. Our family also enjoyed the welcoming hospitality of some great neighbors and an occasional "pig pickin'," where a whole pig was barbecued on a spit. You just walked up and tore off a hunk of pork.

Hungry for more

Dead set on growing his agency, Gene Lewis was forever pitching new business. This meant a ton of extra work for the creative folks, and I was already struggling to get my regular work done. Sure, it's exciting to come up with campaign ideas; it's fun to write clever new ads and commercials. But this is exhausting when your regular workweek is 50 plus hours. And all of the work we did on a new business pitch was done on spec, meaning the agency didn't get paid a penny for it. When we pitched Smithfield (the outfit that makes country hams) I worked until 3 a.m. cleaning up radio scripts and TV storyboards. Then I pedaled home on my bike to catch a few hours of shuteye. I thought we had a good chance of landing that account, but it didn't happen. Working late on another night, I had to finish a group of radio scripts for a local bank. I typed them rough, made hand-written corrections then retyped them a couple of times. During this process things started developing – like a sheet of photographic paper in the soup. The spots got better and better. One of them, featuring Dr. Frankenstein and Igor, was the spot that won an Andy award in New York. The extra effort I put in that night paid off.

Where's the beef?

Lewis had a local supermarket client that ran weekly price-and-product TV spots. Part of my job was producing them at a TV station in Durham about 60 miles from Rocky Mount. The client stuffed the products for the commercials into a large cooler and left it on the ground outside their warehouse. I drove over after work, loaded the cooler into my trunk and headed for Durham. The TV studio was in an old building that had once been a schoolhouse. Inside, I had to set everything up in a hurry and shoot it before the anchorman showed up to do the ten o'clock news. With no time to waste, it was a challenge to make those spots look good, but the client was pleased with them.

The first time steak was a featured item I removed it from its plastic wrapping, videotaped it and put it back in the cooler afterward. Not wanting to waste good beef, I took it home and stashed it in the freezer. My family and I ate it for supper the next night. A day or two later the client phoned the account exec at the agency, asking what had happened to the meat. Buddy, the account man, relayed the question to me. "The meat? I ate it," I told him. "Well, the client wants it back," he said. "You're joking!" Buddy assured me that was no joke. *"Talk about miserable!"* I barked.

With Thanksgiving approaching, turkeys were on special. I knew one would be packed into the cooler waiting for me at the warehouse. Wanting to make a good presentation on TV, I borrowed an elegant china platter from home. Mary surrendered it reluctantly with a warning, "Don't break this! It belonged to my grandmother!" At the studio I removed the bird from its plastic bag, set it on the platter and shot it buck naked and uncooked. A few days later, after he got a phone call from the client, Gene Lewis walked into my office and asked: "Whatever possessed you to show a raw turkey in a food commercial?" I couldn't think of an answer.

Sad news

Early in February I got call from my sister Joan, who told me that our uncle Mike had died, and that his funeral would take place in a couple of days. I booked a flight to Chicago and arranged to stay overnight at my brother Dan's apartment, just north of downtown. At work the next morning I told my art director/boss John that I needed a day off so I could fly to Chicago for the funeral. "Sure," he said. Just then Don

Williams, co-owner of the agency, walked into my office. I told him I'd be gone the next day and explained why. "Take an extra day," he said. "You'll want to spend some time with your family." I phoned the airport to check on my departure time. Sure enough, my flight to Chicago would take off at 5 p.m. I called Mary and told her I'd be right home to grab my suitcase and say "goodbye" to everyone. In the parking lot I started my car, backed up too fast and got stuck in a muddy rut. Unable to free my rear wheels, I went back inside and asked John for help. He came out and pushed as I stepped on the gas. His third push freed the car. "Thanks John!" I shouted through my open window. His shoes and pants were covered with mud and he looked pissed. "Be careful on your trip," John cautioned. "This ugly start bodes ill!"

Hurry! Hurry!

At home I changed into a suit and I checked the suitcase Mary had packed for me. Everything was there, even my harmonica, which Mary included whenever I took a solo trip. Before closing the bag I tossed in a cassette holding a few TV spots and a reel of radio commercials – all stuff I'd done since leaving Chicago. Something told me to add these items – some vague notion that somehow I might be able to show them to someone in Chicago. Experience had taught me that in advertising anything could happen at any time.

On the plane I thought about my Uncle Mike, Mom's bachelor brother. He often visited our house on Saturday mornings when I was a kid. He liked to chat with Mom and he loved kids. Mike was never shy about taking us to task if we were getting out of line, wasting our time or not helping Mom. He didn't suffer fools gladly and didn't give a damn about pop culture or new-fangled fads. If I mentioned the Beach Boys or the Beatles, he'd come back with, "Those goofy bastards? They just make a lot of bad noise," or something like that. As a young man Mike was a Marine serving in the Philippines. Like my dad, he was a pipefitter, but being a bachelor, he was free to find work in warmer climes during the winter. Over the years, he sent us postcards from

Los Angeles, Las Vegas and Hawaii. When Mike returned he brought presents for everyone. He was an admirable character. I was going to miss him.

When I landed at O'Hare my brother Dan was there to pick me up. It was great to see him despite the somber circumstances. Taking in the scene as we drove toward downtown, I felt more and more energized. We stopped for dinner at the Red Star Inn, an old German restaurant that served terrific food. Over sauerbraten and red cabbage we reminisced about our colorful uncle, agreeing that we hadn't appreciated him enough while he was with us. At his apartment Dan showed me to an extra bedroom, where I quickly fell asleep. In the morning my brother went off to work, so I was free for most of the day. I thought of the broadcast samples in my suitcase and then called Ed Bresnan at D'Arcy MacManus & Masius Advertising downtown. Having interviewed with him a year earlier, I hoped he'd remember me. Luckily, he did. Ed sounded upbeat and glad to hear from me. I asked him if he could look at my TV and radio stuff in the afternoon. "Sure," he replied. "Your timing is perfect – a writer just gave his notice today!" Encouraging words.

After lunch I took the El downtown to the Washington subway stop. From there it was a short walk to the new, 80-story Standard Oil Building, nicknamed "Big Stan." Shooting skyward just east of Michigan Avenue, it was easy to spot. I rode a zippy elevator up the 71st floor, home to D'Arcy's creative department. Behind floor-to-ceiling glass doors a granite monolith stretched 20 feet across. In the center the DM&M logo stood out boldly in chrome. The scene was impressive but intimidating, suggesting that D'Arcy was a place where big, important things happened. One of the two female receptionists manning this command post buzzed me in. I told her I had an appointment with Ed Bresnan. She phoned him, announced my arrival and told me how to find his office. It was good to see Bresnan again. I remembered him as a bright, unpretentious man with a good sense of humor. When I apologized for not having a résumé, he said he was more interested in viewing my TV reel and hearing my radio spots. As we listened to the radio stuff he laughed out loud a couple of times. So far so good.

*The Standard Oil building looked rock solid, but
slabs of its original marble facade were falling off.*

The suspense mounts

We walked back to the agency's in-house TV studio, where Bresnan
played my cassette of TV spots. I was proud of the commercials I'd done
for the National Coal Association, and I thought Peter Graves did a nice
job on the Carolina Telephone spots. Ed's only comment was. "Wait
here – I'll get Valtos." A few minutes later he returned with Bill Valtos,
the creative director on several accounts, including Amoco. Ed played
my TV cassette for his boss, who watched in silence. As the three of us
walked back to the creative department, Ed told me to wait in his office.
He and Valtos strolled down the hall. Ten minutes later Ed returned,
offering me a job at more money than I was making in North Carolina.
I accepted with glee and we shook hands. Looking back, I think it was
those TV spots that got me the job.

It was great seeing Mom, Dad and all my siblings that night at Uncle Mike's wake. I told everyone that Mary and I would be moving back to Chicago. They were so happy to hear the news that watching them choked me up. At the funeral the next day Mom and Dad looked much less hearty than I'd remembered them. It was a gray, biting-cold day at the Catholic cemetery in Gary, Indiana. A thin crust of ice covering the grass made the footing slippery. I could see that my parents were having a tough time keeping their balance as they walked to the gravesite. It was comforting to know that my young family would soon be living near them.

TWENTY-TWO

GOOD TO BE BACK

"I saw a subliminal advertising executive,
but only for a second."
– Stephen Wright

RESETTLING IN OAK PARK, WE were lucky to find a home just a block from the rapid transit tracks that ran east to Chicago's Loop. I could usually find a seat on the morning train and read, doodle or sleep on my way downtown. It took about 30 minutes to reach my stop. Then it was a short walk to my job in the Standard Oil Building. Nearing that new skyscraper, I was dazzled by its pristine appearance. Clad in white Italian Carrera marble, it struck me as being the handsomest structure on the lakefront.*
All the window offices at D'Arcy were occupied by folks who had bigger jobs than mine. My immediate boss, Ed Bresnan, was upbeat and fun to work for. The first writing assignment he gave me was a corporate ad for Amoco. At that time the thrust of Amoco's advertising was their search for new sources of domestic oil. The main headline in every print ad was followed by a subhead echoing the television message: **All over America, Amoco is working to make our country less dependent on foreign oil.** With every ad repeating this message, it was hard to make

---

*   When completed in 1974, the Standard Oil building was sheathed with 43,000 slabs of Italian Carrera marble. During construction in 1973, a 350-pound slab detached from the building and penetrated the roof of the nearby Prudential Center. An inspection in 1985 revealed numerous cracks and bowing in the marble cladding. Later, between 1990 and 1992, the entire building was refaced with white North Carolina granite at an estimated cost of more than $80 million. Source: buildingfailures@wordpress.com

one sound different from another. Still, it felt good to be working on such a prestigious, big-bucks account. Most of the Amoco writing I did was industrial trade: ads for plastic resins, like polypropylene and polystyrene. The basic product came in the form of little pellets that looked like rabbit food. But the ads showed attractive finished items in four-color splendor – storm doors, plastic plates and toy trucks – all made from Amoco resins.

Plastic pellets aside, it felt great to be back in Chicago. I connected with Fred Sherwood, who was still at Weber Cohn & Riley, and we went to lunch. Fred caught me up on the local scene – what accounts had moved to which agencies and where people we knew were now working. Fred told me that the Chicago Transit Authority was now one of Weber Cohn's clients. He described a TV spot he'd written for the CTA based on the lunch trips to the Chinatown Garden Restaurant we'd taken when we worked together at Weber Cohn. The spot, which aired for months, followed us as we caught a CTA train in the subway downtown, rode to Chinatown, chowed down on a buffet luncheon, and then traveled back downtown, each paying just a single fare. How could this happen? We bought nickel transfers that let us reverse directions within a one-hour time span.

In addition to Amoco, I worked on Rust-Oleum coating systems – an array of products used to cover everything from storage tanks to airport towers to truck fenders. I enjoyed writing an ad that featured the space shuttle, which was coated with Rust-Oleum epoxy. The headline read: **Tough enough for space.** And I got to write some ads on the regular Rust-Oleum that homeowners use on their lawn furniture. One day Bresnan needed some blue-sky concepts for a Rust-Oleum consumer TV spot – a rare chance to have some fun. I came back to him a few days later with some ideas, one of which showed Mr. Rust out in the yard throwing rust flakes all over the patio furniture. I wanted to use Rip Taylor, a comic whose shtick was throwing confetti. At that time he was hosting a silly show entitled, *The Dollar Ninety-Eight-Beauty Pageant.* I worked with Pat Daley, a talented lady illustrator, to make a key frame (a poster-sized illustration) of Mr. Rust, which Bresnan presented to the creative biggies at D'Arcy. Sadly, the idea didn't click with them. *Way too much fun.*

Another TV opportunity presented itself on Amoco's China Foam plastic plates. I wrote a spot staged in a Greek temple. An elderly mentor presents a lesson in economy to a young boy by using disposable picnic plates. He demonstrates how the paper plate sags when full, and how the pulp plate sogs. But the China Foam plate doesn't sag *or* sog. The enlightened boy comments, "You know much about plates." His mentor responds, "That's why they call me Plato." Management didn't think we needed to go back in history to make a point. *Deadheads!* Despite the stodgy management at D'Arcy, we "creatives" found ways to inject a little levity into our days. Ed Bresnan and Don Pausback, a young writer in the cube next to me, maintained an ongoing caption contest. Every Monday morning Ed or Don tacked up a picture from a newspaper or magazine near the coffee machine. Attached to it was a blank sheet to hold captions submitted by people in the office. Bresnan usually won. It surprised me that management allowed this tomfoolery to continue. It was fun, and fun seemed to be the dirty "F" word at D'Arcy.

Meanwhile, I was adjusting to the high-rise work environment at D'Arcy. Windy days scared me. The floor undulated like a blanket being shaken by some colossal cleaning lady. At the same time, the elevator cables made loud slapping noises: *WHAPAPAPAPAPAP....* It took a while to get used to this, but eventually I could laugh about it. However, one thing that gave me ongoing grief was my cubby's corner location at the junction of two busy hallways and adjacent to the noisy secretarial pool. Girls chattering office gossip and blathering about their boyfriends made it hard to concentrate. *I left my big office with a door to sit here listening to this drek?* Lunchtime provided welcome relief. I joined a little diner's club made up of Ed Bresnan, co-writer Don Pausback, art director John Doering and Ann Wojik, a perky blonde media buyer. We often ate at a cozy restaurant in the Pittsfield Building (a structure my dad helped to build in the thirties). Ed and Ann argued good-naturedly but constantly. Their lively banter kept our group entertained. Doering called them "The Bickersons," alluding to the 1940s comedy radio duo. Other bright spots of my job at D'Arcy were a couple of nifty Amoco items I was able to take home. One was a wallet made of a flexible plastic that had the look and feel of buckskin. Its rough texture made it hard to stuff into my pocket. But that roughness made the wallet pickpocket-proof, which I appreciated as a public transit passenger. I also got a deal on a handsome Amoco tank truck made of steel. It was silver with a red cab, and its thick rubber wheels rolled smoothly. At Christmas I gave it to my five-year-old daughter Bridget, who seemed to enjoy this boy toy as much as her new dolly.

I'd been at D'Arcy a few months when I got a phone call from the ANDY advertising show in New York. "Congratulations," a pleasant female voice informed me. "Your commercial, *Solar Connection*, won an ANDY award!" It turned out that a 60-second radio spot I'd written and produced in North Carolina had won the top award in the comedy category. "It's the 'Head' award," she assured me, "The big one." *WOW! I won! I won!* My mind was doing cartwheels. The lady caller gave me the date, time and other details about the award ceremony in New York City. I thanked her, but said I wouldn't be able to attend. "No problem," she continued, "we can mail your award to you." I gave her the address of my folks' house where I was staying. Before ringing off she hinted that there might be a cash prize coming as well. Two weeks later Mom phoned me at work and told me that a box from New York had come for me in the mail. I left my cube at five o'clock sharp and went straight home. With my parents watching I tore open the box and pulled out a gleaming chrome bust with my name on it. I also found a check for $250 and a letter of congratulations. My aging parents beamed with pride. I was so happy I got all choked up.

Things could be better

After another few months at D'Arcy, the agency's stodgy character was wearing on me. It was impossible to get the go-ahead on anything fun or clever. I began setting up lunchtime job interviews. Of course, I had to be careful. There was no way I could walk into the office carrying my portfolio. So on my way to work in the morning I stopped at the Trailways bus terminal on Randolph and stashed my bag in a storage locker. At noon I left work, picked up the bag and carried it to my interview. Then, on my way back to work, I returned it to the locker. This system worked well until one winter afternoon when I interviewed at a big agency in the John Hancock Building. My appointment was with a full-fledged creative director. We shook hands. I took a seat. "Why don't you just open your book here on the floor," he suggested. I unzipped my portfolio and folded it open onto the carpeting. A plump cockroach scrambled out of it and onto the toe of my interviewer's shoe. He kicked it off, jumped to his feet and stomped on it a few times. Then, smiling, he sat back down and flipped through my samples. I told him the bug must have come from the bus station where my bag had been stashed. "Don't worry about it," he said good-naturedly. When he finished viewing my stuff he looked up and said he'd keep me in mind. "And if we ever get the Raid account," he added, "you'll be the first guy I'll call."

Eyes on the prize

One day at lunch I told John Doering that I was tempted to drop off my résumé at Campbell-Mithun Advertising, even though it wasn't likely to land on the desk of anyone who could hire me. Scratching his chin thoughtfully, John told me about a writer named Dave Lieberman, who had moved from D'Arcy to Mithun a year earlier. He said Dave was a real human being – someone who might actually put my résumé on the creative director's desk. Without delay I phoned Lieberman and asked him if he could get my sheet into in the hands of someone qualified to judge it. Dave was pleasant and sympathetic, promising to do what he could. Per his instructions, I dropped off a copy of my résumé marked to his attention. A day or two later I got a call from Joe Berner, a full-fledged creative director at Mithun. He asked me to come over with my portfolio.

Paunchy, middle-aged Berner struck me as being a good listener. He liked my TV reel, which was now enhanced by a couple of Amoco spots. He asked me what kind of opportunities I was looking for. "More broadcast, especially TV," I answered. Berner listened quietly as I vented my frustration at not being able to produce commercials at D'Arcy. He told me that my job at Mithun would be mostly writing industrial trade ads. I said that would be fine as long as I got to work on *some* broadcast. He assured me that broadcast would be part of the mix, but there wouldn't be a whole lot of it. Regarding salary, I asked for a couple grand more than I was making at D'Arcy. I left the interview feeling optimistic. A few days later Berner called me at home after supper and told me that I had the job. I thanked him heartily, hung up the phone and literally jumped for joy. "I'm outa D'Arcy!" I shouted gleefully.

A cordial start

On my first day at Campbell-Mithun I was surprised by the convivial atmosphere and tickled to have an office of my own. I was still unpacking when Dave Seibel, president of the agency, walked in. He shook my hand and welcomed me warmly. Seibel seemed genuinely happy that I'd come on board. At noon a group of creative folks heading out to lunch stopped by my office and invited me to come along. We went across the street to an Italian restaurant where I got acquainted with the group. They were all like me – married with wives and kids and mortgages. Conversations had little to do with advertising. It was very refreshing.

I didn't see much of Berner for a while. He was the creative director on G. Heileman, brewers of Old Style beer. At that time Heileman was turning out more than 50 brands of beer and ale, and using several ad agencies to produce their broadcast. Although Campbell-Mithun handled about a dozen Heileman brews, Old Style was the flagship brand, brewed with virgin clear spring water and "fully krausened." Other brands included Special Export, Blatz and Mickey's Ale.

My one, for-sure broadcast assignment disappeared just days after I arrived at Campbell-Mithun. Their brand-new food account, the Dubuque Packing Company, said "bye-bye" and took their their *Plumpers* hot dog advertising to another agency. Even in the topsy-turvy world of advertising, this was a sudden turn of events. So I focused my efforts on print ads for Cutler-Hammer, maker of electrical equipment like switches and circuit breakers. Then my past came flying back at me. I was assigned to the Automatic Electric account and found myself working on the same products I'd written about at the company's Northlake offices a decade earlier. The creative work had been moved to Mithun and a bigger budget meant the ads were now in four-color instead of black-and-white.

As fate would have it, Bert Hansen, my old boss at Automatic, was still working there. In fact, Bert was the agency contact. The challenge on this account was to come up with compelling visuals because many of the products were racks filled with wires and switches – not much to look at in black-and-white or four-color. But undaunted, my art director, Bill Hurthle, and I came up with ads that combined strong headlines with fetching visuals. Hansen was tickled pink with the stuff we were doing. He commented to the account exec that the new writer was "spot-on" with everything. In fact, he wanted to meet him. At that point I told the account man that I'd worked for Hansen years earlier, and confessed that my parting words to Bert were real bridge burners.

"So who gives a rat's ass?"

That was Bill Hurthle's comment when I told that I'd just rubbed elbows with Bob Elliot, the radio funny man. I'd passed Eliot walking across the Michigan Avenue Bridge at lunchtime. It was the thrill of a lifetime for me but it left Bill flat. *You probably don't who Bob Elliot is*, I thought. He was, in fact, Bob of Bob & Ray, the comedy duo famous for their hilarious radio sketches and commercials. *Well, maybe Bill didn't hear me right*, I decided. He was in a hurry to finish an ad layout so we could get started on some beer storyboards.

On a Monday morning Joe Berner had enlisted three writer/art director teams to submit concepts for a Blatz Light beer commercial. I sat in Bill's office that afternoon and we bounced ideas off each other. Our concepts drifted from beer cans orbiting the earth to historical character endorsements to a talking blues guy on camera. Over the next few days we came up with more ideas, churning out one storyboard after another. (A storyboard is a series of little framed drawings with words beneath them that mimic a finished TV spot.) I liked working with Bill. He could draw sharp, clear frames with blazing speed. At the end of the week we went into a meeting where all three teams showed what they'd come up with. The other teams each presented two or three boards. We pinned up ten, one of which, the talking blues spot, won. Bill got the frames colored and I polished up the words. Berner sold the spot to Heileman and he let Hurthle and me handle the shoot.

RICK: Of all the beer joints in all the towns in the world you walk into mine.

ILSA: Rick, I was thirsty.

Storyboard for beer TV commercial by Bill Hurthle.

Beer poster for college market. Art director, Terry Sirrell.

My standing at Campbell-Mithun improved when the agency held their 1979 Christmas party at Febo's, a family-run Italian restaurant on south Western Avenue. Jim Tomazin, the senior writer in Berner's group, recommended the place, promising everyone that the food and the atmosphere were great. He was right. Waiting for dinner I loosened up with a couple of vodka martinis. Once we were seated, Berner started calling on people in his group to stand up and make toasts. When he got to me, I said something silly that got a few laughs. *Whew!* I was glad that was over. But a few minutes later he called on me again. *Oh boy!* I stood up and made another humorous toast, which garnered more laughter. The boss asked for toasts from a few other folks, then called on me a third time. By then those martinis had sunk in and my fear of speaking was gone. I tried hard to enjoy the food but it wasn't easy. Berner kept asking me to make toasts. When the party was over I'd made seven of them. As everyone was leaving, the president of the agency came up and shook my hand. "You're a delight!" he said. "You've showed us a different side of Joe Murphy today." *Wow, this is good,* I thought. *Somebody up there likes me!* The next day at work Al Swanstrom, one of my favorite art directors, asked me to repeat some of my funny toasts, but I could only recall the first two. Things got even better for me when Berner asked all the writers to submit radio scripts for Freshlike canned vegetables. I turned in a half dozen humorous scripts, and the client signed off on three of them. Before long there was another call for radio scripts, this time for the California Egg Board. Berner and the account man liked my scripts and read them to the client. The Egg Board folks bought five of them. Even better, I got to fly out to Hollywood with the boss and produce them.

Just for laughs

After working at Mithun for a few months I met Ed Azevedo, an art director with a black push broom mustache and a quirky sense of humor. Ed was a hard worker but he managed to squeeze some fun into everything he did. He furnished humorous illustrations for memos announcing company events like the Christmas party and annual picnic. Over a weeklong stretch he drew large caricatures of everyone in our creative group. They gave us all some morale-boosting laughs. Ed had worked with Tim Kazurinski at Leo Burnett before Tim left to join the cast of Saturday Night Live in New York. Soon afterward, Ed came to work at Mithun. On mornings when we weren't too busy, Ed and I walked the underground passage from our building in Illinois Center over to Lower Level Louie's, a small breakfast nook in the basement of the 333 North Michigan Building. Over coffee we'd talk about our kids, home repair projects and humorous ideas. Sometimes we'd try to come up with funny sketches like the ones airing on Saturday Night Live each week. We developed humorous storyboards with my words and Ed's drawings, which Ed sent to Kazurinski at NBC in New York. Tim looked at our stuff and got back to Ed, commenting that he liked some of it, but reminding him that SNL did not accept unsolicited material. Well, so what! We had fun churning out those comedy sketches even if the laugh was on us. I still have some of Ed's storyboards and cartoons in my file cabinet at home.

Lunching

A group of us from Mithun would sometimes walk south to Weiboldt's Department Store on State Street for lunch. There was a restaurant on the top floor where the food was decent and cheap. Our favorite waitress was Eileen, an energetic blonde lady who was always as happy as a lark. And no matter how many were in our group, she gleefully took our orders without writing anything down. At first we thought she was crazy, but she never made a mistake. Everyone got just what they ordered, and fast. In winter I'd hang my parka in the cloakroom, where the while-tiled floor was accented with little black swastikas. The building had obviously been constructed before Hitler had made that design the insignia for his Nazi regime and cast a lasting stigma on it.

On other days a few of us would walk up to Ohio Street to lunch at the Inn of Chicago. I think my art director, Al Swanstrom, liked the place because it appealed to the gambler in him. You could leave your business card in a fish bowl next to the register and have a chance to win a free lunch; there was a drawing each week. Swanstrom left a card every time we ate there, but he never won, whereas I kept winning again and again. It seemed like every other week I'd get a letter telling me that I'd won a free lunch. It got to the point where this was driving Swanstrom nuts.

Occasionally we'd hike up to Jerry's on Grand, a raucous deli where owner Jerry Meyers and his staff yelled at you. "What the hell to do *you* want!" You could count on being yelled at when you walked in. And then came, "Come on, I haven't got all day – WHAT – DO – YOU – WANT! Customers loved Jerry's loud verbal abuse. This shtick always got us laughing. Jerry and his boys got away with it because a herd of regular customers ate it up. But I saw this routine backfire on one occasion. A young lady walked in and stopped to look up at the menu board. Jerry bounded into view shouting, "What the hell to do *you* want!" His greeting paralyzed her. When he kept yelling at her she started to cry. He backed off, but it was too late – the girl turned and ran out of the place.

In warm weather a jaunt to the Berghoff was fun. That great old German restaurant was on Adams, seven blocks south of Mithun. Three or four of us would hoof it down there for sandwiches in the brass-laden "Men's Bar," a good-sized section on the east side of the restaurant. Skillful carvers wielding huge knives sliced a variety of juicy sandwiches – roast beef, ham, turkey, tongue.... You'd stand in line and watch your sandwich being assembled. Then, with luck, you might find a seat at the bar. Fat chance. We always wound up standing at a tall mini-table. The Berghoff bar served its own brewed-in-Wisconsin beer. The atmosphere was totally male. I never saw a woman in the bar, even though ladies had been admitted since 1969, when members of the National Organization for Women (NOW) marched in and demanded service. Soon afterward, feminist Gloria Steinem stopped by for a drink. Today women visit the bar without trepidation, although they remain a definite minority.

Hooray for Hollywood!

A week or two into the New Year, Berner officially invited me come along on a trip to the coast to produce the Egg Board radio spots. The weather in L.A. was perfect: 70 degrees and surprisingly smog-free. We spent a week in La-La Land making six radio spots. Our leisurely schedule allowed us time to get the job done each day and have time left over to goof off. One morning Berner and I had breakfast at Schwab's drug store on Sunset Boulevard, where Lana Turner was allegedly discovered while sitting at the soda fountain.

We spent a day auditioning folks for the voice parts, and picked some big-time talent, including Alan Reed, the voice of Fred Flintstone and Jack Riley, from the cast of *The Bob Newhart Show*. When we recorded the scripts the next day Berner pretty much turned the producing duties over to me. His confidence in me was reassuring. Things went well; the humor I'd written into the spots came through. A day or two later we worked in the studio with Chicago music jingle wizard Dick Boyell as he recorded six musical stings – a different one for the end of each radio spot. The next day he recorded half-a-dozen separate vocal treatments of the *Incredible Edible Egg* jingle and joined them with the music. Then everything (dialogue, sound effects and music) came together in the final mix. I'd never seen so much time, care and expense go into making radio commercials.

When I got back to the agency, Bill Hurthle updated me on the trade advertising we'd been working on. The Automatic Electric ads had been winning readership awards aplenty, but suddenly the account was gone. GTE, the parent company, decided to move the account to Doyle Dane Bernbach in New York. That agency was already producing GTE's corporate advertising; now they'd be handling the whole ball of wax. Oh well, Hurthle and I still had plenty to work on. Bill was a storyboard wizard; he could he draw faster than I could write, and he often drew things from memory. If a TV storyboard required a car, Bill would draw one from memory. "How 'bout a '36 Cord Beverly Sedan?" he might suggest. Two minutes later that very car would be parked on a storyboard frame in stunning detail.

Greetings!

At Campbell-Mithun I met Terry Sirrell, a talented young art director with a unique cartooning style. He and a couple of friends had produced a line of greeting cards using simple cartoon illustrations on the front and just a few words inside. Terry told me that the cards would be selling better if they were for sale in more locations and venues with higher traffic. He mentioned a hot new line of cards called "California Dreamers." Produced in Chicago, the cards were selling like gangbusters all over the country, thanks to great distribution.

Terry described a typical California Dreamer as very slick, with a photographic image on the front and one short, catchy line inside. As it turned out, the studio churning out these alluring cards was just a few blocks away from Campbell-Mithun. Some of Chicago's top photographers were shooting the images, and the lines were coming from freelance writers. Terry suggested that I call Jim Lienhart, the outfit's creative director, and try to drum up an interview. Without delay I phoned Lienhart and asked him if I could show him some humorous samples and maybe submit a few lines for his cards. He invited me to come over with my portfolio.

After work I hiked north on Michigan Avenue a few blocks to Erie Street and headed west a short distance to a row of old buildings that housed several small "creative boutique" ad agencies. Before long I found Murrie White Drummond and Lienhart studios. In his immaculate office, Lienhart viewed my samples; a few of my headlines made him smile. He showed me a batch of colorful California Dreamers. The photos up front were stunning and the clever lines inside played off those images well. Lienhart explained that the writers he used worked on spec and received royalties in line with how well their cards were selling. Writers submitted rough layouts with a graphic concept indicated on the outside and a short line written on the inside. He gave me a few weeks to come up with some ideas – a lot more time than I ever got on my regular job. On presentation day I showed up with a big envelope full of layouts. He sifted through them for twenty minutes or so, and picked a dozen from the sixty I'd submitted. "I like these ones," he said. "I'll show them to my partners. As we shook hands he reminded me that the okay had to be unanimous. I felt great walking to the subway. *Way to go!* I said to myself sitting on the train bound for Oak Park. I flipped through the rejected layouts, thinking that Lienhart had nixed some of my best ideas.

"HEARTLESS, BART."

HE WAS NOBODY'S VALENTINE.

My humorous concept illustrated by Terry Sirrell.

A month or so later I got a call from California Dreamers. The pleasant perky voice of Lienhart's female assistant told me that four of my card ideas had been selected for production. I was ecstatic. Waiting to see the finished product was agonizing. After two weeks I phoned her for an update, "Your three cards are looking great!" "What?" I asked. "I thought four cards made the cut." "Well, there was another review session, and one of your cards was dropped." "Humph," I groaned, thinking of all the time I'd put in on those concepts.

Fortunately, a new interest brought me some positive feedback. I started taking classes in improvisational theater. Rick Thomas, a relative and friend of mine, told me about an improv class he was teaching at Victory Gardens Theater on Lincoln Avenue near Wrigley Field. Rick's background included a long stretch as a cast member at Second City in Old Town. His class was very rewarding. Rick had a relaxed, informal teaching style that put everyone at ease and produced great results. I met some interesting folks in that class. The experience of interacting with them boosted my self-confidence and improved my presentation skills at work.

Déjà vu all over again

A few years later I was working at an agency that handled several small brands of beer. The client contact was Stan Atkins, a brand manager who had started in the beer business driving a delivery truck. I met Stan at a brief meeting where our creative director, Joe Butler, introduced him to my art director, Jerry Eifrig, and me. Stan struck me as a friendly, easy-going guy. He said he liked country music and I could see that he liked to eat (he must have weighed 400 pounds). Stan said he needed a few funny commercials fast. He gave us two weeks to show him some ideas. Jerry and I got right to work. We dreamed up some humorous approaches and showed them to Butler, who picked a few that he liked. So Jerry put them into storyboard form for presentation day, which arrived all too soon. We pinned up our concepts in the conference room for Stan to review. He liked three of our ideas, but felt that one of them needed his magic touch. The storyboard showed two buddies in small boat fishing in a north woods setting with cattails in the background. One of them keeps grumbling about how he's dying for an ice-cold Kurst beer. His pal listens patiently and finally pulls up on his rod. A six-pack of Kurst is hooked to his line. I was about to read the words that buttoned the spot when Stan interrupted: "I think ya oughta put a mermaid in there, Murph!" "A what?" I asked in disbelief. "A mermaid. Yeah, he hooks a big, sexy mermaid!" Butler rolled his eyes, but we wound up injecting a well-endowed mermaid into the spot. She pops up out of some lily pads holding a six-pack and sys something like, "Hi guys, how 'bout a beer?" Pure genius.

That was one of four spots we made for Stan out in the Pacific

Northwest. The trip began on a frosty February morn when Butler, Stan and I met at O'Hare and boarded a plane bound for Oregon. The forecast was warm but wet; February is rainy season out there. We were flying all that way because the brewery told us to; we had no say in the matter. The client-agency relationship had deteriorated to a deplorable state. The beer folks were used to kicking the agency around.

Drizzling rain made life pretty soggy throughout the 11-day shoot. Anticipating this scenario, the studio set things up so we'd be shooting all our commercials inside. That mermaid spot was a doozy. The studio built a mini lake, constructing walls three feet high and lining the enclosure with plastic sheeting. The local fire department filled it with water from a hydrant outside on the sidewalk. Our actors sat in an aluminum boat with dozens of lights hanging overhead. I feared that they would both be electrocuted. The only person in a worse spot was the mermaid. She was a pretty young gal in an iridescent outfit that covered most of her body and flared into a huge tail. That poor girl had to stay submerged for each take – until someone cued her to pop up by poking her with a stick. And that water was COLD. After four or five takes her voice was trembling and she looked blue. Two strong members of the film crew pulled her out of the water and wrapped her in a blanket. After a short break she returned to the drink. And, luckily, after a few more takes we got a good one. The shuddering fish lady was quickly escorted to a dressing room.

I didn't have time to goof off on that shoot. The days in the studio ran long. And afterwards, my boss and the brewery boys went out for big dinners with drinks and desserts. They wouldn't get back to our hotel till 9 or 10 p.m. Meanwhile, I was in my room working on a sales video for one of Stan's brands. He wanted this video to be a spoof on *Monday Night Football* with actors playing Don Meredith and Howard Cosell. We planned to intercut shots of Cosell and Meredith in the booth with actual clips from National Football League games. Stan gave me a huge reel of 16mm film, a collection of action clips from NFL games. I was told to pick out some funny ones and find a way to combine them with Cosell and Meredith doing the play-by-play, which had yet to be videotaped. I managed to shanghai a projector from the hotel and viewed the film in my room.

Returning to Chicago, I had the film transferred to tape, which made choosing the right clips easier. Then I had one whole day to write a script. "Impossible!" I screamed at maximum volume. With my office door closed, I cranked away – straight through lunch, past quitting time and beyond dinnertime. Butler's secretary stayed to do the final typing. We finished the script at 7 p.m. and dropped it into a FedEx box on our way out of the building. The next day, senior art director Don Smedley and I auditioned a colorful array of actors for the booth announcer parts and picked two guys who did great comic imitations of Cosell and Meredith. And, per Stan's instructions, we found a model to play a female part he had injected into the script to spice things up.

But wait, there's more!

In the midst of this mayhem Stan needed a slew of jingles for all of his little brands of beer. I banged out the words for eight or nine different jingles and worked with Shelly Elias at Elias/TMK Music to make a demo tape at warp speed. Shelly took my lyrics and put together a great-sounding reel. I sent it straight to Stan, hoping he could find a few minutes to listen to it. I wondered what else he wanted to beat out of me. Oh yeah, he needed a batch of animated TV spots designed to promote beer specials.

I found an outfit in New York City that specialized in simple, neon-like animation and was soon on a flight to the Big Apple with a few sample scripts. In a cramped little loft of an office I met with two young animation gurus and showed them my scripts. They explained what was doable considering my bare-bones budget. These animated spots included a middle section designed to show in-store displays of beer cases stacked into pyramids. Stan would have to ship cases of beer (for several brands) to the studio. Of course, he would have enough sense to send flat, unassembled boxes. But no, he sent a truckload of full cases. With zero room to spare in the tiny studio, all those cases for all those brands were unloaded onto the sidewalk in midtown Manhattan.

When I got back Chicago, Smedley told me that Stan had approved the video script. *Thank God.* Don and I worked together, directing the Cosell/Meredith/blonde babe sequence in the agency's AV department. When we walked in at 9 a.m. the on-camera trio was fired up for the big game. Things progressed slowly. It was a long day of shooting and by 5 p.m. everyone was spent.

Don and I pulled everything together and FedExed a videocassette of our efforts to Stan. The next morning my phone rang. It was Stan. *"I didn't want to talk to you!"* he whined. We both knew which Joe he wanted to dump on, but my boss made sure the call was switched over to me. Stan fumed about one thing after another. Things that were supposed to be funny left him befuddled or just plain pissed. The bizarre changes he demanded and his nasty tone really frosted me. When he hung up I threw the receiver in my hand at the wall. Then, the morning after the sales meeting, Butler gave me a report: the video was a dog. The whole thing only got a couple of laughs. Stan was embarrassed and fuming mad. And guess who took the rap for this mess? In a way I was glad to see Stan's cheap-ass tactics backfire on him. I stayed out of sight while a young agency producer recorded all the jingles whose lyrics I'd written. I was through working with Stan, but I was happy to learn that Stan's boss at the brewery said the finished jingles were terrific.

TWENTY-THREE

WHY WOULD I LIE?

*"Truth is stronger than fiction.
Fiction has to make sense."*
– Leo Rosten

Loitering in the Loop

AFTER CATCHING A MATINEE AT the Woods Theater with my brothers Jim and Dan, we bummed around awhile taking in the downtown scene – tall buildings, big stores, swanky hotels and hordes of yellow taxis. Noise from traffic congestion and El trains thundering overhead added to the lively ambience. We walked over to Treasure Chest on Randolph Street. It was an amazing place, filled with pinball machines and countless other coin-operated amusements. Entering the store, you passed counters on the left and right loaded with magic tricks, games and curios. It was hard to walk by without playing with a Chinese finger trap or Magic 8 Ball.

The main area was a gamester's paradise filled with pinball machines of every ilk. What's more, you could play pachinko, test your aim at a shooting gallery or entertain yourself with dozens of other noisy mechanical diversions. You had to use tokens, purchased from a cashier, to use any of the devices. At that time the machines were electromechanical, made of metal springs, gears and pinions. They clicked and clacked and dinged and rattled. The sounds were crisp, lively and real, unlike the synthetic humming, buzzing and beeping emanating from today's electronic amusements.

We wandered over to Marshall Field's on State Street, passed under the store's huge clock jutting from the building's corner, and entered. Inside, we browsed some goods on the first floor: leather luggage, jewelry, cosmetics, cameras … the prices seemed astronomical. I was ready to leave, but Jim wanted to ride the escalator, so we took it all the way to the top, grabbing quick glimpses of the merchandise on each passing floor. Then we caught an elevator down and walked a block north for one more look at bustling Randolph Street. Trekking west, we enjoyed cool breezes that cruised between the buildings. Blasts of cold air shot up from the subway through huge steel grates on the sidewalks.

Marshall Field's iconic clock at Washington & State has been part and parcel of Macy's since 2005.

A man with his head bent downward approached us on the sidewalk. He was looking into a waist-high camera hanging from his shoulders. As he passed us, he handed me a little brown envelope. Printed on it were instructions for mailing it with a dollar inside to get a copy of the photo he'd snapped. It stirred the faintest memory of the same scene occurring years earlier, when I was a little kid walking with Mom and Dad downtown. A photographer handed Dad something small and brown. Mom explained what it was, but I was too young to understand. Those sidewalk shooters had been clicking away year after year while I was growing up. I wondered how many thousands of folks they'd photographed over that stretch of time.

The tall, tall bus

Whatever possessed me to take that insane job? I was panic stricken the second I took a seat behind the wheel. Hell, I'd never driven a bus in my life, but here I was doing just that on this dark, dreary afternoon. Heavy sleet pelting the windshield blurred my vision as I inched along the slush-smeared street. Trying to navigate through downtown traffic in those conditions was a hellish nightmare. Vehicles trying to turn were held back by throngs of pedestrians oblivious to traffic signs and signals. They just kept coming, right in front of cars that were stuck halfway into their turns. Horns blared, angry motorists shouted, rude pedestrians yelled back at them.

I was finally nearing the busy corner where I had to turn left. *God help me,* I prayed. This situation would test the mettle of a top-flight driver maneuvering a normal CTA bus. But my bus was quite different; it was five stories high! I was sitting 60 feet above the street doing my best to guess my way through the tangled Loop traffic below. My view of the street began half a block away. I had no idea of what was right in front of me at ground level. People could be darting across the street inches from my front bumper and I wouldn't know it.

I pressed the gas pedal and started my turn. *Too fast!* I hit the brake and sat there frozen with fear. An insistent finger tapped me on the shoulder.

I turned and yikes, there was Bob Tomaska, downtown inspector for the CTA, staring me in the face. "Whacha stop for Murphy?" he snapped. "You shoulda made that corner by now!" Panicking, I pressed the gas pedal, but too hard. The bus swayed drunkenly to the left. *Oh shit!* I swung the steering wheel right, but it was too late. We were tipping ... tipping over. *Oh God! We're going to die!* "Whoa!" an urgent voice resonated in my left ear. Jim Rogers, a pre-med classmate, stopped me from toppling over into the pew. We were sitting inside Madonna Della Strada Chapel at Loyola, making a mandatory retreat. I'd drifted off during a lecture by Father Filas, who was talking about the Shroud of Turin. He was convinced that this cloth had covered the body of Jesus as he lay in his tomb. Filas had hung full-size copies of the shroud from several statues, creating an atmosphere that was both eerie and laughable. He was attempting to use the shroud to demonstrate the real presence of Christ in our lives. For me it was quite a stretch; I didn't get the connection. The scene was just as strange as my bus dream, maybe stranger.

Uncle Sam calls

I'll never forget the day I took my pre-induction physical to satisfy the Selective Service Board. It was January 1966 and bitterly cold outside. I'd just graduated from college, which made me fair game for the draft. Along with scores of other young men, I reported to a big, old building downtown at 6 a.m. We started by taking a multiple choice IQ test. When we got the graded tests back I noticed that the kid across from me got the same score that I did, and he didn't look too bright. Next, we candidates had to strip down to our jockey shorts for the long battery of physical tests. Each of us was issued a small paper bag in which to carry our wallets and watches from one test to another.

I began the day convinced that I couldn't possibly pass the physical. My feet were as flat as the floor and my eyesight was lousy. Hell, my neighborhood optometrist told me that my left eye was legally blind. But the testers were very forgiving of minor flaws like these, sending me on to the next test. *Holy shit*! *I'm going to pass this damned physical*! It wasn't until the very last station when I learned that I might get a chance to flunk after all. A uniformed army sergeant said, "Anybody with a letter from your doctor, move over to this side." A few of us formed a short line. A young MD read my letter, then told a technician to take a couple of X-rays. The results came out fast. The doc viewed the scans and wrote a note that read something like, "This inductee has suffered multiple pelvic fractures. He is likely to require corrective surgery in the future." I presented the note to a young soldier in full dress uniform seated a small desk. He read it, looked up at me and, in a sincere voice, said, "I am sorry to inform you sir, that you are unfit for military service." Totally crushed, I headed for a nearby lounge and celebrated with a vodka martini.

The telltale toilet

Mary was about to move out of her apartment when her roommate dropped something onto the ceramic lid on the toilet tank in their bathroom. It broke cleanly into two almost equal parts. I intended to glue them together seamlessly with epoxy; the repair would be invisible. Unfortunately, the landlord made an impromptu inspection of the apartment the next day. Spotting the broken top, he decided to keep the security deposit that Mary and her roommate had put down when they moved in. Mary decided to take this schmuck to small claims court. I went with her on a cold winter day to lend some moral support. She presented her argument convincingly and won. Mr. Landlord reluctantly wrote her a check for $150. Hooray!

We celebrated by walking over to Fritzel's Restaurant on Wacker Drive. Seated at a table set with a fancy tablecloth and thick cloth napkins, we both ordered soup – the only thing we could afford without cashing that $150.00 check. It was delicious soup, served in large, ornate bowls; even the spoons were oversized. The victorious occasion and cold weather outside made our dinner all the more warming and delicious. What a memorable experience! Right from its earliest days in the thirties

Fritzel's was a first-class place, offering services like car hops, doormen and cigarette girls. It was frequented by celebs from all over the country. At the time of our visit in 1972, Fritzel's was the home of three-hour lunches for big shots, show people and columnists like Irv Kupcinet, who once described the restaurant as Chicago's version of Toots Shor's in New York.

Bye-bye, disco

Disco meant dancing. What was so bad about that! Pop culture had all but killed dancing until disco came along in the early seventies. Here was music with melody and a beat that folks (who knew how to dance) could enjoy. Dancing had slid a long way downhill, starting with Chubby Checker and "The Twist." Any moron could do that dipshit dance. It took more skill to keep a Hula-Hoop spinning around your waist. Soon after the twist, dancing sank to an all-time low. Now two people facing each other shaking, shrugging and flailing their arms were considered to be dancing. It looked pathetic. Going out dancing throughout the sixties was a bizarre exercise. Masses of young males and females congregated, drank and "danced," displaying a pitiful array of spastic contortions. Couples faced each other but never touched. Rock music assaulting their ears at a deafening volume made it impossible to for them hear each other speak. Maybe some of them communicated via lip reading or some kind of sign language that I had not been introduced to.

The disco movement was a reaction to the prevalence of rock and a distain for dance music. Disco had a good run during the seventies, but its popularity declined toward the end of the decade. On the night of July 12, 1979, Chicago disc jockeys Steve Dahl and Gary Meier staged a volatile, anti-disco protest entitled "Disco Demolition Night" at Comiskey Park, home of the White Sox. This event was intended to "end disco once and for all" that night in center field. Fans could get tickets to a doubleheader against the Detroit Tigers at the box office if they brought 98 cents and a disco record. After game one,

Dahl gleefully blew up a crate filled with disco records. KABAAM! Thousands of fans stormed the field, chewing up the turf, burning signs and flinging records. The playing surface was damaged so badly by the explosion and the rowdy fans that the Sox had to forfeit the second game to the Tigers. Nice going, Steve.*

Miracle on Pico Boulevard

"Type this thing so I can read it, and make it fast," my boss ordered, handing me the script for an Old Style beer commercial. It was riddled with the edits I'd made in order to cut the narration to 30 seconds. The original script was running 15 seconds long! *Unbelievable! Who wrote this?* I asked myself. *And how the hell did it get approved?* My scribbled edits had made the script hard to read, so now I had to retype it. I rushed to the studio's office and asked the secretary if I could borrow her typewriter for a few minutes. She said she didn't have a typewriter. *What?* I told her there had to be someone in that big building who used a typewriter. She couldn't think of a soul.

I reported this news to my boss. His response? "That script is unreadable. Get it clean typed, I don't care how you do it!" I wondered how I got into this dilemma. I didn't even work on the Old Style account. My role on this shoot was to produce commercials for some of Heileman's lesser brands. I decided to take my typewriter search outside the building. The bright sun on Pico Boulevard was blinding as I walked past one storefront business after another. (The strip reminded me of 95th Street in Oak Lawn, near my folks' house on Chicago's far South Side.) *On a busy street like this there's got to be an outfit with a typewriter.* Aha! An insurance office! I entered and explained my predicament to a nice lady, who let me use her typewriter. She even made a couple of photocopies for me, and refused to accept payment for the help she'd furnished. Very classy.

Walking back to the studio, I pondered this surreal scenario. Everyone at the studio – my boss, the director, the client, the talent, the

---

*   Copyright © 2016, *Chicago Tribune*

cameraman, the grips – all of them were suspended in time and space until I got back with a few flimsy sheets of paper. The Old Style spot was a simple narration from a bartender, and the actor who played the role was perfect. He nailed it on the first take. Of course, we got several more takes – maybe a dozen – and each one was better than the one before it. When the agency presented the finished commercial to Heileman they rejected it. They wouldn't even pay for the production costs.

Will the real genius please stand up?

Intellectual property? What's that? The first time I heard the term I pictured a vacant lot with furrowed terrain resembling the surface of a human cerebrum. The phrase's real meaning didn't concern me at the time. But when I started working in advertising, "intellectual property" became something very real – something that could directly affect my livelihood. It turned out that ideas for ads and commercials dwelt in the foggy netherworld of intellectual property. When I started working for D'Arcy McManus & Masius in Chicago (a good sized ad agency) the first thing I encountered was intellectual property. I had to sign a confidentiality agreement, which stated that all the advertising ideas that I created while working for D'Arcy were their property now and for all eternity. Signing that agreement gave me a strange feeling – like I was signing my soul over to the agency. But once on the job, I didn't worry about it. I worked at D'Arcy for year and then moved to Campbell-Mithun, where I immediately signed another confidentiality agreement. This time the situation was less intimidating. I was resigned to the fact that signing such a document was a pro forma thing that creative folks had to go along with.

Working on ideas for GTE, one of Mithun's clients, I sometimes wondered if a particular idea that came to me might be one that I'd already thought up for some other client at some other agency. Hell, I'd written on the same GTE products a decade earlier when I worked at Automatic Electric Company, part of GTE. Beyond that, I'd written on dozens of accounts at different agencies, not to mention numerous after-hours freelance clients. Over the previous decade I'd thought up thousands of ideas, 95% of which were rejected and never used. That's the way things go in advertising. At Mithun I agreed that all ideas I generated while working there belonged to them. But I wondered: *Suppose I come up with a campaign concept that one of their clients really loves? And what if it happens to be an idea I'd had at D'Arcy, only to have it rejected? Did the ungrateful folks at D'Arcy own that idea even though they'd nixed it way back when? Or can Campbell-Mithun now claim ownership? Who's the real owner? My past employer? My current employer? Me? Captain Kangaroo?* And what about the years that followed? I worked for other agencies after leaving C-M. Maybe some of the ideas I came up with while self-employed were the same ones I'd come up with long ago at Mithun or D'Arcy or some other agency. I might have unwittingly revived some long-forgotten ideas, thinking they were brand new ones. Could an agency I worked for long ago (or one of their clients) rouse me from my dotage, drag me into court and sue me? Can someone give me the name of a good lawyer?

THUG 1: We heard you didn't sign the Confidentiality Agreement.

THUG 2: Not good.

Storyboard frame from humorous sketch by
art director Ed Azevedo reflects his attitude
toward confidentiality agreements.

Rumble at the car wash

I was in Cicero on a pleasant spring day talking to a young man who needed some advertising help. He asked me for ideas on how to sell his oversized cookies, which were delicious. I told him that I'd work on some approaches and get back to him. Munching on one of his cookies, I drove south on Cicero Avenue toward home. I braked sharply when a car pulled in front of me exiting a car wash. It looked so spotless and shiny, I decided to stop and surprise my dirt-caked Toyota with a good bath.

I asked the man up front for a regular wash. "You want the car waxed too?" "No, just a wash." "Can we clean the undercarriage?" "No, just a standard wash." "Steam clean the engine for ya?" "No, just a wash – that's all I need." "OK. Should be done in 20 minutes." I sat down and flipped through a two-year old edition of *Motor Trend* magazine. After 25 minutes I asked the man at the counter how things were going with my car. He looked at his watch and scratched his chin. "Let's give the boys a few more minutes," he said. I went back to my magazine for a while, and then asked about my car again. "Hang on, I'll go check on things."

After five more minutes he hadn't returned, so I decided to go back and see what the hell was going on. Walking through a set of big swinging doors, I couldn't believe my eyes. Two full-grown men, who were supposed to be washing my car, were fist fighting. The man who'd gone to check on them was trying to break up the contest. (As it turned out, he owned the car wash.) "You're both fired!" he shouted. "Get the hell out of here and don't come back!" Turning to me he offered to finish the car himself. "Just have a seat up front," he said calmly, so I went back to reading *Motor Trend*. After a few minutes the boss came back, apologizing for the fisticuffs episode. He didn't charge me for the wash. In fact, he gave me a coupon good for another free wash and told me to have a nice day.

Chicago Trivia True or False

                                                                 T   F

1. The Chicago Playboy Club was on Rush Street.   __ __

2. The 16" softball was invented in Chicago.   __ __

3. The Wrigley was the first air-conditioned office building.   __ __

4. Historic Route 66 starts downtown on State Street.   __ __

5. In Chicago it is illegal to fish in your pajamas.   __ __

6. Grant Park is part of the Magnificent Mile.   __ __

7. The Chicago River is the only US river that flows backwards.   __ __

8. Chicago is home to the world's first skyscraper.   __ __

9. Invented in Finland, the cell phone was perfected in Chicago.   __ __

10. Chicago was the setting for "The Bob Newhart Show."   __ __

Answers: 1- F, 2- T, 3-T, 4-F, 5-T, 6-F, 7-T, 8-T, 9-F, 10-T

TWENTY-FOUR

AIMLESS ENCOUNTERS

"I go from stool to stool in singles bars hoping to get lucky,
but there's never any gum under any of them."

– Emo Phillips

THE STONE CONTAINER BUILDING AT Wacker & Wabash was one of my favorite downtown structures, mainly because it housed the London House right at street level. At 5 p.m. you could walk in and listen to jazz greats like Charlie Byrd and Dizzy Gillespie making great music. On a brisk, fall morning I strode into the Stone Container lobby to drop off some freelance copy I'd written the night before. Spotting an open elevator, I dashed toward it. A hand was holding the door for me, and it wasn't just any hand. It belonged to radio legend Paul Harvey.

Harvey was a conservative who voiced his right-wing opinions with exaggerated pronunciations and pregnant pauses for dramatic effect. His messages included folksy observations and heartwarming tales of Americana. He started every show with a hearty "Hello Americans, stand by for news!" and signed off with "Paul Harvey ... good day! I loved his stories and the way he praised his sponsors' products. Harvey could sell the hell out of anything, but claimed to endorse only products he believed in. He was quoted as saying, "I'm fiercely loyal to those willing to put their money where my mouth is."

As the elevator started its ascent I told Mr. Harvey how much I enjoyed his broadcasts, and asked how he found the material for his numerous *The Rest of the Story* segments. He said his son had been doing the research for them. I mentioned that I was a writer and said it must be fun to dig up stories like those. He invited me to unearth a few, type them up and send them to him. I meant to follow up on his offer, but freelancing kept me too busy to work on spec.

The Queen of Folk

It was dark and my frozen ears were stinging. I feared that touching one of them would break it like a potato chip. A long photo session had kept me in the Rush Street area late. Walking north on Dearborn toward the parking lot where I'd left my car that morning, I spotted the Barbarossa, a great place to hear live folk entertainment. It looked warm and inviting, so I crossed the street and went in.

Sitting at the bar, I couldn't see a thing through my fogged-up glasses. After I'd wiped them clean and ordered a drink I noticed a girl sitting on the stool next to me. *No way,* I thought. *It can't be her!* Mustering every molecule of courage in my gut I babbled, "Excuse me, are you Bonnie Kolak?" She turned toward me and answered, "Yes I am." My heart jumped into overdrive. I was talking to the queen of Chicago folk music! Trying to disguise my panic, I told her that I'd heard her sing at the Earl of Old Town a few times. "You have a wonderful voice," I assured her.

I kept heaping compliments on her until she spoke again (probably to shut me up). The folk goddess asked me what brought me into the Barbarossa so early in the evening and all by myself. I told her I'd been working downtown that day and stopped in to warm up. My honesty paid off. She felt like talking, and somehow our conversation took a personal turn. I told her that being in a place like the Barbarossa by myself was a lonely deal. She alluded to a breakup with some guy she'd really liked. I was amazed that someone like her could be telling me something so personal! Minutes later she went onstage to sing, backed up by a couple of musicians. Bonnie was great. I stayed for the whole set, hoping she'd rejoin me at the bar. Sadly, that didn't happen, so I left, found my way to the parking lot and paid a staggering sum to get my car. I drove back to the South Side, still lonely, but with a good, warm feeling inside.

A brief brush with fame

My feet were killing me. I'd been hauling my portfolio around the Loop for hours on a gray November afternoon when I spotted a sidewalk bench near Wacker & Wabash. Sitting there in a semi stupor, I gazed at the Jewish Theological Seminary across the street. Its round design and modest height contrasted with the straight lines of the tall buildings next to it. After a few minutes a beat-up bag lady sat down next to me. I'd seen her before, but always from a distance. "Are you an artist?" she asked. "I see you have a portfolio." I told her that I was an advertising writer. "*I'm* an artist!" she stated emphatically. "Would you like to see one of my drawings?" "Sure," I said, just to humor her. She unrolled a large scroll of thick, white paper that held a childlike drawing of a woman with huge blue eyes and bright yellow hair. Lying, I told her it was beautiful. She said she earned a living by selling her drawings in the downtown area. I said that I couldn't afford one of her pictures because I was broke and looking for work. We chatted a bit longer before I left her sitting on that cold bench and hoofed it to the train.

It was decades later when I learned what a celebrity I had rubbed elbows with that day. Her name is Lee Godie. And it turns out that over the years she has attracted quite a following throughout the Loop. She's sold hundreds of drawings, many for prices approaching $100. Today art critics rave about her work; some even compare her to Grandma Moses. According to one well-respected Chicago critic, "She's far more interesting than Grandma Moses, far bolder and stronger." Serious art collectors value her creations to be great examples of "naïve and outsider art." And here I had judged this lady to be an eccentric, no-talent street person.

Howling on the bridge

"He stinks!" I said aloud the first time I heard him play. This huge hulk of young humanity was standing on the Michigan Avenue Bridge making god-awful noises with his saxophone. I figured he was playing some form of far-out jazz; the sound was unmusical, unpolished and repetitive. I soon got used to hearing it however, because working in the Wrigley Building I walked by this incessant noise polluter day after day. He seemed to be a permanent fixture on the west side of the bridge spanning the Chicago River. On a sweltering July afternoon he'd be standing in the same spot, his instrument case lying open at his feet. Even on subzero days I'd see him on the bridge with his sax, white steam billowing from his mouthpiece. This cacophonous character called himself "Little Howlin' Wolf." I learned from my co-workers that he'd been part of the scene long before I came along. And, as it turned out, he was still there making his unique music long after I'd moved on.

In fact, ten years after leaving my job in the Wrigley, I read a newspaper article that said Howlin' Wolf was still blowing his sax on the west side of the bridge. However, another sax player had suddenly appeared, setting up business on the bridge's east side opposite the Wolf Man. This intruder was Yusef Watts from Providence, Rhode Island. Howlin' Wolf was clearly pissed. He'd been playing on the bridge since 1968. To him it was a matter of principle. "Look at these hands," he said to a reporter. "I've been out here every season … this cat comes to this place and plays, like, 'The Prime of Miss Jean Brodie' in my face." Wolf said he believes jazz musicians should compose their own music. He called his own style "free-form hokomo."*

Hustlers from Hell

Strolling on a lightly trafficked downtown street, my peaceful isolation could be invaded by the Processarians, young people in black-hooded

---

*   *Chicago Tribune* article, *It's Dueling Saxes On Michigan Avenue Bridge*, May 9, 1995 by Barbara Brotman

robes who pitched their strange beliefs with bloodhound tenacity. I could easily spot a pair of these dark figures coming toward me from a block away. And knowing how persistent they were, I'd cut across the street. If they crossed as well, I'd switch sides again. The hooded hawkers would remain on the opposite side until we were almost passing each other, and then dash across to attack me with their religious pitch. They tried to sell me a hardcover book as thick as a novel. The cult was often viewed as Satanic on the grounds that it worshipped both Christ and Satan. Processarians believe that Satan will be reconciled to Christ when they come together at the end of the world to confront humanity, Christ to judge and Satan to execute judgment.

And then there were the Hare Krishna people with their shaved heads, orange raiment and incessant drumming. I'd see a bunch of them on State Street at lunchtime dancing and chanting ecstatically. They belonged to a Hindu sect that says we're living in an evil age. But fear not, we can be saved through permanent "Krishna-consciousness." These young folks were annoying but appeared to be harmless. They seemed lost and totally brainwashed, chanting the same phrases over and over all day. What a mind-numbing waste of youth and potential. I wondered where they went at night and who took care of them.

The least annoying of the holy hustlers were the Jews for Jesus. These sidewalk evangelists handed out little pamphlets that were well illustrated, hand lettered and remarkably down to earth. I enjoyed their informal tone and sense of humor. The young volunteers who dispersed these pamphlets were pleasant and upbeat, and they didn't try to sell me anything. Hallelujah! After working downtown for a few years I had acquired a nice collection of their brochures. The Jews for Jesus claim to hand out eight million of them a year. The last time I checked their reach had extended to New York City, Toronto, Paris, London and Moscow.

The colossal Indian

The weather had sure fooled me. I was in Minneapolis making some TV spots for Blatz Light beer. When the day's shoot was over I walked back to my hotel, flopped onto the bed and fell asleep. Half an hour later my growling stomach woke me up. Luckily, I knew of a decent restaurant just a few blocks away. The temperature outside was balmy, so I decided to walk. After ingesting a savory sirloin I started back toward my hotel, but the weather picture had changed; now it was dark and downright chilly. A few raindrops hit my face, followed shortly by a few more. Seconds later I was caught in a fierce downpour. Just my luck. Seeking cover, I ducked into a doorway and found myself standing next to a massive Native American. He was about seven feet tall, built like an oak and dressed in rags. Looking down at me, he asked in a gravely voice if I could spare some change. Afraid to refuse him, I scrounged in my pants pockets without any luck. Next, I checked the pockets in my jacket. Nothing there either. The huge Indian grunted. I looked up at his scowling face and shuddered. My wallet was the last resort. I took it from my back pocket, hoping to find a single or two, but my smallest bill was a fiver. I placed it in the Indian's oversized hand, excused myself and jogged through the rain to my hotel.

RETRO DOWNTOWN CHICAGO FACTS-IN-FIVE GAME

	BUILDINGS	EATERIES	STREETS	STORES	ATTRACTIONS
M					
T					
P					
F					
W					

**Use your memory to fill in the squares or
borrow from the answers below.**

Peacock's Marina City Fannie May Wendella Tribune Tower Taylor
Top of the Rock Miller's Pub Polk Walnut Room Magnificent Mile
Picasso Statue Prudential Franklin Wrigley Marshall Field's Talbots
Washington Fine Arts Tad's Steaks Wieboldt's Pump Room Forum
Field Museum Madison

TWENTY-FIVE

FREELANCING

*"The freelance writer is a man
who is paid per piece or perhaps."*
– Robert Benchley

THROUGH THE EARLY YEARS OF my writing career I'd seen creative folks (both writers and art directors) devoting time during work hours to projects that had nothing to do with their jobs. They were freelancing (aka moonlighting) to earn extra bucks. During this period, my household was in dire need of a cash infusion. Mary and I had two kids and a shack of a house that begged for major repairs. The battered Ford Fairlane we were driving coughed black smoke and wouldn't stay put at stoplights. Any extra money would make our lives easier and safer. Spurred by these circumstances, I decided to try my hand at a little freelance work. I wanted to start with some small jobs, knowing that they would help pay a few bills. And I thought that the experience gained through this effort might help me land a better full-time job with more money and better things to work on.

While holding down a nine-to-five agency job, I furnished concepts and headlines for Simmons Advertising, an industrial agency just off Michigan Avenue. Marty Simmons, who owned the outfit, liked my stuff; we got along fine. I never asked him for a full-time job. I guess he assumed that I would have preferred to work on consumer advertising and TV accounts. He surprised me one day with this comment: "I just couldn't see you working here. It would be like hitching a thoroughbred race horse to a junk wagon." I appreciated the compliment, but didn't know how to reply.

While working at an ad agency that specialized in real estate I wrote a campaign for a development in a western suburb called Green Glen. Our media buyer left and moved to another small agency. Soon afterward, we lost Green Glen to that shop. I was shocked because that client seemed very happy with the work we were doing for them. A few weeks later I got a call from our ex-media buyer. She said that her new employer wanted me to write the Green Glen ads for them on a freelance basis. Very surprised, and jittery about the right course of action, I told her I'd think about it and get back to her. I missed writing the Green Glen account. Their campaign was based on a nostalgic Americana theme: *Small Town America is Calling You Home.* This ghostwriting opportunity boosted my ego, but it scared me. I'd be working for a client that was competing with my employer. But my curiosity was aroused. The next day I had an after-work chat with the agency's creative director. He was a hulking young huckster who looked as if he might have played nose tackle in college. His suit, shirt and tie all looked a little tight on him and his skin was unnaturally red. Sitting behind a huge glass table he used as a desk, he boasted shamelessly about his agency's rapid growth. What an ego! This character thought he had the world by the ass.

He said that an associate had given him my name, adding that "In this business it's who you know that counts." After praising my work on the Green Glen ads, he asked if I'd be OK with writing them for his agency. We both knew that doing work for a shop that's competing with the one you're working for is dishonest and dangerous. It can get you fired. *What an asshole!*

Starting toward the door, I told him I'd have to think about his offer. "Hang on," he urged. "Right now I'm just looking for some broad concepts – just to give me an idea of the way you think. I'd pay you, of course." This blue-sky exercise seemed a bit shady but it wouldn't be like blatantly writing ads. Besides, doing conceptual work was more fun than cranking out copy. So I agreed to dream up a few ideas for him. A week later I came back with a half dozen concepts. Mr. Big Shot seemed very impressed. He told me to send him a bill, which I did in short order. I waited patiently for payment, but after 30 days I got itchy. Doesn't prompt service deserve prompt payment? I phoned my media buyer friend and told her about the delay. She promised to look into the matter. A few days later my check arrived in the mail. Thus ended my Green Glen moonlighting career.

The Big Four Oh!

With my 40th birthday approaching, I thought about where my advertising career was headed. Way off track, I concluded. Where were the big-bucks TV accounts I'd hoped to work on? Where were the clients who wanted my funny radio spots? I was stuck writing print ads for banks, phonograph cartridges and two-way radio systems. The fun factor of my job was close to zero. My title, associate creative director, was misleading. I wasn't doing creative work or directing much of anything.

My big birthday at the office was a silent disaster. I waited anxiously for the customary card signed by everyone at the agency. It never came. *What the hell?* I always made an effort to write something fun on every card that came across my desk. Now on my 40th birthday – a really special one – it looked like nobody gave a shit about me. A week later, the boss' secretary who kept track of birthdays, discovered that mine had escaped her notice. She apologized profusely, telling me that she couldn't understand how she'd missed my birthday. I lied, telling her it was no big thing and not to worry about it. But the incident reminded me that even the things we take for granted are never really for sure. After working in the agency business for a decade, the glitz and glamour were gone. I knew that nothing better was on the horizon. It was up to me to make something happen. Moonlighting over the years had expanded my writing experience in several areas. I felt I could do a good job on just about any advertising project. And so, armed with a potent new pitch sheet outlining my full range of skills, I left Michigan Avenue and headed home to embark on a career in freelance writing.

Whole new ballgame

When I became a full-time freelancer in the fall of '84 I presented myself as a versatile, all-purpose writer – a pro who could write everything from humorous one-liners to annual reports. The eclectic assortment of writing jobs I worked on resulted mainly from the cold calls I'd made. I'd just knock on a door and introduce myself, right out of the blue. This approach scares the hell out of some freelancers, but I liked it, figuring what have I got to lose? If folks would drop what they were doing for twenty minutes to look at my samples, they were my kind of people. Often, someone just took my résumé, assuring me that it would get to the right person. At small outfits the owner was likely to be out and about – maybe hustling business like me. If nobody answered my knock, I'd write a note on my sheet and slip it under the door. Leaving résumés here and there gave me the Johnny Appleseed feeling that some of them were bound to bear fruit. A person reviewing my background could see that it covered a lot of ground. He or she might make a note that I could be useful on some upcoming project.

When I started hustling business downtown in the fall of '84, the breezes off Lake Michigan were cool and refreshing. But before long, brisk winds from the lake were landing with a sting. Schlepping my portfolio along Boul Mich gave me a new appreciation of the term, "cooler by the lake." When it got really cold and windy, hauling a briefcase and a big portfolio was hard work. On some winter days stiff gusts were strong enough to lift both of my bags like wings. I felt like I might go airborne while crossing the Michigan Avenue Bridge and land in the Chicago River. Sometimes I'd cut inland hoping for kinder, gentler weather but there was no guarantee. Wind squeezing through the Loop's concrete canyons can pick up gale force before it punches you in the face. In subzero weather the blast hitting your forehead can give you a splitting headache. I found that the best protection against this assault is a wool stocking cap from the Army Surplus store – an official U.S. Navy watch cap. It's warm and clings snugly to your cranium. But winter, spring, summer or fall there are places downtown where winds can slow your progress to a snail's pace. I remember trudging north on Wabash toward Wacker Drive on a warm day in May. It was like climbing a steep hill. I felt that if I tried to fall forward, the rush of fierce, Loop-funneled wind would hold me upright.

This is war

To keep from missing meetings and due dates I mounted a huge plastic-coated calendar on the wall in my basement office. It was my WAR BOARD. Every project, large or small, was marked on this erasable calendar, which I updated from day to day, week after week, month after month. I couldn't afford to screw up, even if some of the jobs I took on were insane. And some were.

About a third of my business resulted from making cold calls. If I had to pick up or drop off a job in a downtown building I checked the lobby directory to see if any potential customers might be listed. If I spied an ad agency or art studio I'd knock on their door. That approach brought me an eclectic mix of jobs. During my freelance days I wrote brochures on banking, boilers, hospitals, shopping malls and other local businesses; humorous sketches for conventions and roasts; radio spots for car dealerships, books on tape, bubble gum and appliances. I even wrote a few menus for restaurants. I spent half a year flying around the country for Motorola, talking to customers who used Motorola communications systems. I interviewed people, took their pictures, wrote up their stories and messengered everything to Motorola headquarters in Schaumburg, a bustling northwest suburb of Chicago.

Those testimonial brochures helped get my freelancing career off to a strong start. They explained how Motorola two-way radios and pagers were boosting efficiency and profits for all kinds of businesses. The most memorable of these stories concerned a limousine business. All the cars were white Lincoln Town Cars equipped with Motorola two-ways. Better yet, all the drivers were young blonde ladies. "We don't drive hearses," boasted Dan, the young owner. I sat down with him and got the story on how Motorola two-way radios were helping his business. He asked me to hold off on picture taking until late afternoon. He had a special locale in mind he said – one that would show off his cars and drivers to best advantage.

This setting turned out to be the grounds surrounding the state capitol, about ten miles away. We waited till the building closed for the day and then drove to the capitol in a caravan with me following a couple of stretched white Lincolns. They pulled right onto the lawn; a uniformed young blonde exited each vehicle. Of all the shots I took, my favorite was Dan with a pretty blonde driver on each arm. Everyone was smiling. We were finishing up when Dan got a call from one of his drivers. She was stuck in an alley waiting for a male customer to come out of an X-rated bookstore. He'd entered the place two hours earlier, leaving his briefcase in the car and telling her to wait. Now she was on her two-way radio asking the boss what to do. Dan told her to drive straight over to the Capitol. A few minutes later the limo dispatcher called Dan relaying a message from the bookstore customer, who was furious. He claimed that his lady driver had ditched him and taken off with his valuable briefcase. Just then that same driver pulled onto the Capitol grounds. Dan checked the briefcase. It was stuffed with thousands of dollars in cash. At that point I had to leave for the airport to catch my plane back to Chicago. Just when the fun was starting.

Stretch Armstrong to the rescue

Another offbeat job was for an outfit that created hand-scraped wooden floors. The owner asked me to write a small paragraph about how hand-scraped floors were inspired by the druids. According to legend, these elf-like critters inhabited the forest way back in the misty past. I forget the connection between them and beautiful handcrafted floors, but my client insisted that hand scraping produced the best-looking, longest-wearing wood floors on earth. The men who worked for him knelt on their knees and scraped away, using flat steel blades. The boss explained that this old-world technique removed the soft grain, leaving only the longwearing hard grain. He saw his workers as artists. Every one of them, he claimed, left a different signature on a wooden floor.

He could look at a hand-scraped floor and tell which one of his men had done the job.

And then there was that bizarre assignment to write a brochure promoting kids' baseball cards as a savvy investment. It explained how purchasing the cards in huge lots from outfits like Topps and Fleer would pay off in the long run. Just buy tons of cards and store them someplace – maybe in your basement or attic. They would increase in value with each passing decade. *Yeah, right.*

Unbelievable!

Through a referral one afternoon, I got in touch with a small agency that needed a radio script. They wanted me to write a sample commercial to help them land a new client. No problem. I typed up a humorous dialogue script requiring a male and a female voice and faxed it to the agency. The owner phoned me – he loved the spot and wanted it recorded ASAP. CLICK! He hung up. *Wait a sec!* A few minutes later the phone rang again. This call was from a recording studio I'd never heard of. A man's voice told me I should be at his place at 6 p.m. that same night. *What? I'm supposed to* produce *this spot?* This was news to me. Production is a whole different ball game, requiring time and travel. The voice gave me an address – it was way out west in the super boonies. *What the hell is going on here?* It was now past 5 p.m. I phoned the agency to get more info. Nobody answered. It was the end of the workday and I was suddenly forced into making this commercial out in the middle of nowhere. *How did I get myself into this?*

I grabbed the script and drove west, wondering what the next surprise would be. The engineer, who was also the studio's owner, met me at the door. After we'd introduced ourselves I asked, "Where's the voice talent?" "We're it," he answered. "What? I'm no radio voice!" I bellowed. "Neither am I!" He calmly replied. *What kind of crazy con game is this?* I wondered. "One of the voices is supposed to be a woman," I said. The guy shrugged his shoulders and offered to put on a high voice. He seemed to be taking this mess in stride, as if it were all part of a normal day's work. I started to question him, but he urged me to hold off until we laid something down on tape. We went through the script and recorded take one. He played it back. Truly horrible! His female voice sounded like a sissified Sly Stallone. We switched parts, so I was doing the woman. Take two made the first take sound good. It was obvious that we had to go with two male voices, but that meant changing the script. I did some fast editing and we recorded a few takes until we got one that wasn't completely awful. The engineer promised to get the tape to the agency in the morning. "Wait," I implored him, "I need to know a few things!" "So do I," he answered. Anxious to get going, he said the agency we were dealing with did everything at the last minute. Chaos was their MO. He told me to check with them about getting paid as he ushered me to the door.

Moments later I was on the Eisenhower heading home and feeling like I'd escaped from a nuthouse. *Did that really happen? Impossible! Better get home and get some sleep.* I billed the so-called ad agency $100. A few weeks later, a check arrived in the mail. Written on the bottom was, "Really Joe, this is pretty stiff!" *Are you joking?* After writing and rewriting the spot, producing it, performing in it and putting 20 miles on my car, I should feel bad about charging $100? I'd easily put $400 worth of time and sweat into the demo. That episode was one of several that showed me the kind of bush-league advertising outfits that were operating just a few miles from downtown Chicago. I guess there will always be plenty of schlock shops like these out there – light years away from good writing, professional art direction and quality recording studios where talented voice people work for union rates.

Who is this character?

I returned home one night after going out to buy a newspaper. Seated on the couch was an elderly gent with a fat briefcase perched on his lap. His name was Jerome Schulman and he needed my help. While I was out he had phoned my home, spoken to Mary and told her that he wanted some advertising written pronto. He introduced himself to me and said he needed two commercials for his product – one for TV and one for radio. Both of these spots were scheduled to air in a few days. I had come home expecting to relax in my Barcalounger and read the paper, but this complete stranger wanted to put me to work. We got right down to business. "I make Shane Toothpaste, the best toothpaste in the world," he declared.

Spreading pages of test results on the carpet, he explained that along with a hefty dose of fluoride, Shane contained aloe. So along with whitening teeth and removing plaque, it helped to heal sore gums. His toothpaste was selling for twice the price of popular brands, but Shulman convinced me that it was in a class by itself. We went over the studies and test results for two hours. I kept reminding him that everything had to boil down to 30 seconds in a finished commercial. Around midnight he seemed confident that I knew what he wanted. I agreed to write the scripts and deliver them to him in the morning. Bright and early the next day I drove to Shulman's office in a South Side industrial park. Sitting at his desk, he read the scripts quickly and looked up at me. "These are right on target," he said crisply. "How much do I owe you?" I told him. He wrote me a check and handed it to me. *Good deal!* I drove straight back to my basement headquarters in Oak Park.

No job too small

The phone rang. I picked up the receiver. "Are you the fellow who writes funny speeches?" a man's shaky voice asked. Someone I had written a few humorous lines for had referred this gentleman to me. I said I might be able to help him if he explained what was needed. It turned out that the caller was a friend of Morrie Mages, the Chicago sports equipment mogul. He'd been invited to a roast for Mages and was expected to make a funny toast. I asked him a few questions and then typed up a speech that poked fun at Morrie in a good-natured way. Then I walked down the street to a local stationery store and faxed the spiel to my client. A few days later he called me back, reporting that the short speech was spot-on. "It got some big laughs!" He thanked me for helping him on such short notice and sent me a check forthwith.

One final fun job was for an ad agency with a client who owned a car dealership. The agency asked me for a series of humorous ads tracing their client's travels throughout the Soviet Union. The project sounded so absurd that I couldn't resist taking a crack at it. The episodes started out silly and got more and more ridiculous each week as the intrepid traveler progressed from St. Petersburg to Moscow all the way to Vladivostok. The agency liked the ads so much, they called me on a few other occasions to write ads with a humorous twist.

TV ad campaigns: fill in the banks

1. I'd walk a mile for a _____.
2. The best part of waking up is _____ in your cup.
3. Where's the _____?
4. See the USA in your _____.
5. Fly the friendly skies of _____.
6. Like a good neighbor _____ _____ is there.
7. It's _____ time.
8. Plop plop, _____ _____, oh what a relief it is.
9. Have it_____ _____ at Burger King.
10. There's always room for _____.

Answers: 1. Camel 2. Folgers 3. Beef 4. Chevrolet 5. United 6. State Farm 7. Miller 8. fizz fizz 9. your way 10. Jell-O

TWENTY-SIX

BRAVE NEW WORDS

"Don't fear change – embrace it!
– Anthony J. D'Angelo

I WORKED AS A FREELANCE writer for quite a stretch and enjoyed a flexible schedule that let me attend grade school plays and concerts that my kids were involved in. Depending on where in the Chicago area a job took me, I could stop into a neighborhood bakery or coffee shop. Or browse at a hardware store or video shop. If I were downtown I might stop into Hammacher Schlemmer to marvel at their newest electronic gizmos or walk up to Water Tower Place and play with the expensive toys at FAO Schwartz. When I was out in the western burbs I'd sometimes park along Route 45 and walk a mile to my favorite greasy spoon. On the way I'd find parts that had been shed by speeding cars and trucks: wheel covers, lug nuts, pieces of broken leaf springs and shiny trim parts that had miraculously escaped any damage. At home I found time to patch the rust holes in my Toyota wagon and make a balance beam for my gymnast daughters. In summer I got up early, turned on the lawn sprinkler and went for a bike ride that often included coffee and Danish at the Seneca Restaurant in Berwyn.

I didn't like being stuck at home; it was easier to work on ideas and first drafts at coffee shops or the library. In the morning I wrote the headlines and body copy longhand in a notebook; after lunch I typed them into my little Panasonic computer at home. Sliding a floppy disc into the machine, I kept my fingers crossed as it burped and moaned, finally managing to boot up. The public library in Oak Park was a pleasant place to work and close to home, but for a change of pace I'd drive to the library in Forest Park or Berwyn. Eventually I found the library at Rosary College in River Forest. It was the best – quiet and classy with lots of natural light. I loved its dramatic spiral staircase.

Some of the freelance jobs I wrote were for thriving downtown ad agencies. I was flattered when creative directors at two different shops asked me if I'd be interested in full-time employment. A couple of agency folks I'd worked with on Michigan Avenue called me occasionally to write humorous radio spots. Great fun. I wish more jobs like those had come my way. A few of my client contacts said they envied me for being a freelancer. "I'd like to be doing just what you're doing" one pretty young lady confessed to me. I could have told her stories about the downside of freelancing, like waiting and waiting to get paid. (Folks who want work delivered overnight are usually the ones who take forever to send a check.) Or setting up a meeting in a downtown restaurant and waiting for a client who doesn't show.

Was it worth it?

When I first started working for myself I cranked out a slew of items for Dr. Scheider, a local audiologist. He asked for ads, brochures, sales letters, even a logo and a name for his business. I delivered the work in a timely fashion and waited patiently for payment. After three months he sent me a check for $300 – one-third the amount on my bill. Included was a snotty note telling me that $300 was all my efforts were worth. My head felt hotter and hotter as the blood in my brain boiled. I took this character to Small Claims Court, where he showed up with a professional witness – a "writer" friend of his.

I made a presentation to the judge showing all the work I had done for my client. Everything was mounted on illustration boards. I argued that the audiologist didn't seem to have any idea of what professional writers charge for their work. Dr. Scheider swore that I was incompetent, insisting that the work I'd done for him was unprofessional. The "professional" witness he brought with him corroborated his opinion. The magistrate asked this "witness" what kind of writing he did. He claimed to write articles for magazines like *Time* and *Newsweek*. "Then you don't know a lot about promotional writing, do you?" His Honor asked. The witness was silent. The judge knocked $100 off my bill, so subtracting the $300 I'd been paid, Scheider still owed me $500. The dynamic duo turned to leave. "Where's my check?" I asked. "It's in the mail!" snarled Scheider as he and his professional pal bolted for the door.

Three months later I still hadn't been paid. I contacted the court and set up a second hearing, convinced that my unworthy opponent would have to appear. I showed up in good faith, but the audiologist was nowhere to be seen. After waiting for two hours while case after case was called, I wound up sitting by myself and feeling stupid. Finally, I walked up to the bailiff and asked him why my case hadn't been called. Had there been some kind of a mix-up? I gave him my name and the other info he asked for. "You should have spoken up sooner," he said. "I thought you were the defendant." This was infuriating. I rode the El back to Oak Park, fuming all the way. Scheider was going to make things as tough for me as he could. But his imperious attitude made me white-hot. I knew that getting the $500 he owed me was going to cost me plenty of aggravation, but I was dead set on winning this contest of wills.

Trying hard to remain calm, I phoned the good doctor and reminded him that he hadn't showed up in court. "That's contempt of court," I said. He hung up on me. Again I contacted the court and arranged for another hearing. I called Scheider's office, reached his assistant and gave her the new court date, recommending that her boss play it smart and show up. Our day in court arrived a few weeks later. As I waited in the hall outside the courtroom, who should approach me but Scheider accompanied by a lawyer. Legal Man pleaded that we could settle the matter right there without going before the judge. "No way!" I shouted. Looking my audiologist adversary in the eye I said, "You've been jerking me around for six months. I want to hear the judge tell you that you have to pay me!"

Before the bench I explained the bizarre chain of events leading up to my third court appearance. "Can you please explain to Dr. Scheider that he has to pay me the money he owes me?" I asked the judge. "Yes," he answered. "The doctor has to pay you or he'll go to jail." *Hooray!* Feeling vindicated, I tuned out on what the lawyer mumbled to the judge – something about scheduled payments. As it turned out, I was paid the hefty sum of $20 a month for two years. The arrangement was pathetic, but the thought of Scheider having to write a check to me every month made me smile. Looking back, was suffering through all that bullshit worth it? Yes! I had just begun my freelance career and thought that getting screwed right off the bat would not bode well for my future success. Over the next five years I worked for hundreds of clients, having trouble getting paid only three times. Nothing used up my time and sapped my energy like chasing down those deadbeats.

Time for a change?

After half a decade on the freelance trail, the grind of hustling business, cranking out the work and waiting for payment was wearing on me. I was paying a hefty chunk each month to keep myself and my family covered by health insurance. Mary could see that this routine was taking a toll on me. Then, one spring afternoon in 1990, she reminded me that Dave Lieberman, with whom I'd worked in the agency world, was now a writer at Lands' End, the mail order clothing company. "Maybe he could help you get a job there," she suggested. (Dave had helped me get hired a decade earlier at Campbell-Mithun.) I phoned and asked him if Lands' End could use another writer. Just like before, Dave was only too happy to help. I drove up to Lands' End headquarters near O'Hare Airport and talked with him. After we'd reminisced about our agency days, Dave looked at my portfolio and liked what he saw. Then he surprised me with the news that Lands' End would soon be moving its headquarters from Chicago to Dodgeville, Wisconsin. I'd never even heard of the place.

Getting hired would mean relocating. *Maybe you're moving to Dodgeville, but not me,* I thought. Then Dave told me that even with all my experience I'd have to take a copywriting test. "Are you joking?" I gasped. "No," he said, assuring me that the test was mandatory. He'd had to pass the same test in order to get hired. Well, I knew there was no way I'd ever move to Dogpatch or whatever that Wisconsin town was called, but I brought the test home anyway. After a few days I sat down, completed it and mailed it back to my old friend.

A week or so later Lieberman phoned. He told me that his boss, Don Carlson, wanted to see me. Back at Lands' End I spoke with Dave again. He prepped me for my interview, stressing that I shouldn't worry about money. Good raises and hefty bonuses would be coming, he promised. Dave also said that every writer would enjoy a window office in the spectacular new building that was waiting for us in Dodgeville. He made it sound like Shangri-La. Then I talked with Carlson, a pleasant middle-aged gent. He was impressed with what I'd done on the test and liked the samples in my portfolio. Don offered me a job and I accepted, figuring I'd work at Lands' End until their big move, but stay in Chicago and hunt for a full-time job on my home turf.

Within a few days I was working in the round, modern building that housed Lands' End. The offices were arranged around a central hub, so the main hallway was a circular path. It took some getting used to. My trip to work was a pleasant drive north on River Road, but I had the option of walking a block to the Rapid Transit station. It was a cheap ride but a long one – all the way downtown, through the entire Dearborn Street Subway, onto the elevated tracks and northwest almost to O'Hare. (I could read the paper and finish the crossword.) Exiting at Cumberland, I was stone's throw from Lands' End.

I started on a Monday early in May and went to work writing about men's tailored clothes. I was amazed at all the features that went into a pair of tailored pants: French fly, lined crotch, Ban-Rol® waistband, center back belt loop.... And there were so many fabrics: twill, poplin, gabardine, corduroy, whipcord, moleskin.... While I was studying up, droves of employees were leaving the company. Most of the staff had opted to stay in Chicago and find new employment there. Every Friday at noon sizeable groups headed out to goodbye luncheons. I attended a few of these send-offs for creative folks I'd just met.

On weekends, Mary and I drove to Wisconsin in search of a house. (Don Carlson lined us up with a Dodgeville real estate agent on my first day at work.) We headed west on I-90, which was under repair and down to one lane. On our first trip torrential rain pummeled us all the way, but we managed to hook up with the real estate man, a portly, middle-aged fellow who chauffeured us to five homes. The best of the bunch was a five-bedroom farmhouse that was far too big for us and beat-up beyond repair. After a few more house-hunting sorties, our tireless realtor showed us two places in Mount Horeb, a town of about 4,200, located halfway between Dodgeville and Madison. Mary and I liked both houses, one of which had a permanent swimming pool. The kids went bonkers over it and lobbied hard for their choice: "The one with the pool! The one with the pool!" They won, but we had to wait until November to move in.

One advantage to living in Mount Horeb was its nearness to Madison. Mary and I and the kids had discovered Madison a couple of years earlier after a family picnic in Lake Geneva. Heading west in search of a motel, we drove from town to town with no luck. Everything was booked. It was prom night in one town, a clogging convention had taken over the next one, and the one after that was hosting a wrestling meet. We finally spent the night at the Concourse Hotel in downtown Madison. In the morning we looked at the city and fell in love with it. Now, two years later, we thought that living halfway between Madison and Dodgeville would give me a reasonable commute to work and allow the kids easy access to Madison.

Hard to say goodbye

Our house in Oak Park sold in a flash. After a bidding war, the winning buyer hired an inspector to check the place out. He inspected the house from top to bottom and said it was the cleanest place he'd ever seen. Everything worked. Nothing needed fixing. The movers took everything except some cans of paint. On my last trip to our Oak Park house I met with Mary's dad and brother, who came to take that paint off my hands. Gallon-sized cans, about 20 of them, were lined up on the workbench. My helpful in-laws assured me that they could put them to use. Good luck, guys.

I brought my camera with me because Mary had asked me to take some pictures of the empty house. It was a lonely assignment. I snapped a photo of the art glass windows she was so fond of. And as I moved from room to room, memories came flooding in: birthday parties and graduations, Thanksgivings and Christmases … family and friends smiling, joking, laughing, hugging…. I heard notes from a piano; one of the girls was practicing "Spinning Song." Kids were running through the hall, shouting and giggling. Upstairs I took a few shots of the antique bathroom where I had redone the woodwork and Mary had added brass fixtures and ornate stenciling. On the front porch I snapped a picture of the two bench swings that faced each other. Every kid on the block loved those swings. And outside I took a shot of the long, green side yard, shaded by trees the kids and I had planted.

B and E were dead set against moving from urban Oak Park to a remote rural setting. Mom and Dad could haul them there, but they would drive right back home, they promised. Their angst gave me guilt pangs. Lands' End put us up in temporary lodging in Madison for a few weeks. Then our realtor got us into a first-floor apartment in Mount Horeb for two months. Facing a cornfield, our kitchen window gave us front-row seats to a terrific light show furnished by the headlights of nocturnal harvesters. We moved into our house just in time for Thanksgiving, grateful that our relocation odyssey was over. Mary liked our vast bedroom that opened to the deck/swimming pool area and she loved the deluxe kitchen. The kids were off to a good start at Mount Horeb High School. Bridget, a senior, made the pom-pom squad and sophomore Eileen was welcomed warmly by the girls' basketball team.

On our first weekend in Mount Horeb Mary and I looked around downtown, where the area's Norwegian heritage was proudly displayed. We walked the main drag, known as the "Trollway," viewing several trolls carved from tree stumps that were still rooted in the ground. We browsed a few antique stores and stumbled upon a quirky Mustard Museum housed in a guy's garage. At a nearby grocery store we found flat, circular coffee cakes called kringles and odd-looking cheese curds that squeaked when we chewed them. One Mount Horeb grocer furnished meat trimming and sausage making for deer hunters. We drove by the famous Gonstead Chiropractic Clinic, a sprawling complex of low buildings with an airstrip to accommodate emergency patients.

At home our monthly phone bills were over $100 for quite a while. Breaking away from their Oak Park friends was a slow grieving process for the kids. At school they were shocked at the hair dos girls were wearing: teased and sprouting bodacious bangs up front. "Big hair," they called it or "Berwyn hair," alluding to the coif favored by girls in Berwyn, a blue-collar city bordering Oak Park. The Murphy sisters were among a handful of girls at school with "straight" hair.

Our whole family got a kick out of the local restaurants. At most of them we entered through a huge, lively bar area. The dining area seemed to be an afterthought. Broasted chicken was a favorite menu item and nearly every eatery hosted a busy Friday fish fry. On weekends I sometimes visited the Cenex store, browsing exotic lubricants for farm machinery, Bag Balm for sore cow udders, chick brooders and mysterious cow magnets.

Better days ahead

The road to Lands' End took me through a rolling landscape of green pastures, cornfields and dense clumps of oak and evergreens; it was a pleasant, twenty-five-minute drive. On my first day at work Dave Lieberman welcomed me with open arms. He showed me to my roomy office and gave me a tour of the brand-new atrium building. Designed with a nautical theme, it really knocked me out. One side of my office bordered a carpeted veranda that circled a central atrium. This broad balcony was furnished with tables and upholstered chairs for meetings and informal gatherings. Standing at the railing you could look down and watch the activity on the first floor.

At lunchtime Dave took me next door to the company's huge recreation center. Unbelievable! It was built with a 25-meter pool, indoor running track, gym with basketball court and workout machines, racquetball courts, rooms for aerobics and dance classes – you name it. The place was jumping with employees using their lunch hour to work out. In the afternoon Al Shackelford, the creative director, introduced me to Shirley Ross, who would be my art director on men's tailored clothing. Al gave me some background on the category and encouraged me to wear test the slacks and sport coats I'd be writing about. My limited wardrobe would appreciate the upgrade. Lieberman dropped by again, apologizing because I didn't get the window office he'd promised me when we talked in Chicago. I told him truthfully that I was quite happy with my new digs. Before he left, Dave asked me if I would read the script for a play he'd written. He handed it to me saying he'd appreciate my comments. I gazed through the glass wall of my office at the unoccupied floor, wondering what was destined to fill that vast, gray space. Minutes later I learned that the smooth expanse out there was covered by large carpet tiles. An electrician arrived and pulled one of them up, revealing a hollow space underneath. Then he removed a squat, wheeled robot from a box and attached a wire to it. Curious, I walked over for a closer look. Now he was directing the little vehicle by remote control as it pulled the wire to some distant spot beneath the floor. Amazing!

Shirley found me. We were due at an input session on men's tailored clothes. Heading back to my office, I spotted a carpenter at work. He was giving the wall next to an elevator a broad round corner, gluing a sheet of dark mahogany veneer onto an understructure of wooden strips. As he stretched the thin sheet over the framework, the dramatic, rounded corner took shape. He called it "voodoo carpentry." Fascinating! There must have been a dozen other craftsmen like him working throughout the building, adding finishing touches to its unique decor. I felt a strong urge to walk around and look in on them, but it was time for my meeting. I reviewed a list of questions I'd prepared about the components of a fully lined crotch. The phone rang. It was the product manager calling about our meeting. "Where's your office?" I asked. "Straight across from yours," he answered cheerfully. I looked up and saw him smiling and beckoning to me from the opposite side of the atrium. He could have been a neighbor waving me over to check out his new Chevy. *This is a really friendly outfit,* I thought. *With luck I'll be working here for a good long time.*

Pieces of the not-too-distant past